Foreign Intervention in Africa

Foreign Intervention in Africa chronicles the foreign political and military interventions in Africa during the periods of decolonization (1956–75) and the Cold War (1945–91), as well as during the periods of state collapse (1991–2001) and the "global war on terror" (2001–10). In the first two periods, the most significant intervention was extracontinental. The United States, the Soviet Union, China, Cuba, and the former colonial powers entangled themselves in countless African conflicts. During the period of state collapse, the most consequential interventions were intracontinental. African governments, sometimes assisted by powers outside the continent, supported warlords, dictators, and dissident movements in neighboring countries and fought for control of their neighbors' resources. The global war on terror, like the Cold War, increased the foreign military presence on the African continent and generated external support for repressive governments. In each of these cases, external interests altered the dynamics of internal struggles, escalating local conflicts into larger conflagrations, with devastating effects on African peoples.

Elizabeth Schmidt is Professor of History at Loyola University Maryland. She is the author of *Cold War and Decolonization in Guinea, 1946–1958* (2007), which received the African Politics Conference Group's 2008 Best Book Award, and *Mobilizing the Masses: Gender, Ethnicity, and Class in the Nationalist Movement in Guinea, 1939–1958* (2005), which received Alpha Sigma Nu's book award for history in 2008. Her 1992 book, *Peasants, Traders, and Wives: Shona Women in the History of Zimbabwe, 1870–1939*, was awarded a special mention in the Alpha Sigma Nu book competition for history, was a finalist for the African Studies Association's Herskovits Award, and was named by *Choice* an "Outstanding Academic Book for 1994."

New Approaches to African History

Series Editor
Martin Klein, University of Toronto

Editorial Advisors:
William Beinart, *University of Oxford*
Mamadou Diouf, *Columbia University*
William Freund, *University of KwaZulu-Natal*
Sandra E. Greene, *Cornell University*
Ray Kea, *University of California, Riverside*
David Newbury, *Smith College*

New Approaches to African History is designed to introduce students to current findings and new ideas in African history. Although each book treats a particular case, and is able to stand alone, the format allows the studies to be used as modules in general courses on African history and world history. The cases represent a wide range of topics. Each volume summarizes the state of knowledge on a particular subject for a student who is new to the field. However, the aim is not simply to present views of the literature, it is also to introduce debates on historiographical or substantive issues and may argue for a particular point of view. The aim of the series is to stimulate debate, to challenge students and general readers. The series is not committed to any particular school of thought.

Other Books in the Series:

1. *Africa since 1940*, by Frederick Cooper
2. *Muslim Societies in African History*, by David Robinson
3. *Reversing Sail: A History of the African Diaspora*, by Michael Gomez
4. *The African City: A History*, by William Freund
5. *Warfare in Independent Africa*, by William Reno
6. *Warfare in African History*, by Richard J. Reid

Foreign Intervention in Africa

From the Cold War to the War on Terror

Elizabeth Schmidt

Loyola University Maryland

Foreword by William Minter

CAMBRIDGE
UNIVERSITY PRESS

32 Avenue of the Americas, New York NY 10013-2473, USA

Cambridge University Press is part of the University of Cambridge.

It furthers the University's mission by disseminating knowledge in the pursuit of education, learning, and research at the highest international levels of excellence.

www.cambridge.org
Information on this title: www.cambridge.org/9780521709033

First published 2013
Reprinted 2013

A catalog record for this publication is available from the British Library.

Library of Congress Cataloging in Publication data
Schmidt, Elizabeth, 1955– author.
Foreign intervention in Africa : from the Cold War to the War on Terror / Elizabeth Schmidt, Loyola University Maryland.
  pages cm. – (New approaches to African history ; 7)
Includes bibliographical references and index.
ISBN 978-0-521-88238-5 (hardback) – ISBN 978-0-521-70903-3 (paperback)
1. Africa – Foreign relations. 2. Africa – Politics and government. 3. Africa – Foreign economic relations. 4. Insurgency – Africa – History. I. Title.
DT31.S32 2013
327.6009′045–dc23   2012035195

ISBN 978-0-521-88238-5 Hardback
ISBN 978-0-521-70903-3 Paperback

Cover photograph: Angolan soldier with Soviet-made AK-47 Kalashnikov submachine gun, guarding Soviet-made ground-to-air missiles near Cuito Cuanavale, Angola, February 29, 1988 (Pascal Guyot/AFP/Getty Images)

Contents

ILLUSTRATIONS   *page* ix

ACKNOWLEDGMENTS   xi

FOREWORD BY WILLIAM MINTER   xiii

ABBREVIATIONS   xvii

Introduction   1

1 Nationalism, Decolonization, and the Cold War, 1945–1991   18

2 Egypt and Algeria: Radical Nationalism, Nonalignment, and
   External Intervention in North Africa, 1952–1973   35

3 The Congo Crisis, 1960–1965   57

4 War and Decolonization in Portugal's African Empire,
   1961–1975   79

5 White-Minority Rule in Southern Africa, 1960–1990   103

6 Conflict in the Horn, 1952–1993   143

7 France's Private African Domain, 1947–1991   165

8 From the Cold War to the War on Terror, 1991–2010   193

   Conclusion   227

INDEX   231

Illustrations

Maps

0.1 Africa, 1947   *page* xix
0.2 Africa, 2011   xx
2.1 North Africa and the Middle East, 1971   34
3.1 Congo, 1960–65   56
4.1 Portuguese Africa, 1974–75   78
5.1 Southern Africa, 1982   102
6.1 Horn of Africa, 1995   142
7.1 Francophone Africa, 1991   164

Photographs

2.1 Nasser is cheered by a Cairo crowd after the
    nationalization of the Suez Canal, August 1, 1956
    (Hulton-Deutsch Collection/Corbis).   39
2.2 Oil installations burn as British troops advance through
    Port Said after the Anglo-French invasion, November 10,
    1956 (Bettman/Corbis).   41
2.3 Algerian civilians flee a conflict zone under the eye of the
    French military, December 9, 1954 (Bettmann/Corbis). 47
2.4 French men fighting to keep Algeria French receive
    supplies from French women, January 31, 1960
    (Bettmann/Corbis).   53

3.1 Congolese troops loyal to Mobutu manhandle Lumumba
     after his capture, December 6, 1960 (Bettmann/Corbis).   65
3.2 Secessionist leader Moïse Tshombe with Belgian
     commander of the Katanga Army, Lieutenant Colonel
     Jean-Marie Crèvecoeur, February 1, 1961 (Terrence
     Spencer/Time Life Pictures/Getty Images).   66
3.3 Picketers protesting UN and Belgian actions in the Congo
     demonstrate in front of the United Nations, February 1,
     1961 (Yale Joel/Time Life Pictures/Getty Images).   67
3.4 President Kennedy with General Mobutu after their
     White House meeting, May 31, 1963 (Bettmann/Corbis).   71
4.1 UNITA leader Jonas Savimbi with his troops in Nova
     Lisboa, Angola, September 1975 (Patrick
     Chauvel/Sygma/Corbis).   96
4.2 Cuban military officer in Angola, February 23, 1976
     (AFP/Getty Images).   97
5.1 Sign outside the General Motors factory in Cape
     Province, South Africa, January 1, 1956 (Three
     Lions/Getty Images).   107
5.2 Anti-Rhodesia demonstrators in London protesting
     British appeasement of the white-minority regime,
     November 25, 1971 (Frank Barratt/Getty Images).   117
5.3 President Reagan with UNITA leader Jonas Savimbi in
     the Oval Office, January 30, 1986 (Bettmann/Corbis).   133
6.1 Somali residents of Mogadishu protest Soviet support for
     Ethiopia in the Somali-Ethiopian War, April 5, 1978
     (Keystone-France/Gamma-Keystone via Getty Images).   152
7.1 French and African soldiers marching together in Middle
     Congo shortly before independence, August 1, 1960
     (Terrence Spencer/Time Life Pictures/Getty Images).   179
7.2 Cameroonian President Ahmadou Ahidjo, French
     President General Charles de Gaulle, and French Africa
     advisor Jacques Foccart leaving the Élysée Palace, Paris,
     June 21, 1967 (AFP/Getty Images).   183

Acknowledgments

I could not have written this book without the invaluable critique, sharp insights, and sound advice of William Minter, who read every chapter with a fine-toothed comb. A scholar and activist on Africa issues since the mid-1960s, Bill has an extraordinary grasp of the scholarship, the details, and the big picture, and he understands the complexities of the continent better than anyone I know. I owe him an incalculable debt.

This book would not have seen the light of day without the support of Martin Klein, editor of Cambridge's New Approaches to African History series, who invited me to write a different book but enthusiastically supported my proposal to write this one instead. At Cambridge University Press, Eric Crahan, Abigail Zorbaugh, and Paul Smolenski worked tirelessly to bring the project to fruition. I received extremely valuable advice from several Cambridge readers. In particular, I would like to thank Allen Isaacman, who generously read and commented on the entire manuscript, helping me to publish a better book, as he has several times in the past. (I also owe a debt of gratitude to Barbara Isaacman, who pressed Allen to take on this task despite his overloaded agenda.) David Newbury, Mamadou Diouf, and several anonymous readers provided helpful comments on various versions of my proposal.

My manuscript benefited from other insightful critiques. Participants in the African Seminar at the Johns Hopkins University provided many useful suggestions, and Richard Immerman and Petra Goedde, editors of *The Oxford Handbook of the Cold War* (2013), offered constructive comments on my contribution to their volume, which helped me to write a more polished, expanded account in this book. Many thanks to Oxford University Press for allowing me to use excerpts from my contribution to their book in this one.

Other individuals and institutions supported the project in important ways. I would like to thank the staffs of Loyola–Notre Dame Library and of the Library of Congress for their ever-prompt response to my requests for materials and advice. Loyola University Maryland contributed significant financial support. The Research and Sabbatical Committee, the Center for the Humanities, and the dean of the College of Arts and Sciences provided two summer research grants, and the center, the dean, and the Office of Academic Affairs generously helped to pay for the cost of maps and photographs. Cartographer Philip Schwartzberg at Meridian Mapping willingly produced the maps to precise specification, and Ryan Bakerink at Getty Images and Louis Riquelme at Corbis helped me acquire the appropriate photographs. I offer many thanks to the staff at Aptara, Inc., where Peggy Rote expertly supervised the book's production, Katherine Faydash applied her skills as copy editor, and the Help Desk responded to my numerous indexing queries.

I owe an enormous amount to activist academics, friends and colleagues of more than three decades, who taught me how to integrate scholarship and solidarity. In particular, I would like to thank Prexy Nesbitt, my earliest teacher and inspiration, and Bereket Habte Selassie, both of whom were my mentors and colleagues at the Africa Project of the Institute for Policy Studies; Carol Thompson, my teacher in the anti-apartheid and Southern African solidarity movements in Zimbabwe and the United States, whose scholarly activism is a model for us all; Allen Isaacman, my mentor in the Twin Cities, who introduced me to the Mozambique Support Network and encouraged me to participate in engaged scholarship; and Bill Minter, with whom I first collaborated on Southern African research and writing in the mid-1980s.

For their love, support, and encouragement, I thank my parents, Albert and Kathryn Schmidt; my son, Jann Grovogui; and my partner, Mark Peyrot – all of whom kindly tolerated the mood swings that writing a book seems to entail. Finally, this book is dedicated to Prexy Nesbitt, who introduced me to the liberation struggles of Southern Africa and set me on my path.

Foreword

Foreign intervention, as this survey by Elizabeth Schmidt makes clear, is no simple concept to define. The reality is no less complex than the definition. Even in the periods of the slave trade and of established colonial rule, the dominant powers from outside the continent had to take account of local realities. African societies defeated on the battlefield and subordinated to economic coercion found ways to resist, adapt to, or manipulate the presence of outside powers.

From 1945 to 1991, most of the period covered by this book, the Cold War between the two superpowers, the United States and the Soviet Union, dominated world politics. Outsiders often viewed African conflicts as reflecting this global contest. Although superpower competition may have been the dominant factor in European confrontations, in Africa the realities did not fit as easily into a bipolar framework. The colonial powers retained influence and had their own distinct interests as their control over the continent diminished. The Soviet Union led a coherent bloc including most of Eastern Europe. However, other communist powers, including Yugoslavia, Cuba, and China, had their own foreign policies, based on distinct interests in Africa. Most significantly, African nations themselves, along with Asian and Latin American countries, shared an alternate dominant narrative based on anticolonialism and nonalignment between the superpowers. Different nations within Africa, and different political forces within each country, had their own interests, which led them to seek international alliances and sometimes invite external intervention against domestic enemies or neighboring countries.

No continent-wide account of this complex period could even come close to being "complete." However, Schmidt's wide-ranging review of multiple case studies succeeds in paying due attention to nuance without getting bogged down in detailed narratives and academic disputes.[1] In each case, the historical record allows for differences among historians and social scientists in evaluating the scale and character of external intervention and the relative influence by external and internal actors on the outcomes. Assessments of the damage done or the possible positive effects of intervention also vary depending on who is doing the evaluation. Most would probably agree on the horrific negative balance of the slave trade and of colonial rule, particularly when combined with expropriation of land and property by European settlers, and most would probably agree with Schmidt's considered judgment that in most cases external intervention from 1945 to 2010 brought more harm than benefit. However, sharp disagreements will undoubtedly continue in evaluating particular interventions, past, present, or future.

In my personal opinion, the 1979 overthrow of Idi Amin in Uganda by Tanzanian troops, for example, was more justified than would have been a failure to intervene, although subsequent events made clear that it was hardly a solution to Uganda's problems. Similarly, in my judgment, the intervention of Cuban troops in Angola in 1975 to counter Central Intelligence Agency and South African intervention, and their role in subsequent years in protecting Angola against attacks by South Africa and the UNITA rebels, was also justified. Moreover, if the international community had not failed to intervene against the 1994 genocide in Rwanda, hundreds of thousands of lives probably could have been saved.

All such judgments admittedly depend on incomplete evidence and hypothetical reasoning about the options not chosen, as well as on value judgments of both observers and participants. What should be clearly rejected, however, are simplistic accounts that reduce events to a simple story of dueling outside interventions or a clear dichotomy between external and internal causes of conflict. The postcolonial wars in Angola and Mozambique, for example, which I analyzed in *Apartheid's Contras*, were neither simply civil wars nor conflicts among proxies of the United States, Soviet Union, Cuba, and South Africa.

---

[1] Full disclosure: I served as a consultant on this book project, reviewing drafts, discussing the topics, and raising difficult-to-answer questions with the author.

Instead, internal, global, and regional conflicts intersected in complex patterns, which shifted over time. Moreover, as many scholars have demonstrated with more finely grained analyses, in each country these wars featured local realities with their own distinctive features.

For the policy analyst or social justice activist trying to make sense of and support or oppose today's interventions, factual information is almost always incomplete, and the motives of those involved are mixed. There are no simple formulas. Supporting (or opposing) an intervention simply because the United States, the African Union, or the United Nations supports it, for example, would be a recipe for ignoring the realities of particular cases and the contradictions within the policies of these states and institutions themselves. The concept of a purely humanitarian intervention simply to aid innocent civilians, with no political or military implications, is an illusion. An intervention with a limited mandate, such as to protect corridors for relief supplies, may or may not be justified in a particular case. Yet it will have political consequences; it will weaken some forces and strengthen others. So, of course, will unilateral or multilateral interventions designed to combat terrorism, reverse a coup against an elected government, or "protect civilians" against human rights abuses by a repressive regime or a rebel movement. However, ruling out all interventions ignores the fact that inaction also affects the outcome of any conflict, by deferring de facto to the most powerful and ruthless forces on the ground. The balance of forces between governments and rebel movements, whatever their ideological orientation or extent of abuses against civilians, is affected by their structural links to the outside world, including political and economic as well as military ties. Finally, the failure of diplomatic action, which should be the first resort, may also lead to enormous human costs.

There is no alternative to making fallible judgments about particular cases. The human suffering from some conflicts does indeed "cry out" for intervention. Yet the consequences of actual interventions can appall even those who called for the interventions in the first place. It would be easier if there were some formula to tell us which interventions would alleviate human suffering and increase the possibility that people would get a chance for a fresh start and which interventions should be opposed because of ulterior motives or the high probability of making things worse. If, as I believe, such reliable formulas do not exist, it is better to recognize that, and then get on with sorting out our messy and inevitably inconclusive collective judgments on specific cases. As a corollary, we must recognize the likelihood of ongoing dis-agreements among humanitarians, progressives, and people of good-will. If "dialogue" is needed among internal parties to a conflict, it is equally essential among outsiders, including not only representatives of states and multilateral agencies but also national and international civil society.

In the context of the second decade of the twenty-first century, the danger of too much intervention or bungled intervention seems more likely than the danger of no intervention at all. The impetus to inter-vene is coming not only from outside governments, most notably that of the United States, in response to real or imagined terrorist threats. It is also coming from African governments and rebel movements, which are increasingly turning to African regional organizations; the United Nations; and bilateral suppliers of arms, training, and security per-sonnel (both public and private). Increased multilateral involvement in conflicts both within and across borders is no doubt inevitable. However, the outcomes are as uncertain as ever. The consequences are far too great for the decisions to be made by governments behind closed doors, without transparency and input from a wider range of voices, particularly those most affected.

Today, in comparison to much of the period covered in this book, modern communications technologies allow for more transparent decisions, more consultation, and better checks on the ulterior motives of parties to a conflict and of those who volunteer to be peacemakers. Whether this opportunity leads to better decision making depends, first, on the decision makers themselves. It also depends on the capac-ity of media and scholars to provide deeper analysis that rejects sim-plistic solutions and on local and international civil society to sustain the pressure for genuine human security.

William Minter
Washington, D.C., June 20, 2012

Abbreviations

AFDL	Alliance of Democratic Forces for the Liberation of Congo-Zaire
AFRICOM	U.S. Africa Command
ANC	African National Congress (South Africa)
CENTCOM	U.S. Central Command
CFA	African Financial Community
CGT	General Confederation of Labor (France)
CIA	Central Intelligence Agency
CJTF-HOA	Combined Joint Task Force–Horn of Africa
CONCP	Conference of Nationalist Organizations of the Portuguese Colonies
CONSAS	Constellation of Southern African States
DRC	Democratic Republic of Congo
EACTI	East Africa Counterterrorism Initiative
ECOMOG	Economic Community Monitoring Group (Liberia)
ECOWAS	Economic Community of West African States
ELF	Eritrean Liberation Front
EPLF	Eritrean People's Liberation Front
EPRDF	Ethiopian Popular Revolutionary Democratic Front
EUCOM	U.S. European Command
FBI	Federal Bureau of Investigation
FLN	National Liberation Front (Algeria)
FNLA	National Front for the Liberation of Angola
FRELIMO	Front for the Liberation of Mozambique
FROLINAT	Front for the National Liberation of Chad
GUNT	Transitional Government of National Unity (Chad)
IGAD	Intergovernmental Authority on Development
IMF	International Monetary Fund
MDRM	Democratic Movement for Malagasy Restoration (Madagascar)
MNC	Congolese National Movement
MPLA	Popular Movement for the Liberation of Angola

NATO	North Atlantic Treaty Organization
NPFL	National Patriotic Front of Liberia
OAU	Organization of African Unity
OEF-TS	Operation Enduring Freedom–Trans Sahara
PAIGC	African Party for the Independence of Guinea and Cape Verde
PCF	French Communist Party
PSI	Pan-Sahel Initiative
RDA	African Democratic Rally
RENAMO	Mozambique National Resistance
RPF	Rwandan Patriotic Front
R2P	Responsibility to Protect
RUF	Revolutionary United Front (Sierra Leone)
SACP	South African Communist Party
SADC	Southern African Development Community
SADCC	Southern African Development Coordination Conference
SADF	South African Defence Force
SDECE	External Documentation and Counterespionage Service (France)
SPLM	Sudan People's Liberation Movement
SWANU	South West Africa National Union (Namibia)
SWAPO	South West Africa People's Organization (Namibia)
TPLF	Tigray People's Liberation Front (Ethiopia)
TSCTI	Trans-Sahara Counterterrorism Initiative
TSCTP	Trans-Sahara Counterterrorism Partnership
UDI	Unilateral Declaration of Independence (Rhodesia)
ULIMO	United Liberation Movement of Liberia for Democracy
UN	United Nations
UNITA	National Union for the Total Independence of Angola
UNITAF	United Task Force (Somalia)
UNOSOM	UN Operation in Somalia
UPC	Union of the Peoples of Cameroon
USAID	U.S. Agency for International Development
USPACOM	U.S. Pacific Command
WSLF	Western Somali Liberation Front
ZANU	Zimbabwe African National Union
ZANU-PF	Zimbabwe African National Union–Patriotic Front
ZAPU	Zimbabwe African People's Union

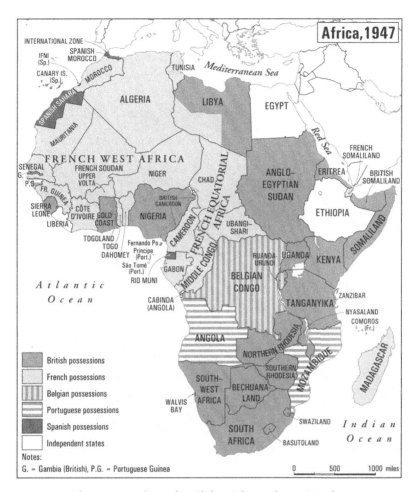

MAP 0.1. Africa, 1947. (Map by Philip Schwartzberg, Meridian Mapping, Minneapolis.)

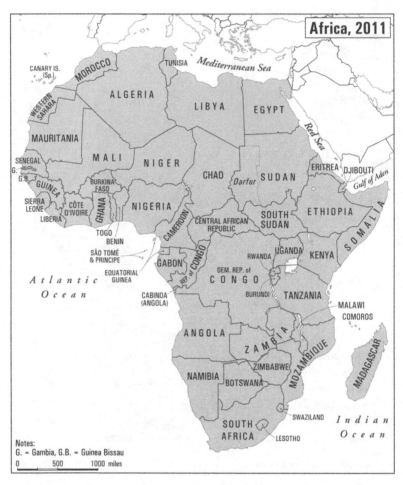

MAP 0.2. Africa, 2011. (Map by Philip Schwartzberg, Meridian Mapping, Minneapolis.)

Introduction

For many outsiders, the word *Africa* conjures up images of a continent in crisis, riddled with war and corruption, imploding from disease and starvation. Africans are regularly blamed for their plight. They are frequently viewed as being intolerant of ethnic and religious differences but accepting of corruption and dictatorship. They are often presumed to be unwilling or unable to govern themselves. This book challenges such popular myths. By examining the historical roots of contemporary problems, the book demonstrates that many of the predicaments that plague the continent today are not solely the result of African decisions but also the consequence of foreign intrusion into African affairs. Focusing on foreign political and military intervention in Africa during the periods of decolonization (1956–75) and the Cold War (1945–91), with reflections on the later periods of state collapse (1991–2001) and the "global war on terror" (2001–10), this book advances four central propositions.[1]

First, as colonial systems faltered, imperial and Cold War powers vied to control the decolonization process. While imperial powers hoped to transfer the reins of government to neocolonial regimes that would continue to serve their political and economic interests,

---

[1] Portions of this book have appeared in my contribution to *The Oxford Handbook of the Cold War* (2013), ed. Richard H. Immerman and Petra Goedde, and are reproduced here with the permission of Oxford University Press. The post–Cold War periods are dealt with more extensively in my book, *From State Collapse to the War on Terror: Foreign Intervention in Africa after the Cold War* (Athens: Ohio University Press, in progress).

1

Cold War powers strove to shape a new international order that instead catered to their interests. Although independence struggles and their aftermath were dominated by local issues, Cold War intervention rendered the conflicts more lethal and the consequences longer lasting. Second, as the Soviet Union collapsed and the Cold War ended, African nations were abandoned by their Cold War allies. They were bequeathed a legacy of enormous debt; collapsed states; and, in many cases, deadly competition for the spoils. While indigenous prodemocracy movements challenged warlords and autocrats, foreign actors both helped and hindered their efforts. Neighboring states and regional, continental, and transcontinental organizations supported opposing sides in the war-making and peace-building processes. Third, the global war on terror, like its Cold War antecedent, increased foreign military presence on the African continent and generated new external support for repressive governments. Fourth, throughout the periods under consideration, foreign intervention tended to exacerbate rather than alleviate African conflicts and to harm rather than help indigenous populations. Even international humanitarian and peacekeeping efforts were marred by conflicting interests that sometimes hurt the people they were intended to assist.

In considering these propositions in relation to the case studies that follow, readers should bear in mind several caveats. Although four discrete historical periods have been described, in reality, events do not fit into neat time frames but progress unevenly. Some African states began to collapse even as the Cold War raged – particularly during the economic crises of the 1980s – and in some areas, the war on terror commenced even before the September 2001 attacks on the United States. Just as historical periodization is necessarily imprecise, terminology can be complicated by multiple meanings. The book's title, *Foreign Intervention in Africa*, refers not only to military terrain and the corridors of power but also to the struggle for African hearts and minds. For the purposes of this study, *foreign* refers to alien political powers rather than individuals. Sometimes these powers are external to the continent. In other instances, the term describes the relationship of one African country to another. *Intervention* implies a relationship with an imbalance of power. It is not synonymous with engagement, involvement, or influence, which reveal nothing about the power dynamics of the relationship. Foreign intervention occurs when a dominant country uses force or pressure to interfere with and exert power over the affairs of a weaker sovereign entity. In many cases, force is employed when political pressure fails. Sometimes intervention can be viewed in a positive light, such as when powerful nations intervene to halt a genocide or to help maintain the peace. More often it has negative connotations, such as when powerful nations intervene to conquer, colonize, overthrow governments, install new ones, or plunder resources.

During the periods of the Cold War and decolonization, the most significant intervention was extracontinental. The United States, the Soviet Union, the People's Republic of China, Cuba, and the former colonial powers embroiled themselves in countless African conflicts. During the period of state collapse, countries outside the African continent continued to implicate themselves in African affairs, often under United Nations (UN) auspices. However, the most consequential foreign intervention during this period was intracontinental. African governments, sometimes assisted by extracontinental powers, supported warlords, dictators, and dissident movements in neighboring countries and fought for control of their neighbors' resources. The African Union and regional bodies regularly intervened to broker, monitor, and enforce peace agreements, their personnel sometimes profiting from the strife. With the onset of the war on terror, extracontinental intervention again became the most salient form. In all cases, external interests altered the dynamics of internal struggles, often escalating local conflicts into larger conflagrations, with devastating effects on African peoples.

Three other points should be borne in mind. First, governments are not sentient beings with desires, will, and the capacity to act. Yet the need for shorthand sometimes leads to the personification of political structures and the occasional reference to governments as actors. Second, governments are not monolithic. There is often dissension within and between branches of government. Policies are contested, and outcomes are the product of struggle. The good intentions of some quarters may be thwarted by the realpolitik of another. Humanitarian rationales may be genuine – or used to mask broader strategic and economic interests. Third, foreign intervention cannot occur without internal collaboration. To effect change in African countries, foreign governments must form alliances with indigenous actors who benefit from the relationship, whatever the cost to the rest of the population.

Historical Background: Situating the Book

Although this book begins with the Cold War, the history of foreign involvement with Africa has deep roots. Africans have engaged with peoples from other continents for thousands of years. Much of this interaction cannot be termed intervention, and much of it was mutually beneficial. The development of commercial and cultural exchanges is a case in point. Nearly 2,000 years before the common era, Egypt participated in a trade and communications network that embraced the Persian Plateau, the Indus Valley, and lands as far away as China. By 800 BCE, Phoenician trade routes spanned from Egypt to Morocco, and by the first century of the common era, Africans on the Indian Ocean coast had developed commercial links with the Arabian Peninsula, the Persian Gulf, and India, establishing a trading complex that eventually extended to China and Indonesia. North Africans were an integral part of the Greek and Roman worlds, where goods, ideas, and cultural practices traveled in all directions and brought many shared benefits. World religions also spread into Africa, transforming the African religious landscape and assuming new forms as they absorbed indigenous beliefs and practices. During the first three centuries of the common era, Judaism expanded into Ethiopia, while Christianity spread into Egypt, Ethiopia, and across North Africa to the Maghreb. In the seventh and eighth centuries, Islam began to take root in North Africa, whereas in later centuries, Muslim merchants extended its reach along the East African coast, into the Sudan and the Horn of Africa, and across the Sahara Desert into West Africa.

Unlike commercial and cultural exchange, other forms of foreign contact clearly involved dispossession and the loss of sovereignty. These unequal relationships can properly be characterized as intervention. Centuries before the common era, Egypt was forcibly incorporated first into the Persian and then into the Greek Empires. By the first century BCE, all of North Africa had been absorbed into the Roman Empire, following the defeat of indigenous rivals. Arab conquests began in the seventh century of the common era. By the middle of the sixteenth century, Turkish conquests had rendered the Ottoman Empire the dominant power in North Africa. During the same period, Ottomans and Portuguese vied for control of East African port cities and the lucrative Indian Ocean trade, bolstering their respective positions by forming alliances with indigenous political forces.

Externally driven slave trades, like conquest, can be considered foreign intervention. They, too, were dependent on African collaborators for success. Beginning in the seventh century CE, Arab-dominated trading networks exported millions of Africans from the northern and eastern parts of the continent to the Arabian Peninsula, Persian Gulf, Indian Ocean islands, and India. Other nexuses transported West Africans across the Sahara Desert to North Africa and the Mediterranean. Arab-led slave trades lasted through the nineteenth century. Meanwhile, the European- and Euro-American-dominated trans-Atlantic slave trade, which spanned the mid-fifteenth to the late nineteenth centuries, forced more than ten million Africans into slavery in the New World. Millions more died in slave raiding wars, in transit to and inside coastal holding stations, and during the treacherous Middle Passage.

The distinction between foreign involvement and intervention can be blurred. Economic interactions have sometimes precipitated foreign intervention. As the trans-Atlantic slave trade waned in the nineteenth century, the Industrial Revolution took off in Western Europe and North America, stimulating a new interest in Africa. Industrial and commercial concerns from the Northern Hemisphere targeted the continent for its rich natural resources and potential markets. While African producers and merchants prospered from the new "legitimate" trade, indigenous strongmen also took advantage of the increased opportunities for wealth and power, which were enhanced by the influx of modern European weapons. Competition among Africans for control of lucrative trade routes resulted in war and instability in many parts of the continent, while heightened demand for labor to produce cash crops generated new forms of indigenous servitude. As European powers vied with one another for control of African resources, government officials worried that informal spheres of influence could no longer protect their countries' economic interests. The Berlin Conference was convened in 1884–85 to stave off the threat of an intra-European war. Without a single African present, representatives of European political and commercial interests mapped out plans to establish "effective occupation" and formal colonial administration throughout the continent, claiming for their countries a share of what Belgian King Leopold II called "this magnificent African cake."[2]

---

[2] Quoted in Adam Hochschild, *King Leopold's Ghost: A Story of Greed, Terror, and Heroism in Colonial Africa* (New York: Houghton Mifflin, 1998), 58.

The scramble for Africa was unleashed with a new wave of foreign intervention. By the first decades of the twentieth century, most of the continent had been conquered, colonized, and placed under European control. France, Britain, Belgium, Portugal, Germany, Italy, and Spain had established regimes to extract African wealth – especially rubber, cotton, minerals, and oils – and to force Africans to provide the labor and taxes necessary to keep the system afloat. Once again, African responses were varied. Indigenous political leaders whose powers were threatened, and peoples whose land, labor, and livestock were alienated, generally resisted the imposition of European authority. Those jockeying for position or those who had been oppressed or marginalized by indigenous rulers or rivals sometimes sought alliances with the new rulers. Responses varied across time and space. Any given individual might resist, acquiesce, accommodate, or collaborate depending on the circumstance.

Focus of the Book

The balance of forces began to change during World War II, sparking the postwar period of decolonization, which encompassed the middle decades of the twentieth century. Wartime exactions had resulted in increased hardships for African populations, as they were forced to provide labor, resources, and soldiers to support the European war effort. Propaganda promoting democracy and self-determination, the experiences of African military conscripts, and economic distress led to widespread resistance after the war. For many European powers, the political and economic costs of colonial rule increasingly seemed to outweigh the benefits. As the "wind of change" blew across the continent during the postwar period, African nations in growing numbers achieved political independence.[3] Although most attained independence in the 1960s, others remained under European rule until the mid-1970s. Majority rule was not instituted in the settler-dominated territories of Southern Africa until the 1980s and 1990s. With varying degrees of success, the former imperial powers attempted to

---

[3] In 1960, British Prime Minister Harold Macmillan famously announced that "the wind of change is blowing through this continent, and, whether we like it or not, this growth of national consciousness is a political fact." Quoted in Frank Myers, "Harold Macmillan's 'Winds of Change' Speech: A Case Study in the Rhetoric of Policy Change," *Rhetoric & Public Affairs* 3 , no. 4 (Winter 2000): 565.

control the decolonization process, just as they had asserted their authority over African political and economic processes during the colonial period.

As colonialism collapsed, the contemporaneous Cold War brought a new surge of foreign intervention to the continent. The Cold War was characterized by political competition, economic rivalry, and military friction between the United States and the Soviet Union, as well as their respective allies. Although direct military confrontation between the two superpowers did not erupt, the Cold War period was punctuated by proxy wars in the developing world, where internal actors were supported by external powers. Just as the periods of decolonization and the Cold War overlapped, so, too, did the major participants. The major extracontinental players in the decolonization process were the colonial powers, in particular, France, Britain, Belgium, and Portugal. During the Cold War these countries were allied with the United States through their membership in the North Atlantic Treaty Organization (NATO). The settler regimes in Southern Africa (South Africa and Rhodesia) played the Cold War card in an attempt to protect their quasi-colonial systems of white privilege. The United States, which hoped to replace the imperial powers as the dominant external force in Africa, bridged the decolonization and Cold War processes. Wavering between its European allies and moderate African nationalists, the United States strove to keep both radical nationalism and communism at bay. The Soviet Union and other communist countries sided unabashedly with African liberation movements, although they differed over strategy and choice of partners. Eastern Bloc nations like Czechoslovakia and the German Democratic Republic (East Germany), which played critical roles as weapons suppliers, followed the Soviet line. Cuba, which was deemed by the West to be no more than a Soviet proxy, often took an independent course. Yugoslavia, though communist, rejected Soviet hegemony, as did the People's Republic of China after the 1960s Sino-Soviet split. Standing apart from both imperial and Cold War powers, Israel followed its own agenda, aligning with the former colonial powers to attack Egypt during the 1956 Suez War, supporting newly independent nations with military and economic aid in the early 1960s and establishing close ties to apartheid South Africa as Israel became increasingly isolated after the June 1967 Six-Day War.

Other countries and international bodies refused to take sides in the East-West struggle yet played critical roles in the decolonization process. The Non-Aligned Movement, composed primarily of developing countries in Africa, Asia, and Latin America, supported the emancipatory program of African colonies, and some member nations gave material support to African liberation movements. The Organization of African Unity (OAU), composed of independent African states, promoted national liberation in territories still under colonial or white-minority rule, providing liberation movements with military, economic, and diplomatic support. The Nordic countries and international bodies such as the UN and the World Council of Churches offered humanitarian and other nonmilitary aid to the Southern African liberation movements, helping to tip the balance toward independence and majority rule.

All of these outside powers became embroiled in the internal affairs of numerous African countries in the decades following World War II. Although domestic and regional conflicts and national liberation struggles centered on local issues, they were played out in the context of the Cold War. External interests altered the dynamics of internal struggles as Cold War tensions were superimposed on local ones. Small-scale conflicts escalated into full-scale wars armed and financed by opposing sides in the geopolitical struggle. The result was widespread destruction and instability, with consequences that continue to plague the continent today.

Some of these interventions resembled past imperial practices, with more powerful nations attempting to exploit Africa and its riches for their own ends. Former colonial powers and the United States tended to support regimes that opposed communism and left colonial economic relationships intact – even when they were corrupt or repressive. Western patronage was often based on the willingness of local actors to serve as Cold War allies and regional policemen, providing military bases for Western use and thwarting radical movements among their neighbors. With fewer means at its disposal and less intrinsic interest in the continent, the Soviet Union generally increased its presence in response to escalated Western involvement. It supported movements and regimes that declared themselves in favor of scientific socialism and a Soviet-style model of development – regardless of their internal practices – as well as radical nationalist regimes that were shunned by the West. Although deemed by the United States to be following the Soviet lead, Cuba often took an independent route, not always to the liking of its Soviet ally. China favored African political parties, movements, and regimes that opposed Soviet influence and ideology.

Their mutual opposition to the Soviet Union sometimes resulted in awkward alliances among China, the United States, and apartheid South Africa.

Although this book focuses on foreign political and military intervention in Africa, the problems that plague Africa today cannot be properly understood if the impact of foreign intrusion into African economies is ignored. Unequal exchange between African commodity producers and industrialized countries is a legacy of the colonial era that has contributed to the deep impoverishment of African populations. The inequality inherent in these economic relationships persisted after political independence in a system that has been characterized as neocolonialism. In the words of Ghana's first president, Kwame Nkrumah, neocolonial states had "all the outward trappings of international sovereignty," while their economies and political programs were "directed from outside."[4] Entrenched economic inequalities were exacerbated by the steep rise in oil prices in the early 1970s and the worldwide collapse in commodity prices at the end of that decade. As exporters of primary products and importers of manufactured goods, African nations suffered severe balance of trade deficits, which were compounded by inflated military budgets, corruption, and economic mismanagement. With few alternatives available, many governments turned to the International Monetary Fund (IMF), the World Bank, and Western governments and commercial banks for assistance.

Foreign aid came with strings attached. Motivated by free market ideologies that were intended to bolster global capitalism, Western-dominated international financial institutions imposed draconian stabilization and structural adjustment programs on African nations as a condition for foreign loans. Private banks generally required the IMF's seal of approval before granting loans of their own. Development agencies attached to Western governments and international nongovernmental organizations dependent on government funds refused assistance to projects that did not conform to free market or "neoliberal" norms. All of these institutions required the implementation of economic development models in which African populations had no say. In what was broadly referred to as the Washington Consensus, in reference to the home of the IMF, the World Bank, and the

---

[4] Kwame Nkrumah, *Neo-Colonialism: The Last Stage of Imperialism* (New York: International Publishers, 1966), ix.

U.S. government, these neoliberal programs curbed government involvement in the economy, ending subsidies, price controls, and tariffs; undermining health and educational services; and destroying social safety nets. Mandated currency devaluations resulted in spiraling inflation and shortages of imported goods. Stipulated privatization programs resulted in widespread layoffs, rising unemployment, and an upsurge in crony capitalism. These measures had devastating effects on the most vulnerable members of society. Moreover, because the structural adjustment programs were imposed from above – and thus were inherently undemocratic – the balance of power was tipped in favor of governments with the coercive means to impose unpopular measures. Foreign intervention in African economies not only resulted in increased economic hardship for many but also stimulated the installation of politically repressive regimes.

The wave of neoliberal economic interventions that began in the late 1970s, like their neocolonial antecedents, constituted a fundamental denial of African sovereignty. More than a decade earlier, Nkrumah had described neocolonialism as "the worst form of imperialism. For those who practice it, it means power without responsibility and for those who suffer from it, it means exploitation without redress." He had warned that "a State in the grip of neo-colonialism is not master of its own destiny."[5] Such characterizations were equally true of the neoliberal policies imposed by Western-dominated international financial institutions, governments, and agencies in a later period and the African states that implemented them.

Massive foreign debts incurred by African governments in the 1970s and 1980s continued to take their toll in the early decades of the twenty-first century. In many cases, the borrowed money was consumed by corrupt leaders, spent on extravagant showcase projects or on military rather than economic development. Nonetheless, successor governments were forced to service the debts with scarce foreign currency, exhausting export earnings, foreign aid, and new foreign loans. Debt servicing to foreign governments, banks, and international financial institutions continued to consume a large portion of African government revenues, which could not be allocated to essential services, let alone economic development. Although foreign intervention into African economies is not a central focus of this book, it is the critical backdrop to the crises of the 1980s and 1990s, which

---

[5] Nkrumah, *Neo-Colonialism*, x, xi

stimulated a new wave of external political and military intervention on the continent.

The late 1980s and early 1990s witnessed the economic and political collapse of the Soviet Union and the end of the Cold War. African dictators, no longer useful to their former patrons, were cut adrift. African nations were left with a legacy of looted resources, massive debt, collapsed states, and multiple regional wars over the spoils. This devastating situation was not solely the result of the Cold War. Distinctions in power and privilege and conflicts over natural resources predated the colonial period. The plundering of African riches through unequal exchange was rooted in colonial economic practices, and ethnic and regional hierarchies established during the colonial period often endured. Internal corruption, mismanagement, and the privileging of some groups over others had resulted in volatile societies characterized by vast disparities in wealth and power. However, the influx of weapons and money during the Cold War entrenched power differentials and rendered local conflicts far more lethal. When the Cold War ended, unstable countries were flooded with leftover weapons that fueled new competition for riches and power. Years of war and repression had destroyed organized political opposition in many countries. Thus, as popular forces ousted Cold War dictators no longer bolstered by outside aid, warlords and other opportunists frequently moved into the power vacuum. Having "won" the Cold War, the United States felt no compelling reason to intervene, and the Soviet Union was no more. A number of wealthy nations turned their backs on Africa in the 1990s. Despite the HIV/AIDS pandemic, widespread poverty, and regional wars, French, German, and American aid declined precipitously, and African peoples were expected to pay off massive debts incurred by Cold War dictators.

Although bilateral intervention by countries outside Africa decreased in the 1990s, multilateral intervention assumed new forms. A number of post–Cold War crises stimulated appeals for foreign intervention – from actors within Africa and supporters in the international community. As a result, UN, African Union, and regional bodies intervened to broker, monitor, and enforce peace accords and to facilitate humanitarian relief operations. These types of intervention were viewed as positive by many African constituencies, although the unequal power differentials meant that African agents frequently could not control international forces once they established themselves on African soil. In some cases, the international community was criticized for not acting quickly or forcefully enough – as in the case of the Rwandan genocide in 1994; the Liberian civil war, which ended in 2003; and the Darfur conflict in Sudan that began in 2003. Condemned for its failure to thwart the Rwandan genocide and under pressure to act more resolutely in Darfur, the UN General Assembly endorsed a document in 2005 that held countries responsible for protecting their citizens from "genocide, war crimes, ethnic cleansing and crimes against humanity" and granted the international community the right to intervene if governments failed to fulfill their "responsibility to protect" (R2P).[6] Supported by 150 countries, the endorsement resolution upended a fundamental precept of international law since the seventeenth century – the principle of state sovereignty – which was enshrined in the UN Charter. Henceforth, respect for "state sovereignty" could no longer be used as an excuse to allow mass killings to proceed unhindered.

Since the dawn of the twenty-first century, foreign intervention in Africa has again assumed new characteristics. The global war on terror and the struggle to secure the flow of oil and other strategic resources have put Africa back on the map. Increased foreign military presence, outside support for repressive governments, and unsavory alliances purportedly established to eradicate terror have brought another round of foreign intervention to the continent. Africa, its people, and its resources have again become the object of internal and external struggles in a pattern that stretches from precolonial conquests and slave trades through the current quest for resources and the war on terror. Once again, local concerns have generally been subordinated to foreign interests. Humanitarian interventions, though well intentioned, have often been ineffective or counterproductive, whereas military interventions, even under the auspices of R2P, have frequently led to regime change with uncertain consequences.

Organization of the Book

The book is organized into eight chapters. The first seven chapters investigate nationalism and decolonization during the Cold War

---

[6] UN General Assembly, "2005 World Summit Outcome," paragraphs 138–139, adopted September 15, 2005, http://www.who.int/hiv/universalaccess2010/worldsummit.pdf.

(1945–91). Chapters 2–7 each focus on a particular geographic region or on multiple regions colonized by a single European power. These chapters examine the ways in which African actors sought outside assistance to bolster their positions in internal struggles and how their external allies introduced geopolitical considerations into local and regional conflicts. Some of these considerations were rooted in past colonial relationships and current bilateral and regional alliances; others were related to the Cold War. Although some local actors initially benefited from outside intervention, the increasingly militarized conflicts were decidedly detrimental to civilian populations, and their negative impact intensified over time. The final chapter considers the period following the Cold War and explores cases from several regions.

To explain why foreign powers became embroiled in these conflicts, Chapter 1 examines the ideologies, interests, and practices of the main external actors, including both former colonial and new Cold War powers. Chapters 2–6 survey major arenas of conflict that are representative of broad trends in foreign intervention during this period. Chapter 2 focuses on North Africa, including Nasser's Egypt, which served as a model of radical nationalism and nonalignment for many African countries, and Algeria, which fought a long war for independence from France. Chapter 3 examines the former Belgian Congo, the site of the first Cold War crisis in sub-Saharan Africa. Chapter 4 investigates the three Portuguese colonies on the African mainland, where decolonization came only after protracted guerrilla war involving outside players. Chapter 5 explores the white-ruled countries of Southern Africa, where indigenous actors backed by external powers engaged in armed struggle against settler regimes. Chapter 6 examines the Horn of Africa, where shifting Cold War and regional alliances and conflicts wrought widespread devastation and instability that have outlasted the Cold War. Chapter 7 takes a different approach, focusing on French intervention in Africa, as France moved aggressively to retain close military and economic ties to its former colonies, to expand its influence into other Francophone countries, and to stave off Anglo-American encroachment.

Chapter 8 explores the aftermath of decolonization and the Cold War, focusing on the periods of state collapse (1991–2001) and the global war on terror (2001–10). As dictators were abandoned by their external benefactors, countries already buffeted by economic and political crises lapsed into violent conflict. Neighboring states intervened to support proxy forces that would allow them to gain control over lucrative resources. After the September 2001 terrorist attacks in the United States, the ensuing global war on terror sparked a new wave of foreign intervention in Africa. American aid became increasingly militarized, focusing on oil- and gas-rich countries and those considered strategic to the American war on terror. A new generation of African strongmen benefited from U.S. military and economic largess, transforming the old rallying cry against "communism" into a new one against "terrorism" – a catchall term used to justify cracking down on a broad range of domestic dissent.

Suggested Reading

The "Suggested Reading" entries at the end of each chapter represent a selection of the most useful sources for readers who wish to investigate particular issues in more depth. The following list includes some of the most important overviews of various themes, historical periods, and foreign actors – and points the way to critical online resources.

Works that explore Africans' interactions with a wider world before colonial conquest include Philip Curtin, Steven Feierman, Leonard Thompson, and Jan Vansina, *African History: From Earliest Times to Independence*, 2nd ed. (New York: Longman, 1995); Bill Freund, *The African City: A History* (New York: Cambridge University Press, 2007); Michael A. Gomez, *Reversing Sail: A History of the African Diaspora* (New York: Cambridge University Press, 2005); and David Robinson, *Muslim Societies in African History* (New York: Cambridge University Press, 2004).

For the periods of decolonization and the Cold War, a number of older but still relevant studies are recommended. Prosser Gifford and Wm. Roger Louis's *The Transfer of Power in Africa: Decolonization, 1940–1960* (New Haven, CT: Yale University Press, 1982) and *Decolonization and African Independence: The Transfers of Power, 1960–1980* (New Haven, CT: Yale University Press, 1988) contain a wealth of articles and bibliographic references on specific colonial powers and regions. For readable overviews covering the entire continent, see Basil Davidson, *Let Freedom Come: Africa in Modern History* (Boston: Little, Brown, 1978) and John D. Hargreaves, *Decolonization in Africa*, 2nd ed. (New York: Longman, 1996). For the Southern African region, see William Minter, *King Solomon's Mines Revisited: Western Interests and the Burdened History of Southern Africa* (New York: Basic Books, 1986).

For a comprehensive study of the Cold War – albeit with relatively little focus on Africa – see Melvyn P. Leffler and Odd Arne Westad, eds., *The Cambridge History of the Cold War*, 3 vols. (New York: Cambridge University Press, 2010). For a brief overview of the Cold War, see David S. Painter,

The Cold War: An International History (New York: Routledge, 1999). Other works explore American and Soviet ideas about anticolonial movements and superpower interventions in Africa. See especially Zaki Laïdi, *The Superpowers and Africa: The Constraints of a Rivalry, 1960–1990* (Chicago: University of Chicago Press, 1990). For Southern Africa and the Horn, see Odd Arne Westad, *The Global Cold War: Third World Interventions and the Making of Our Times* (New York: Cambridge University Press, 2005).

For broad assessments of U.S.-Africa policy during the Cold War, see Peter J. Schraeder, *United States Foreign Policy toward Africa: Incrementalism, Crisis, and Change* (New York: Cambridge University Press, 1994) and Gerald J. Bender, James S. Coleman, and Richard L. Sklar, eds., *African Crisis Areas and U.S. Foreign Policy* (Berkeley: University of California Press, 1985). For the impact of race relations and the civil rights movement on U.S. Cold War policies, see Thomas Borstelmann, *The Cold War and the Color Line: American Race Relations in the Global Arena* (Cambridge, MA: Harvard University Press, 2001); Penny Von Eschen, *Race against Empire: Black Americans and Anti-Colonialism, 1937–1957* (Ithaca, NY: Cornell University Press, 1997); Brenda Gayle Plummer, *Rising Wind: Black Americans and U.S. Foreign Affairs, 1935–1960* (Chapel Hill: University of North Carolina Press, 1996); and Brenda Gayle Plummer, ed., *Window on Freedom: Race, Civil Rights, and Foreign Affairs, 1945–1988* (Chapel Hill: University of North Carolina Press, 2003).

Several recent books investigate Soviet involvement in Africa. Christopher Andrew and Vasili Mitrokhin's *The World Was Going Our Way: The KGB and the Battle for the Third World* (New York: Basic Books, 2005) discusses KGB clandestine operations in Africa. Vladimir G. Shubin's *The Hot "Cold War": The USSR in Southern Africa* (London: Pluto Press, 2008) provides a thorough examination of a major Soviet area of involvement, focusing on Angola, Mozambique, Rhodesia, Namibia, and South Africa. Sergey Mazov explores Soviet activities in the Congo, Guinea, Ghana, and Mali in *A Distant Front in the Cold War: The USSR in West Africa and the Congo, 1956–1964* (Washington, DC: Woodrow Wilson Center Press; Stanford, CA: Stanford University Press, 2010). Aleksandr Fursenko and Timothy Naftali examine Soviet involvement in Egypt and the Congo in *Khrushchev's Cold War: The Inside Story of an American Adversary* (New York: W. W. Norton, 2006).

For China's political and economic relations with African states and liberation movements, see Bruce D. Larkin, *China and Africa, 1949–1970: The Foreign Policy of the People's Republic of China* (Berkeley: University of California Press, 1971) and Alaba Ogunsanwo, *China's Policy in Africa, 1958–1971* (New York: Cambridge University Press, 1974). For an engrossing case study of Chinese aid and its political and economic implications, see

Jamie Monson, *Africa's Freedom Railway: How a Chinese Development Project Changed Lives and Livelihoods in Tanzania* (Bloomington: Indiana University Press, 2009).

For a superb examination of Cuba's involvement in Africa, see Piero Gleijeses's *Conflicting Missions: Havana, Washington, and Africa, 1959–1976* (Chapel Hill: University of North Carolina Press, 2002).

A number of sources focus on foreign intervention in Africa during the post–Cold War period. Ian Taylor's *The International Relations of Sub-Saharan Africa* (New York: Continuum, 2010) investigates the interactions of sub-Saharan African countries with the United States, Britain, France, China, India, the European Union, and international financial institutions. Contributing much-needed internal perspectives, Adebayo Oyebade and Abiodun Alao examine the continent's quest for security in their edited collection, *Africa after the Cold War: The Changing Perspectives on Security* (Trenton, NJ: Africa World Press, 1998), as does Adekeye Adebajo in *The Curse of Berlin: Africa after the Cold War* (London: Hurst & Co., 2010). A number of accounts offer interpretations of recent conflicts and crises. Among the most significant academic studies in this category are Morten Bøås and Kevin C. Dunn, eds., *African Guerrillas: Raging against the Machine* (Boulder, CO: Lynne Rienner, 2007); William Reno, *Warlord Politics and African States* (Boulder, CO: Lynne Rienner, 1998); and William Reno, *Warfare in Independent Africa* (New York: Cambridge University Press, 2011). Well-researched and accessible journalistic accounts include Bill Berkeley, *The Graves Are Not Yet Full: Race, Tribe and Power in the Heart of Africa* (New York: Basic Books, 2001); Howard W. French, *A Continent for the Taking: The Tragedy and Hope of Africa* (New York: Alfred A. Knopf, 2004); and Mark Huband, *The Skull beneath the Skin: Africa after the Cold War* (Boulder, CO: Westview Press, 2001).

Most investigations into international terrorism and counterterrorism and counterinsurgency strategies have paid little attention to Africa. Although lacking an African focus, a good overview of the interactions of local insurgencies, international movements, and the global war on terror is David Kilcullen's *The Accidental Guerrilla: Fighting Small Wars in the Midst of a Big One* (New York: Oxford University Press, 2009). Malinda S. Smith's edited collection, *Securing Africa: Post-9/11 Discourses on Terrorism* (Burlington, VT: Ashgate, 2010), offers a much-needed African focal point that includes diverse regional and national perspectives. The implications of the U.S. Africa Command for African and global security are analyzed in Daniel Volman and William Minter, "Making Peace or Fueling War in Africa," *Foreign Policy in Focus* (March 13, 2009; http://www.fpif.org), and Robert G. Berschinski, *AFRICOM'S Dilemma: The "Global War on Terrorism," "Capacity Building," Humanitarianism, and the Future of U.S. Security*

Policy in Africa (Carlisle, PA: Strategic Studies Institute, U.S. Army War College, November 2007; http://www.strategicstudiesinstitute.army.mil).

Online sources that have not been vetted by experts must be regarded with caution. Online sites that offer high-quality analysis and documentation include the following: *Africa Focus Bulletin* (http://www.africafocus.org) features analysis of current African issues and includes excerpts from African publications, reports by nongovernmental organizations, and so on; AllAfrica (http://www.allafrica.com) distributes news from Africa, posting more than 1,000 stories in English and French each day and offering more than 900,000 articles in its digital archive; "Southern Africa Liberation History" (http://www.noeasyvictories.org/search/smartsearch1.php) provides links to important digital archives around the world that focus on Southern African liberation struggles; the National Security Archive (http://www.nsarchive. org) provides access to declassified U.S. government documents, presidential papers, congressional records, and court testimony that focus on U.S. national security, foreign policy, intelligence, and economic issues.

CHAPTER 1

Nationalism, Decolonization, and the Cold War, 1945–1991

This chapter introduces the major external actors in Africa during the periods of decolonization and the Cold War, examines their motives for intervention, and summarizes the book's case studies. The primary foreign participants in the decolonization process were the European imperial powers: France, Britain, Portugal, and Belgium. Italy, which lost its colonies in the aftermath of World War II, played a lesser role. The key players during the Cold War were the United States, the Soviet Union, the People's Republic of China, and Cuba.

Imperial Actors

As anticolonial agitation swept across Africa in the postwar period, the major imperial powers – France, Britain, Belgium, and Portugal – were forced to respond. Their strategies and policies varied, depending largely on their political and economic circumstances. All the colonial powers faced nationalist resistance, and none agreed without internal pressure to grant independence to their colonies. Most anticolonial movements used nonviolent tactics, although some waged armed struggles for national independence. During the first postwar decade, France and Britain responded to political challenges with repression. Armed uprisings in Madagascar, Tunisia, and Cameroon were brutally suppressed by the French, as were anticolonial activities in Côte d'Ivoire and other overseas territories. Britain employed draconian methods to end the Mau Mau insurgency in Kenya and did enormous harm to the civilian population that lived in rebel-controlled areas. Under duress, both France and Britain ultimately acceded to African demands for independence, confident in their ability to transfer political power to African governments that would protect their economic and political interests.

Weaker colonial powers, in contrast, tended to protect their interests by military means. Incapable of maintaining economic dominance without political control, Portugal fought lengthy wars to resist decolonization. Fearful of losing economic clout and influence, Belgium intervened militarily in the newly independent Congo. The presence of white settlers changed the dynamics of all independence struggles and generally resulted in prolonged wars of national liberation. Such was the case in French Algeria, Portuguese Angola and Mozambique, British Rhodesia, and Afrikaner-dominated South Africa and Namibia. Decolonization conflicts opened the door to Cold War intervention by other powers. The most dramatic Cold War interventions were in territories and nation-states where colonial powers had been the weakest.

British officials recognized the power of African nationalism – and its logical consequences – long before their counterparts in other countries. Given its diminished political and economic stature in the postwar period, and increasingly aware of the high costs of repression, Britain realized that it was more advantageous to concede governing power to trusted African collaborators than to attempt to maintain political control. By the 1940s, the Colonial Office assumed that it was preparing British subjects for eventual self-rule – albeit at some indefinite time in the future. In anticipation, the government instituted programs to reshape African societies in ways that promoted the interests of Britain and the Commonwealth, intending to turn over the reins of government to carefully selected Anglophile elites. Only in Kenya, where an armed insurgency threatened the lives and property of white settlers, did Britain pit the imperial army against the African civilian population.[1] Otherwise confident in its ability to maintain influence in the Commonwealth of sovereign independent states composed of the former constituents of its empire, Britain was less worried than other

---

[1] In the case of Rhodesia, Britain opposed the declaration of independence by the white-settler regime, which refused to concede the principle of future majority rule. Because it failed to follow the British decolonization plan, London did not support the settler cause militarily (see Chapter 5).

imperial powers about its ability to fare well in a free-trade system stripped of protective tariffs. Although the new nations could conceivably choose new economic and political partners, it was highly unlikely that most would reject their imperial mentor.

The government of France, in contrast, was convinced that the maintenance of empire was critical to ensuring the country's standing among the world's great powers. France fought protracted wars against nationalist movements in Indochina and Algeria to prevent their secession. Implementing colonial reforms in the face of war and political unrest, France renovated the empire in an attempt to save it. In the 1950s, Paris conceded the principle of local self-government within the empire but never considered political independence to be a legitimate option. The 1958 French constitution, which laid the foundations for the Fifth Republic, dissolved the great federations of French West and Equatorial Africa in order to divide the transterritorial nationalist movements. Demands for independence remained strong, however, and in 1960, France was forced to yield political independence to most of its African territories. Concerned that it would lose power and influence in the free flow of the market, France negotiated political, economic, and military agreements that guaranteed a strong French presence in the newly independent states.

Belgium and Portugal were even less willing than France to grant political independence to their colonies. They had provided only rudimentary levels of social and economic development in the colonies, and the vast majority of their subjects had little, if any, formal education. As a result, when independence came, the African populations were ill prepared for self-rule. It was not until 1959, when popular unrest forced its hand, that Brussels seriously considered independence for the Congo. In January 1960, the government scheduled Congo's independence for June 30 – with fewer than six months to prepare. Like France, Belgium was determined to maintain control of the political and economic processes before and after independence, guaranteeing its continued access to the Congo's enormous mineral resources. In the months before June 30, Brussels transferred the lucrative holdings of colonial state-run companies to private Belgian concerns. After independence, Belgian administrators remained to protect their country's economic interests, and 1,000 Belgian army officers took charge of the Congolese army. Like Belgium, Portugal had no intention of relinquishing control of its lucrative colonies. An impoverished, partially industrialized country, Portugal could not withstand the competition of the world market. It was determined to maintain political control of its African colonies in order to ensure access to cheap raw materials and markets for its manufactured goods. As a result, it fought long, costly wars against liberation movements in Angola, Mozambique, and Portuguese Guinea, which led to the toppling of Lisbon's authoritarian regime in 1974.

Unlike the other imperial powers, Italy was forced to relinquish its empire as a result of its defeat in World War II. The Italian East African empire, comprising Eritrea, Italian Somaliland, and Ethiopia – which Italy occupied between 1936 and 1941 – was conquered by Britain in 1941. Libya fell to Britain and its colonial and Commonwealth forces in 1943. After the war, the Allies forced Italy to renounce all its colonial claims. France, Britain, the United States, and the Soviet Union – and from 1949, the UN – determined the fate of the Italian colonies. France and Britain took a special interest as the dominant imperial powers in North Africa and the Middle East, while the United States and the Soviet Union positioned themselves for their insipient Cold War competition. Although Moscow lobbied to control a portion of Libya as a UN trust, London and Washington feared the establishment of a Soviet naval base on the Mediterranean, and American Secretary of State James F. Byrnes worried that a Soviet presence in Libya would threaten Western control of the distant Belgian Congo, which had provided the uranium for the first atom bomb. Dominated by the Western powers, the UN thwarted Soviet aims and left Libya under French and British tutelage until 1951, when growing anti-colonial sentiment forced the UN to concede Libyan independence. Ethiopia was administered by Britain from 1941 to 1952 and then returned to the feudal stewardship of Emperor Haile Selassie. The UN transferred the Italian colony of Eritrea to Ethiopia for administration, despite significant popular sentiment in Eritrea for independence. The international body was under tremendous pressure from the United States, which was determined to keep the strategic Red Sea coast under the control of a faithful Western ally. Federated to Ethiopia in 1952 as a semiautonomous unit, Eritrea was annexed outright a decade later. At the behest of France, Britain, and the United States, Italian Somaliland was placed under Italian trusteeship for ten years – despite protests from Somalis and opposition from the Soviet Union. Italian Somaliland was joined with British Somaliland in 1960 as the independent nation of Somalia. The United States again intervened to ensure that the disputed Ogaden territory was turned over to America's Ethiopian ally, despite the fact that it was inhabited primarily by ethnic Somalis.

Cold War Actors

Conflict and instability during the African decolonization process provided an opening for Cold War competition. The United States was the most powerful of the external actors whose ideology and interests shaped Africa's Cold War contests. America's interests and involvement varied across time and space, and its actions were influenced by the concerns of the former imperial powers. Many in Washington preferred that European countries take the lead in their former colonies. Hence, the United States followed Belgium in its determination of a Congo policy and took its cue from Britain on Rhodesia. France remained a formidable force in Francophone Africa and resisted American intrusion in its sphere of influence. Thus, U.S. actions were constrained not only by America's Cold War rivals but also by its allies.

From the end of World War II until the collapse of communism in the early 1990s, the promotion of free market capitalism and opposition to communism were dominant features of American foreign policy. As European nations lost their empires after the war, the United States hoped to gain access to the raw materials and markets previously controlled by the colonial powers. Washington also saw a chance to promote American political and economic ideologies in the newly established nations. Although Europe, Asia, and Latin America were more central to American policy concerns, Africa received considerable attention from successive presidential administrations. High-level officials in the Eisenhower administration, which took office as African nationalist movements gained momentum, viewed nationalism with suspicion, considering anticolonial movements to be the product of external communist subversion. Although in general the United States expected Britain, France, and Belgium to take the lead in ensuring stability and pro-Western governments in their traditional spheres of influence, it broke ranks when – as in the 1956 Suez Crisis – the former imperial powers, by discounting the power and legitimacy of nationalist aspirations, threatened to bring about a major Cold War conflagration. Inside the Kennedy, Johnson, and Carter administrations, minority voices in the State Department stressed the importance of responding to nationalist concerns and befriending the governments of the future. They advocated forging an anticommunist coalition under American leadership that would press for gradual social and political change. However, even these officials opposed political movements that the United States could not control. The maintenance of good relations with European allies and the containment of radicalism remained paramount. In the end, even liberal Democratic administrations backed away from any actions that might threaten these fundamental objectives. The Nixon, Ford, and Reagan administrations were less nuanced in their understanding. Republican administrations were less likely than their Democratic counterparts to court African alternatives. In general, they viewed Africa through the prism of white-minority rights and the Cold War and considered radical nationalist movements to be Soviet proxies.

Despite their differences, Democratic and Republican presidential administrations pursued many common objectives in Africa. All of them sought relations with pro-Western governments that were friendly to American business and foreign policy interests. Because poverty and instability provided fertile ground for communist ideas, successive American administrations strove to thwart communism through economic development. Political stability and governments that favored American economic models were considered prerequisites for success. From the mid-1950s until the end of the Cold War, the United States engaged in a massive transfer of foreign aid to developing countries. It offered assistance to leaders who adopted free-enterprise models, opened their countries to American investment and trade, and agreed to the export of profits on generous terms. In addition, the United States provided military and security assistance to its protégés – to protect them from both domestic insurgencies and international communism.

Although useful for the purposes of analysis, generalizations about Democratic and Republican policies must be employed with caution, as they fail to highlight divisions within the government at any given time. Policy options are contested and debated within and between governmental branches. The final determinations are the product of struggle, representing the victory of one set of concerns over others. Democrats and Republicans in Congress may be at odds, and the legislative branch may be pitted against the executive. Within the executive branch, the National Security Council; Central Intelligence Agency (CIA); and Departments of Defense, Commerce, Treasury, and State may challenge one another. Within the State Department, the Bureau of African Affairs is often more sympathetic to African perspectives than offices operating under different mandates.

Because the balance of forces changes over time and according to circumstances, the United States has pursued contradictory Africa policies. On the one hand, as an early proponent of decolonization, which would open the door to American influence, the U.S. government rhetorically championed freedom, democracy, and self-determination. On the other hand, factions in the government have sympathized with the concerns of white settlers, and at times, their voices were dominant. Pervasive anticommunism in some quarters often led to a misunderstanding of nationalist movements. Radical nationalism was frequently confused with communism – or viewed as an equal threat to Western interests. Fear of communism – real or imagined – led the U.S. government to support many unsavory dictatorships. Although the dictatorships were pro-Western and anticommunist, they did not promote the freedom and democracy that Washington claimed to endorse. In the case of Southern Africa, a region valued for its strategic location and minerals and home to a significant population of white settlers, conflicting American interests led the United States to reinforce, rather than oppose, colonialism and white-minority rule.

The U.S. government's support for European and settler agendas was a contentious issue during the Cold War, as the status quo was challenged by opponents both inside and outside the government. Policy-makers in Washington, who generally hailed from elite, all-white-male backgrounds, often felt more comfortable with European allies and representatives of white-minority regimes than with African nationalists. They shared a common view that sovereignty within a country's borders precluded the interference of international bodies in determining how governments should treat the people residing within them. They were usually supportive of the notion that European colonial powers would pass the torch of their "civilizing mission" to the United States, which would assume the "white man's burden" – fostering Western civilization and economic development – and, in a natural progression, take the lead in fighting communism. During the Truman and Eisenhower administrations, prominent American officials had no qualms about expressing their beliefs in white superiority and racial segregation. Prosegregation advocates dominated the foreign policy establishment and the most powerful congressional committees. However, during the Kennedy and Johnson administrations, African

Americans, who constituted about 11 percent of the U.S. population in 1965, increasingly linked the struggle for civil rights at home to black liberation and national independence abroad. Many were vocal proponents of African decolonization. Simultaneously, a growing number of liberals in the foreign policy establishment argued that racial discrimination at home and support for white-minority and colonial regimes abroad eroded America's moral high ground. How could the United States expect to win friends among newly independent African nations when black Americans were treated like second-class citizens? How could it avoid charges of hypocrisy in its claim that it represented a more humane and democratic society than those of communist states? New power dynamics emerged in the 1970s and 1980s, as the growing number of black elected officials established the Congressional Black Caucus and explicitly linked African and African American struggles for equality and justice. These efforts, which culminated in the African American–led Free South Africa Movement of the mid-1980s and the passage of the Comprehensive Anti-Apartheid Act in 1986, were part of a broad and diverse anti-apartheid movement that engaged millions of Americans.

After the United States, the Soviet Union was the second most important Cold War actor in Africa. Washington and Moscow had very different concerns after World War II. While the American economy had been bolstered by the war, the Soviet Union had lost twenty million people and almost half its economic capacity. Far from being bent on world conquest, the Soviet Union was primarily concerned with securing its perimeters and surrounding itself with compliant regimes that would forestall future invasions. However, the country also took an interest in Third World decolonization, which offered the possibility of new alliances in the struggle against Western imperialism. Arguing that the "backwardness" of emerging nations was the result of capitalist exploitation, Moscow deemed the removal of colonial capitalism necessary for Third World advancement, and the triumph of national liberation over imperialism a precondition for the victory of socialism over capitalism. In keeping with this view, Nikita Khrushchev, who held power from 1953 to 1964 first as Communist Party leader and then as premier, initiated diplomatic and economic relationships with anticolonial and anti-imperialist regimes in Africa, Asia, and Latin America. Khrushchev's goal was not to establish communist states but simply to increase Soviet influence in the new nations and to diminish that of the West. The Soviet Union's involvement in Africa generally occurred in response to the interference of former colonial powers or the intensified activities of the United States or China. When Western powers spurned or undermined African governments with pronounced anti-imperialist rhetoric or programs, the Soviet Union offered economic and military aid. Such was the case in Egypt (North Africa); the Congo (Central Africa); Guinea, Ghana, and Mali (West Africa); and Somalia (Horn of Africa). None of these regimes was communist. In the Horn, Moscow was motivated as much by strategic as by ideological concerns when it came to the aid of Marxist Ethiopia, which was threatened by socialist Somalia.

In the early 1970s, under Communist Party leader Leonid Brezhnev and Premier Alexei Kosygin, Soviet policy entered a new phase. In Southern and West Africa, the Soviet Union began to provide substantial amounts of military aid to Marxist liberation movements fighting intransigent colonial powers such as Portugal (in the case of Angola, Mozambique, and Portuguese Guinea) and white-settler regimes (in the case of Rhodesia, South Africa, and South African–occupied Namibia). In the strategically located Horn of Africa, the United States had long sustained Ethiopian Emperor Haile Selassie's imperial regime, while the Soviet Union supported the socialist-military regime of Mohamed Siad Barre in Somalia. However, after a military coup toppled the emperor and established a Marxist government in Ethiopia, Moscow and Washington swapped partners. Although the Soviet Union established commercial agreements with most African countries and helped build hundreds of industrial and other facilities, it was in the realm of military assistance to radical regimes and national liberation movements that the Soviet contribution was most decisive.

In their competition for Third World allies, the United States and the Soviet Union offered two very different development models. Promoting the free-enterprise capitalist system, the American model depended on the slow accumulation of capital through profits generated by the market. The Soviet model, in contrast, was premised on centralized economic planning. It focused on the collectivization of agriculture, the development of heavy industry, and the advancement of large infrastructure projects. In the eyes of many Third World leaders, development according to the American model would take far too long. The Soviet Union provided an attractive alternative. It had moved rapidly from an agrarian to an industrial society. Its strong state and centralized economic plan had enabled it to engage in a massive redistribution of wealth. All of this was extremely appealing to many Third World nationalists.

Besides its seductive economic example, the Soviet Union had another advantage. Because the Soviet Union did not have extra-continental colonial possessions, African countries did not associate it with exploitative European colonialism. Conversely, the United States, closely aligned with Western European nations, was linked to the powers that had dominated both Africa and Asia. America's continuation of French colonial wars in Indochina and its own history in Latin America provided little reassurance. Thus, many in Africa associated the United States with the poverty and oppression they experienced under the colonial capitalist system, whereas the Soviet Union evoked no such connotations.

The third Cold War actor in Africa was the People's Republic of China. Like the Soviet Union, China saw the African continent as an arena in which to challenge imperialism. However, during most of the Cold War, China and the Soviet Union supported rivals in the struggle for power. Despite Soviet support for the Chinese Communist Party during China's 1945–49 civil war, and the friendship treaty that provided Beijing with critical Soviet technology and economic assistance, the two countries struggled over both ideology and policy and competed for allegiances in the Third World. Between 1959 and 1965, the alliance broke apart as the Soviets criticized Mao Zedong's leadership and policies while Mao decried Khrushchev's goal of "peaceful coexistence" with the West as counterrevolutionary and challenged Soviet political and economic models. In 1959, Khrushchev abrogated an agreement to provide China with modern military technology. In 1960, he recalled more than 1,000 Soviet scientists and industrial specialists from China, while Beijing declared its independence from Soviet international and domestic policies and sought new allies among emerging Third World nations. By 1965, the Soviet Union openly considered Chinese activities in Africa and Asia to be a threat to its interests, and China publicly declared its independence in both domestic and international affairs. The Sino-Soviet split was complete, and the scramble for allies began.

Chinese interest in Africa emerged publicly at the Conference of Asian and African States in Bandung, Indonesia, a decade before the Sino-Soviet split. At the April 1955 conference, representatives of twenty-nine Asian and African nations and territories, as well as those of numerous liberation movements, agreed to oppose all forms of colonialism and imperialism and to promote economic and cultural cooperation. The participants voiced particular support for decolonization

and national liberation in Africa. China played an important role in
the conference and moved to strengthen ties to other developing countries – in what was dubbed the "Third World." Its early focus on Africa
was in the Bandung spirit of African-Asian solidarity and cooperation.
From the early 1960s until the mid-1970s, China sent tens of thousands of "barefoot doctors," agricultural technicians, and solidarity
work brigades to African countries that had declared their opposition
to imperialism and neocolonialism. It offered grants and low-interest
loans for development projects in Egypt, Algeria, Ghana, Guinea,
Mali, Tanzania, and Zambia. Beijing also provided military training,
advisors, and weapons for African liberation movements. Maoist ideas
were prominent in Zimbabwe African National Union (ZANU) doc-
trines during the struggle against white-minority rule in Rhodesia.
Mozambique's Front for the Liberation of Mozambique (FRELIMO)
benefited from Chinese military training and employed Maoist guerrilla strategies to attain independence from Portugal. (FRELIMO
also welcomed Soviet aid, embraced Soviet development models, and
remained strictly neutral in the Sino-Soviet conflict.)

Although Soviet aid to African liberation movements and nations
was more substantial, Chinese ideology often had greater allure. Soviet
ideology, following the orthodox Marxist position, posited that the
level of development of the productive forces determined whether a
society was feudal, capitalist, socialist, or communist. A higher social
form could not be attained if a society's productive forces were not
sufficiently developed. Mao, in contrast, argued that human ideas,
will, and actions were the most important factors in historical change.
He believed that societies could skip quickly through stages of material
development if the people's consciousness was suitably evolved. China
and the Soviet Union also differed in their views of the revolutionary
capacity of the peasantry. Whereas the Soviet Union adhered to the
Marxist-Leninist perspective that had little regard for the rural populace and claimed that the urban proletariat would spearhead the socialist revolution, Mao argued that the rural peasantry, with its innate
wisdom and natural revolutionary consciousness, would lead a country to socialism. This notion dovetailed with Mao's claim that a high
level of industrialization was not necessary for the march to socialism.
All that was required was a revolutionary peasantry. Maoism, with
its emphasis on rapid industrialization and the revolutionary capacity
of the peasantry, had significant appeal in emerging African nations,
where populations were predominantly rural and colonial powers had
done little to develop the productive forces.

Rivalry with China, as well as the United States, became an important stimulus for Soviet involvement in Africa. During the anticolonial struggles of the 1960s–1980s, the Soviet Union and China generally supported competing movements. After the Nixon administration's rapprochement with China in 1972, the United States and China often assisted the same faction, finding common cause in their mutual opposition to the Soviet Union. The Soviet Union aided the struggle of the Zimbabwe African People's Union (ZAPU) against white-minority rule in Rhodesia, while China assisted ZANU's breakaway movement. In Angola, the Soviet Union supported the Popular Movement for the Liberation of Angola (MPLA), while China and the United States supported the National Front for the Liberation of Angola (FNLA) and the National Union for the Total Independence of Angola (UNITA).

Cuba was the fourth Cold War actor in Africa. Although considered a Soviet surrogate by the United States, Cuba followed an independent foreign policy in Africa, often straining its relationship with the Soviet Union. Fidel Castro and his associates believed that Cuba could serve as an example to oppressed peoples in Latin America and Africa. The tiny Caribbean island had thrown off an exploitative dictatorship and stood up to the United States in the process. In January 1966, Cuba hosted the Tricontinental Conference, at which the Organization of Solidarity with the Peoples of Asia, Africa, and Latin America was founded with the pledge to support national liberation and economic development on the three continents. Cuba's subsequent involvement in Africa was very much in keeping with the revolutionary vision articulated at the Tricontinental Conference.

Although Cuba's African focus stemmed from the belief, shared by all the Cold War powers, that decolonization provided a new arena for the struggle between socialism and capitalism, this was not the whole story. Like African Americans in the United States, Cuba also had an emotional link to Africa. Approximately one-third of all Cubans could boast some African blood. Many were inspired by the desire to liberate their African brothers and sisters from colonialism and imperialism and to share the fruits of the Cuban Revolution with them. In consequence, tens of thousands of Cuban health, education, and construction workers, and tens of thousands of Cuban soldiers, served in more than a dozen African countries during the periods of decolonization and the Cold War – all expenses paid by the Cuban government. Africans were generally impressed by Cuba's willingness to donate military, medical, and educational assistance without expectation of future reward.

The Case Studies

The six Cold War and decolonization case studies featured in this book include countries from each of Africa's five geographic regions. They represent territories formerly controlled by the four major imperial powers and demonstrate a range of motivations for foreign intervention. Chapter 2, which focuses on Egypt and Algeria from 1952 to 1973, examines decolonization in North Africa, where the British and French imperial powers were the key external actors. Instability in this strategic region, which Britain and France could no longer control, stimulated the involvement of the American and Soviet Cold War powers, while Israel's involvement in the 1956 Suez War was sparked by regional political concerns.

Chapter 3 examines decolonization in the Central African nation of the Congo from 1960 to 1965. As the former colonial power with significant economic interests in this strategically located, resource-rich country, Belgium was the primary external actor. Although Brussels intervened shortly after Congolese independence, primarily to protect Belgian mining interests, Belgian settlers, and their property, the situation was far beyond Belgium's capacity to control. Threatened by the radical nationalism of the new government, which Washington viewed as pro-Soviet, the United States was quickly drawn into the imbroglio, which in turn galvanized the Soviet Union and Cuba. The UN, at that time dominated by American foreign policy interests, was also an important actor.

Chapters 4 and 5 examine decolonization and the Cold War in Southern Africa, where the presence of white settlers and/or a weak colonial power prolonged the decolonization process, led to greater postcolonial conflict, and opened the door to intervention from external Cold War powers. The fourth chapter, covering the period 1961–75, focuses on the Portuguese colonies of Angola and Mozambique (as well as Portuguese Guinea in West Africa), where a weak imperial power fought to maintain the political control of territories it could not dominate through neocolonial economic mechanisms. The presence of Portuguese settlers in both Angola and Mozambique further complicated the situation. National liberation wars implicated Portugal's NATO allies – notably, the United States – and wars of destabilization before and after independence drew in other external actors. The United States, the Soviet Union, South Africa, and Cuba took sides in the Angolan wars, while South Africa waged postcolonial wars of destabilization in both Angola and Mozambique (explored in Chapter 5).

The fifth chapter examines the white-minority regimes of Rhodesia, South Africa, and South African–occupied Namibia from 1960 to 1990. As white settlers fought to retain control of the countries they considered theirs to rule as they saw fit, they were opposed by African liberation movements that received military aid from the Soviet Union, Eastern Europe, and China – as well as humanitarian support from Nordic countries and nongovernmental organizations like the UN and the World Council of Churches. As the former colonial power, Britain framed the Western response to the rogue regime in Rhodesia. Although the United States generally followed Britain's lead on Rhodesia, its policies toward South Africa and Namibia were governed by both Cold War and domestic political concerns. Along with Britain and the United States, France and Israel provided significant support to South Africa's apartheid regime, even as they publicly criticized its racial policies.

Chapter 6 focuses on the Horn in East Africa from 1952 to 1993. Following Somalia's independence in 1960, Britain and Italy departed, and Ethiopia stood alone as the region's last imperial power. Having conquered and ruled territory inhabited by Somalis and other ethnic groups and annexed the former Italian colony of Eritrea, Ethiopia was challenged by internal rebellions, an independence war, and armed conflict with neighboring Somalia. Regional strife took on a Cold War hue as the United States, the Soviet Union, and Cuba became embroiled in the conflagrations.

Chapter 7 focuses on French involvement in its colonies and former colonies, primarily in West and Central Africa, from 1947 to 1991. After independence, economic and military agreements bound the new nations to the former imperial power. This chapter stands apart from the others in that it examines the aftermath of decolonization with relatively little reference to the Cold War. In fact, France's involvement in the affairs of its onetime protégés was unique. No other imperial power remained as deeply entrenched in the postindependence politics of its ex-colonies or engaged with such frequency in military interventions to prop up or overthrow African governments. Only Cuba, a major Cold War player, had more troops on the continent during the postwar periods of decolonization and the Cold War.

These case studies represent only a fraction of the many instances of foreign intervention in Africa during the years 1945–91. Rather than offering a comprehensive overview, they provide evidence of patterns that transcended time and space. Although they constitute some of the most significant cases with the broadest ramifications, they are by no means the only ones of consequence. Space constraints preclude a more thorough examination of other critical cases, such as Britain's military intervention in Tanganyika, Kenya, and Uganda in January 1964, following mutinies in all three national armies and a popular revolt on the neighboring island of Zanzibar; the role of foreign governments and private interests in the Nigerian Civil War of 1967–70, which prolonged the war and contributed to the deaths of some two million civilians; and the role played by Israel in the 1971 military coup that brought Idi Amin to power in Uganda and the support given by Israel and Britain to his brutal eight-year dictatorship.

Suggested Reading

A number of readings referenced in the introduction are also included here.

For the periods of decolonization and the Cold War, a number of older but still relevant studies are recommended. Prosser Gifford and Wm. Roger Louis's *The Transfer of Power in Africa: Decolonization, 1940–1960* (New Haven, CT: Yale University Press, 1982) and *Decolonization and African Independence: The Transfers of Power, 1960–1980* (New Haven, CT: Yale University Press, 1988) contain a wealth of articles and bibliographic references on specific colonial powers and regions. For readable overviews covering the entire continent, see Basil Davidson, *Let Freedom Come: Africa in Modern History* (Boston: Little, Brown, 1978) and John D. Hargreaves, *Decolonization in Africa*, 2nd ed. (New York: Longman, 1996). For the Southern African region, see William Minter, *King Solomon's Mines Revisited: Western Interests and the Burdened History of Southern Africa* (New York: Basic Books, 1986). For books that focus on particular imperial powers, see Ronald Hyam, *Britain's Declining Empire: The Road to Decolonisation, 1918–1968* (New York: Cambridge University Press, 2006); Caroline Elkins, *Imperial Reckoning: The Untold Story of Britain's Gulag in Kenya* (New York: Henry Holt and Co., 2005); Tony Chafer, *The End of Empire in French West Africa: France's Successful Decolonization?* (New York: Berg, 2002); and M. D. D. Newitt, *Portugal in Africa: The Last Hundred Years* (London: Longman, 1981). For Israel's involvement in Africa, see Zach Levey, *Israel in Africa, 1956–1976* (Dordrecht, the Netherlands: Republic of Letters, 2012) and Sasha Polakow-Suransky, *The Unspoken Alliance: Israel's Secret Relationship with Apartheid South Africa* (New York: Pantheon, 2010).

For superpower attitudes toward African anticolonial movements and intervention in Africa, see Zaki Laïdi, *The Superpowers and Africa: The Constraints of a Rivalry, 1960–1990* (Chicago: University of Chicago Press, 1990) and Odd Arne Westad, *The Global Cold War: Third World Interventions and the Making of Our Times* (New York: Cambridge University Press, 2005).

For broad assessments of U.S.-Africa policy during the Cold War, see Peter J. Schraeder, *United States Foreign Policy toward Africa: Incrementalism, Crisis, and Change* (New York: Cambridge University Press, 1994) and Gerald J. Bender, James S. Coleman, and Richard L. Sklar, eds., *African Crisis Areas and U.S. Foreign Policy* (Berkeley: University of California Press, 1985).

Several recent books investigate Soviet involvement in Africa. Christopher Andrew and Vasili Mitrokhin's *The World Was Going Our Way: The KGB and the Battle for the Third World* (New York: Basic Books, 2005) discusses KGB clandestine operations in Africa. Vladimir G. Shubin's *The Hot "Cold War": The USSR in Southern Africa* (London: Pluto Press, 2008) provides a thorough examination of a major Soviet proving ground, focusing on Angola, Mozambique, Rhodesia, Namibia, and South Africa. Sergey Mazov explores Soviet activities in the Congo, Guinea, Ghana, and Mali in *A Distant Front in the Cold War: The USSR in West Africa and the Congo, 1956–1964* (Washington, DC: Woodrow Wilson Center Press; Stanford, CA: Stanford University Press, 2010). Aleksandr Fursenko and Timothy Naftali examine Soviet involvement in Egypt and the Congo in *Khrushchev's Cold War: The Inside Story of an American Adversary* (New York: W. W. Norton, 2006).

For China's political and economic relations with African states and liberation movements, and see Bruce D. Larkin, *China and Africa, 1949–1970: The Foreign Policy of the People's Republic of China* (Berkeley: University of California Press, 1971) and Alaba Ogunsanwo, *China's Policy in Africa, 1958–1971* (New York: Cambridge University Press, 1974). For an engrossing case study of Chinese aid and its political and economic implications, see Jamie Monson, *Africa's Freedom Railway: How a Chinese Development Project Changed Lives and Livelihoods in Tanzania* (Bloomington: Indiana University Press, 2009).

For a superb scholarly examination of Cuba's involvement in Africa, see Piero Gleijeses's *Conflicting Missions: Havana, Washington, and Africa, 1959–1976* (Chapel Hill: University of North Carolina Press, 2002) and his more popularly written *The Cuban Drumbeat: Castro's Worldview: Cuban Foreign Policy in a Hostile World* (New York: Seagull Books, 2009).

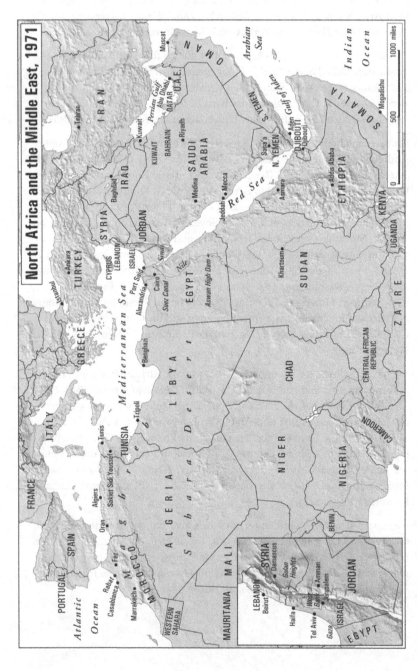

MAP 2.1. North Africa and the Middle East, 1971. (Map by Philip Schwartzberg, Meridian Mapping, Minneapolis.)

CHAPTER 2

Egypt and Algeria

Radical Nationalism, Nonalignment, and External Intervention in North Africa, 1952–1973

American pressure on the old imperial powers began during World War II. In exchange for wartime assistance, the United States sought access to European colonies for raw materials, markets, and military bases. After the war, the United States continued to wave the banner of free trade as it strove to replace France and Britain as the dominant power in Africa and the Middle East. Yet in the Cold War context, Washington was also concerned about maintaining the strength and good will of its NATO allies while pressing for imperial reforms that would thwart the spread of radical nationalism and international communism. In Egypt and the Middle East, radical nationalists challenged the repressive royalist regimes that had remained in power largely as a result of British and American support. In Francophone North Africa, Algerian nationalists waged a war for independence that threatened to disseminate the radical message throughout the region. Although the Soviet Union was anxious to gain a foothold in these Western strongholds, it was not willing to risk war with the United States to do so. It courted radical movements and regimes but also attempted to rein them in, wary of being drawn into conflicts that were not of its own making.

This chapter focuses on foreign intervention in Egypt and Algeria during the period 1952–73, when these countries were central to the political dynamics of North Africa and the Middle East. Events in Egypt and Algeria did not occur in isolation; they were intimately connected to circumstances elsewhere in the region, which was experiencing an upsurge in radical nationalism and regime change.

Both countries figured prominently in the 1955 Conference of Asian and African States in Bandung, Indonesia. Refusing to take sides in the Cold War, participants in the Bandung Conference focused their attention on the Southern Hemisphere. They voiced their opposition to all forms of racialism, colonialism, and imperialism, and they pledged support for emancipatory movements throughout the developing world. Egypt played a leading role in the conference, which specifically endorsed the Algerian independence struggle. In the years that followed, Bandung participants formed the core of the intergovernmental Non-Aligned Movement and the nongovernmental Afro-Asian Peoples' Solidarity Organization, which was headquartered in Cairo. With the addition of Latin American membership in 1966, the latter became the Organization of Solidarity with the Peoples of Asia, Africa, and Latin America.

Once again, external response was inspired by both colonial and Cold War concerns. Of the contested territories undergoing decolonization after World War II, those in North Africa and the Middle East were closest geographically to Europe and the Soviet Union. They were strategic both because of their location and because of their wealth in oil. Britain and the United States had considerable investments in Middle Eastern oil that predated the war, and rich new deposits were discovered in Algeria and Libya in the 1950s. North Africa and the Middle East also figured in Cold War calculations, as the United States and the Soviet Union strove to gain preferential access to a strategic region in the throes of nationalist upheaval.

Egypt, 1952–73

Although Middle Eastern militancy in the 1950s is often associated with Egypt's pan-Arabism, radical nationalism first emerged in Iran. In 1951, the democratically elected Iranian prime minister Mohammad Mossadegh nationalized the Anglo-Iranian Oil Company (now BP), terminating Britain's control over Iran's enormous oil wealth. Iran then appealed to the United States for technical assistance so it could free itself of British dependence. Unwilling to jeopardize its relations with Britain and convinced that Iranian nationalists were a front for the Soviet Union, the United States instead terminated military assistance, drastically reduced economic aid, and supported Britain's boycott of Iranian oil. As the Iranian economy collapsed, the

American CIA and the British Secret Intelligence Service promoted political unrest and encouraged Iranian army officers to overthrow the Mossadegh government. Claiming a communist threat to Western oil supplies, the CIA, supported by British intelligence, organized and financed the 1953 coup d'état. While Britain responded as an imperial power whose assets were threatened, the United States reacted as a Cold War power determined to thwart a communist menace to a commodity that was critical to the West.

As nationalist sentiment surged in Iran, and with it, the desire of the Iranian people to control their own territory and resources, similar sentiments were emerging in Egypt, a country that transcended the boundaries between Africa and the Middle East. In the early 1950s, a broad-based popular movement, including leftist, radical nationalist, and Islamic groups, demanded the withdrawal of 85,000 British troops from the Suez Canal Zone and the transfer of the canal to Egyptian control. In July 1952, middle-ranking military officers, led by Lieutenant Colonel Gamal Abdel Nasser, overthrew the corrupt monarchy of King Farouk. In the months following the coup, Nasser, a militant nationalist, asked the United States for help in pressuring Britain to leave the canal zone. Although Washington had presented itself as an alternative to old-style colonialism, it stalled. Distrustful of Nasser and his radical agenda, the Eisenhower administration was unwilling to jeopardize its relations with Britain to favor such an unpredictable maverick. Washington refused to provide Egypt with military assistance – even after Israel, using French equipment, attacked Egyptian military bases in the Gaza Strip in February 1955.

Meanwhile, the United States and Britain collaborated in the establishment of a series of regional military alliances that protected Western strategic and economic interests and contained Soviet influence. In February 1955, the Baghdad Pact was established by nations along the Soviet Union's southwestern border.[1] The Eisenhower administration had initially wished to include Egypt in the pact, both in the hope of taming it and because it was one of the most influential countries in the Middle East. However, London protested and insisted that Iraq be invited to join instead. Led by the conservative regime of

---

[1] The Baghdad Pact's founding members included Britain, Turkey, Iraq, Iran, and Pakistan. The United States, which signed bilateral agreements with each of the member states, participated in the pact as an observer and joined its military committee in 1958.

King Faisal II, Iraq was Egypt's primary antagonist and a contender for dominance in the region. Furious at British and American meddling, Nasser considered the Baghdad Pact to be another example of Western imperialism and a serious obstacle to Arab unity. He convinced Lebanon, Syria, and Jordan to refuse to join.

In April 1955, as Egyptian-American relations continued to sour, representatives from African and Asian nations, colonies, and liberation movements met in Bandung, Indonesia, to forge a third way between East and West. Nasser emerged as a transformative figure at the conference. He helped to formulate the philosophy of neutralism and nonalignment, which was rapidly embraced by leaders across the African continent and in other parts of the developing world. Concerned that the conference had taken place without Western guidance and disturbed by the prominent role played by the People's Republic of China, the Eisenhower State Department expressed wariness of both Afro-Asian autonomy and the potential for communist influence. Failing to make clear distinctions between communism and nationalist forces that demanded political, economic, and social transformation, the State Department deemed most opposition to its allies to be communist inspired, if not communist directed. Convinced that nonalignment was merely a facade for reorientation toward the East, the United States rebuffed the countries associated with the new movement. The Soviet Union, in contrast, seized the opportunity to establish political and economic ties in regions that previously had been beyond its reach. No longer holding to the Stalinist creed that only Marxist-Leninist parties were worthy of support, the Soviet Union under Nikita Khrushchev declared that movements for political and economic independence were anti-imperialist by definition and, thus, deserving of Soviet assistance.

While Moscow actively courted Nasser and other Arab nationalists, hoping to further their common goal of undermining Western imperialism in the Middle East, Soviet officials remained ambivalent about the Egyptian leader and his potential for progressive change. Nasser was staunchly anticommunist and considered Egyptian communists to be rivals for power and influence. He worried that the presence of large numbers of Soviet technicians and military experts could undermine his authority in Egypt and the region. Even as he negotiated an arms deal with the Soviet Union in June 1955, Nasser arrested key leaders of the Egyptian Communist Party.

For Nasser, the fundamental issue was decolonization, not the Cold War. His primary objective was the eradication of British imperialism

PHOTO 2.1. Nasser is cheered by a Cairo crowd after the nationalization of the Suez Canal, August 1, 1956 (Hulton-Deutsch Collection/Corbis).

from the Middle East. Nasser had hoped to avoid reliance on the Soviet Union by obtaining assistance from the United States. Only after Washington resisted his appeals, on the grounds that aid to Egypt would antagonize its British and Israeli allies, did Nasser turn to Soviet Union. In September 1955, the Western military monopoly in the Middle East was destroyed when Egypt signed an arms agreement with Czechoslovakia, the Soviet Union's primary weapons conduit. The arms deal – which provided Egypt with artillery and eighty MiG-15 fighters – marked the beginning of a flow of military and economic aid from the Eastern Bloc to Egypt.

In November 1955, two months after the conclusion of the Czech arms deal, Nasser demonstrated his ability to play East against West. Determined to balance the influence of the superpowers, Nasser asked the United States to help finance the Aswan High Dam project, which was designed to increase the amount of arable land available for culti-vation and to provide the energy necessary for industrialization. Con-cerned that Nasser would carry out his threat to turn to the Soviet Union if the answer were no, Britain had urged the Eisenhower admin-istration to grant his request. After much internal debate, Washington agreed. However, in July 1956, after Egypt recognized the People's Republic of China in lieu of the Taiwan-based Republic of China,

Congress barred the use of American funds for the dam. In response, Nasser nationalized the Suez Canal Company, which was dominated by French and British investors, asserting that canal revenues would henceforth be used to finance the dam. "Thirty-five million Egyptian pounds has [sic] been taken from us every year by the Suez Canal Company," he declared. "We shall use that money for building the High Dam.... We don't have to seek American or British aid for building the High Dam. We will build it ourselves and with our own money."[2]

In nationalizing the Suez Canal Company, Nasser had acted without Khrushchev's knowledge – and counter to his advice. The Soviet Union had courted Nasser, hoping that a closer relationship with Egypt would serve as a gateway to greater Soviet influence in the Middle East. However, Khrushchev, like his Western counterparts, was wary of Nasser's drive for regional dominance. He was not prepared to fight a war on Nasser's behalf, thereby provoking Israel and the Western powers when he was preoccupied with political unrest in Poland and Hungary. Nasser's nationalization of the Suez Canal was just the sort of aggravation that Khrushchev did not need.

Despite their common fear of Nasser's growing influence, the Western powers were divided in their response. Britain and France responded as old-style imperial powers. Threatened by Nasser's approach to decolonization, they were determined to overthrow him. Britain worried about the vulnerability of its royal protégés and its enormous investments in the oil-rich countries of the Middle East, whereas France was concerned about Nasser's support for nationalists who were fighting an independence war in Algeria and his growing influence in other parts of Francophone Africa. Britain and France thus initiated plans for a military attack. For this task they enlisted the support of Israel, which was motivated by its own regional concerns. The United States, in contrast, saw the conflict as one rooted in the Cold War. In Washington's view, the refusal of Western powers to embark on programs of decolonization played into Soviet hands. Moreover, any threat to Egypt would strain relations with Arab countries and jeopardize American access to oil. Finally, the Eisenhower administration was not prepared to go to war in the Middle East just before the November 1956 presidential elections. Though no friend of

---

[2] Quoted in "Egypt Nationalizes Suez Canal Company; Will Use Revenues to Build Aswan Dam," *New York Times*, July 27, 1956.

PHOTO 2.2. Oil installations burn as British troops advance through Port Said after the Anglo-French invasion, November 10, 1956 (Bettman/Corbis).

Nasser, Eisenhower concluded that as long as Egypt agreed to pay for the Suez Canal Company and to permit international navigation on the canal, it had the right to nationalize the company. On this issue, the American and Soviet positions were nearly identical. The United States thus refused to join its allies in military action against Egypt, and the CIA declined an invitation by the British Secret Intelligence Service to join a plot to assassinate Nasser.

In late October, Israel used French planes and tanks to attack Egypt and occupy the Sinai Peninsula, thus instigating the Suez War. Under enormous pressure from African and Asian countries, Washington broke from its allies and introduced a UN Security Council resolution calling on Israel to withdraw from Egypt and other nations to refrain from military intervention. Moscow supported the American resolution, whereas Britain and France vetoed it and then bombed Egyptian military installations and invaded the country by air and sea. Condemned by the UN General Assembly and members of the British-dominated Commonwealth, Britain, France, and Israel were eventually forced to withdraw from Egypt. The denouement of the Suez War was a major victory for Nasser. He had successfully pitted the Cold War powers against the imperial ones, promoting Egyptian claims in the process. His prestige among Arab nations, and nonaligned countries in general, grew enormously. Among emerging nations, the Soviet Union and the United States were applauded for their anti-imperialist stance.

The United States soon squandered this goodwill through its support for repressive oligarchies across the Middle East. Patronage of unsavory governments was a by-product of the 1957 Eisenhower Doctrine, which authorized U.S. military intervention in nations "requesting such aid against overt armed aggression from any nation controlled by international communism."[3] Worried about the power vacuum left by departing colonial powers and the increased stature of the Soviet Union in the aftermath of the Suez War, the Eisenhower administration was determined to undermine radical influence and secure access to the region's oil wealth. Apart from the Soviet Union, Nasser's Egypt was perceived to be the biggest menace to American interests. Under Nasser's tutelage, Egypt had given support to indigenous movements that threatened repressive pro-Western regimes in Iraq, Lebanon, Jordan, Saudi Arabia, Yemen, and Kuwait. Nasser was also a vocal proponent of Palestinian rights and a critic of the state of Israel.

The United States invoked the Eisenhower Doctrine to invade Lebanon in 1958, with the first of more than 14,000 Marines landing on July 15. Lebanon's Christian president, Camille Chamoun, had angered the Muslim population by supporting British and French actions during the Suez War, British and American plotting against

---

3 "The Eisenhower Doctrine, 1957," http://history.state.gov/milestones/1953-1960/EisenhowerDoctrine.

the pro-Nasser government in Syria, and American military support for the unpopular royalist regime in Jordan. In the face of escalating domestic unrest during April and May 1958, Chamoun had requested U.S. military aid, claiming that Egypt and Syria (recently joined together as the United Arab Republic) were behind the uprising.[4] On the pretext that the Lebanese situation was the result of Nasser's machinations and that radical nationalism was being manipulated by international communism, Eisenhower ordered American Marines to invade Lebanon, suppress opposition to Chamoun's pro-Western regime, and pave the way for a less controversial successor.

Washington was careful to pick its battles. Although it intervened to support a strong Christian ally in Lebanon, it failed to invoke the Eisenhower Doctrine in neighboring Iraq. On July 14, as American troops were preparing to land in Lebanon, a nationalist coup by pro-Nasser military officers led by Brigadier General Abd al-Karim Qasim, toppled the pro-Western monarchy in Baghdad. Motivated in part by opposition to the Baghdad Pact and Iraq's role as the linchpin, the new regime withdrew from the controversial alliance within six months. Although Britain initially proposed a joint military action against the new government, London and Washington quickly concluded that neither Nasser nor the Soviet Union had been involved in the coup and that Western oil interests were safe for the time being. Hoping to court Qasim and to use him as a counterweight to Nasser, the Eisenhower administration rejected military intervention in 1958. When the Qasim government came to be viewed as a threat in its own right, it was the Kennedy administration that promoted regime change. In 1963, the CIA, backed by Britain and Israel, helped to foment the anticommunist Ba'ath Party coup that overthrew the Qasim regime – and paved the way for Saddam Hussein's eventual assumption of power.

Meanwhile, in Egypt, Nasser attempted to counter U.S. intervention in the Middle East by appealing to the Soviet Union. Initially, Moscow responded with military and economic assistance. However, by 1958, the relationship between the two countries was strained. Nasser actively opposed communist parties throughout the Middle East, considering them a threat to his power base. In 1958, he outlawed the Egyptian Communist Party and launched a campaign of

---

[4] The United Arab Republic was a political union of Egypt and Syria, which existed from 1958 to 1961, when Syria seceded. Egypt continued to use the name until 1971.

persecution against its former members. Although Nasser's negative attitude toward communism caused considerable tensions in his relationship with the Soviet Union, Moscow continued to finance the Aswan High Dam and other infrastructure projects during the 1960s. The Soviet Union also established air bases in Egypt and rebuilt the Egyptian military following its destruction by Israel during the June 1967 Six-Day War, providing money, equipment, and some twenty thousand advisors.

Egyptian opportunism vis-à-vis the Soviet Union continued under Anwar Sadat, who became president after Nasser's death in 1970. Sadat, like Nasser, used the Soviet Union to promote his own agenda – and he was willing to stand up to Moscow if necessary. He expelled the military Soviet advisors in 1972, believing that they would obstruct his attempt to regain territory lost to Israel in the 1967 war. In the ensuing 1973 Arab-Israeli War, the Soviet Union became a reluctant player, providing military supplies and helping to orchestrate a ceasefire after massive U.S. military support tipped the balance in Israel's favor. Following a dangerous game of nuclear brinksmanship, both Moscow and Washington pressed their respective allies to settle, thus avoiding a Third World War over the Middle East.

Algeria and Francophone North Africa, 1954–62

Nasser's Egypt was the link between radical nationalism in British and French North Africa. Following the establishment of the Baghdad Pact and French provision of tanks and planes to Israel in 1955, Egypt began to supply military matériel to the National Liberation Front (FLN), which was fighting for Algerian independence. The FLN, like Nasser's Egypt, viewed itself as a leader in the broader movement for the emancipation of all colonized peoples in the European empires of Africa and Asia. Independent Algeria, like Egypt, would become a mecca for liberation movements from two continents.

As in Egypt, the crisis in Francophone North Africa began as a conflict over decolonization, with Cold War issues introduced only secondarily. At stake was Western political influence in North Africa and the Middle East and control over the region's enormous oil resources. Since the North Africa Campaign of World War II (1940–43), France had worried about American encroachment on its imperial domain. The United States had established air bases in French Morocco and Italian Libya during the war, all of which remained critical for

European defense in its aftermath. After the war, the United States sought to retain these military bases and to establish new ones – threatening to replace France as the new great power in the region. The discovery of oil in the Algerian Sahara in the mid-1950s only increased French wariness of American intentions. Until the Suez Crisis of 1956, Washington tried to balance support for its NATO allies and the demands of African nationalists, privately prodding France toward eventual self-government in its North African territories. However, Suez was a turning point. As the crisis intensified, the Eisenhower administration urged Britain and France to reform their imperial practices and embrace moderate nationalists – or risk being overwhelmed by radical forces that were beholden to international communism.

From the close of World War II to the Suez Crisis, the United States and the Soviet Union followed similar policies in French-ruled North Africa. Both superpowers preferred continued French rule in the region to the emergence of a power vacuum that might be filled by their Cold War rival. Both were more interested in protecting their respective relationships with France than in supporting the independence movements in French-controlled territory. France was a key prize in the postwar European theater. The Soviet Union sought an ally with a common interest in maintaining a weak Germany and minimizing American influence in Europe. The United States, in turn, considered France to be critical to European reconstruction and defense. It sought an ally that was securely grounded in the American camp – supportive of German reindustrialization, rearmament, and integration into NATO as a bulwark against Soviet communism. Given the strength of the French Communist Party (PCF), which had spearheaded domestic resistance to Nazi occupation, and the pervasive French fear of American domination, a Franco-American alliance was not a foregone conclusion. Despite its misgivings, France ultimately chose the American camp in exchange for badly needed military and economic assistance. The enormous quantity of American aid provided under the Marshall Plan allowed France to reassert control over its empire in the immediate postwar period.

After the Suez War, Soviet and American policies in French North Africa parted ways. The Soviet Union increasingly favored African nationalists, while the United States privately pressured France to implement reforms to avoid pushing the nationalists into the communist camp. Once it became convinced that Algerian independence was a foregone conclusion, Moscow began to provide indirect material support to the nationalist cause. However, it avoided sending

volunteers to a territory that was considered an integral part of France
and was, thus, covered by the NATO treaty. It would not go to war
with the United States over Algeria, just as the United States had
refused to engage the Soviet Union over Egypt.

French policy in North Africa was deeply influenced by two blows
to the French empire in 1954. In May, the French armed forces suffered a catastrophic defeat at the hands of Vietnamese nationalists
at Dien Bien Phu, resulting in France's decision to withdraw from
Indochina. Six months later, war broke out in Algeria. The Algerian independence war, which would consume nearly one million
lives and render homeless twice that number, would last until 1962.
Although nationalist unrest also challenged French rule in the protec-
torates of Tunisia and Morocco, Algeria was far more important to
France. As subordinate territories, Tunisia and Morocco were members of the French Union, a political association loosely modeled on
the British Commonwealth. Algeria, in contrast, was considered an
integral part of the French Republic. One and a half million people of
French descent lived in Algeria, and French investors held substantial
investments in Algerian mining and agriculture. Two years after the
war erupted, significant oil and natural gas reserves were discovered
in the Algerian Sahara, potentially lessening France's heavy dependence on Middle Eastern oil. Paris was determined that Algeria would
remain French.

The Algerian war was preceded by political and labor unrest in
Tunisia and Morocco, which were racked by strikes and demonstrations after World War II. Following a turbulent period in 1952, French
authorities imprisoned Tunisian nationalist leader Habib Bourguiba,
who had already spent a decade behind bars for his political activities. The following year, France deposed and exiled Morocco's sultan,
Mohammed ben Yusuf, and imprisoned a number of Moroccan political activists. The United States was concerned that French repression would play into the hands of the Soviet Union, pro-Nasser Arab
nationalists, or Nasser's radical Islamic opponents. Noting that the
Tunisian and Moroccan nationalist movements were generally pro-
Western and anticommunist, the Eisenhower administration urged
France to implement political, economic, and social reforms. In 1954,
as political strife spread from the urban areas to the Tunisian countryside, France released Bourguiba and his colleagues from prison,
unbanned their party, and granted amnesty to rural guerrillas. In 1955,
Tunisia was granted local self-government, and the sultan of Morocco

PHOTO 2.3. Algerian civilians flee a conflict zone under the eye of the French military, December 9, 1954 (Bettmann/Corbis).

was permitted to return from exile. Unable to focus sufficient attention and resources on the Algerian crisis while distracted by protests in adjacent territories, Paris cut its losses and in 1956 ceded complete independence to Tunisia and Morocco.

Washington and Moscow were quick to court the fledgling nations. Hoping to prevent Tunisia and Morocco from establishing diplomatic relations with the Soviet Union, the United States provided military and economic assistance. While tilting toward the West, both countries carefully guarded their independence. Morocco allowed the U.S. Strategic Air Command to keep five bases on Moroccan soil, where it stockpiled nuclear weapons and maintained communications facilities. However, Rabat also signed a trade agreement with the Soviet Union and established diplomatic relations with that country in 1958. When France attempted to retain control of six military bases in Tunisia after independence, Tunis claimed that Paris was violating its sovereignty. Similarly, when France refused to sell military equipment to Tunisia on the grounds that it would find its way into the hands of Algerian nationalists – or be used against French troops that were violating Tunisian borders in pursuit of FLN guerrillas – President Bourguiba threatened to turn to Egypt or the Eastern Bloc. The United States was less concerned about the possibility of Soviet subversion than the radicalizing influence of Egypt, which had aided both Tunisia and Morocco in their struggles against France. To prevent Nasser from gaining a foothold in the region, the United States stepped into the breach, providing small arms to Tunisia despite French resistance.

More concerned about American encroachment in North Africa than Algerian aspirations for independence, communists, whether Soviet, French, or Algerian, endorsed the Algerian independence struggle only belatedly. When the Algerian independence war began in November 1954, the Soviet Union did not support it, fearing the consequences for North African stability and distrusting the FLN for its peasant base and anticommunist orientation. Although Moscow criticized French repression and urged UN involvement in promoting peace, it was careful not to tip the balance against France. The PCF, though sympathetic to the Algerian uprising against more than a century of colonial oppression, objected to the FLN's methods, which it characterized as terrorism. The Algerian Communist Party, the majority of whose members were of French origin, initially followed the PCF's lead. However, following its banning in 1955, the Algerian Communist Party increasingly deferred to the FLN, accepting a subordinate role in the nationalist struggle. It was not until October 1960, six years after the onset of the independence war, that the Soviet and French Communist Parties openly supported Algerian independence under FLN auspices.

Throughout most of the war, the PCF rejected the notion of Algerian independence, asserting that African emancipation could occur only within the framework of French governance. Steeped in paternalism, party members generally believed that Algerians' lack of experience would make them easy prey to American imperialism and international capitalism, which they considered a far greater threat than French colonialism. Only the PCF's rise to power in France, and the subsequent transformation of the economy to benefit the French working class and all colonized peoples, would bring true emancipation. Algeria, as an integral part of France, would be a key beneficiary. French communists were also troubled by the role of religion – in this case, Islam – in the Algerian nationalist arsenal.

Disappointed by the communists, Algerian nationalists initially looked for support from the United States, where it presumed that its anticommunist orientation would generate a sympathetic response. The nationalists had additional reasons for expecting American support. The United States had provoked early discussions of decolonization in 1941, when it joined Britain in signing the Atlantic Charter. Besides addressing American economic concerns, the charter declared "the right of all peoples to choose the form of government under which they will live" and the "wish to see sovereign rights and self-government restored to those who have been forcibly deprived of them."[5] France and Britain envisioned the restoration of those rights in European countries that had been overrun by Axis powers and the return of imperial territories that they had lost. The United States, which sought an open door to world trade, asserted that old-style imperialism and free trade were not compatible. Washington thus implied that self-determination might also apply to European colonies.

Perceiving the disjuncture between French and American interests, Algerian nationalists hoped to drive a wedge between the two countries. However, during the first Eisenhower administration (1952–56), the United States took its cue from France, which considered Algeria to be an internal French problem rather than an international one. Although it encouraged France to implement reforms, thus taking the wind from nationalist sails, Washington also provided its NATO ally with helicopters, bombers, and weapons. The Eisenhower administration even permitted NATO troops to be used against Algerian rebels and their civilian supporters on the specious grounds that France was fighting a communist insurgency. Having failed to gain American backing, the FLN looked for support in the UN, where Arab, other Asian, and Eastern Bloc countries took the lead in promoting the Algerian cause. The United States supported the French position that Algeria was a domestic matter and, thus, outside the UN's purview. However, because of its concern for African and Asian sentiment, the Eisenhower administration refused to grant Paris the blank check on Algeria that it so desperately sought.

The Algerian crisis intensified in 1957, when the ten-month-long Battle of Algiers overshadowed all else. As Eisenhower began his second term, more than 500,000 French troops worked to suppress the nationalist insurrection. As the FLN attempted to implant itself in the capital city, French paratroopers established tight control over the civilian population by recruiting informers, collaborators, and auxiliary forces, and by systematically using torture to uncover and demolish rebel cells. By the year's end, the local FLN leadership had been decimated, the leaders either imprisoned or killed.

---

[5] "The Atlantic Charter," August 14, 1941, http://www.nato.int/cps/en/natolive/official_texts_16912.htm?selectedLocale=en.

Some 4,000 people had disappeared, and nearly 10 percent of the capital's population had been herded into internment centers. Publicly, the Eisenhower administration withheld criticism. Privately, the American president was furious that France had put his country in such a bind. French intransigence on Algeria was threatening the Western alliance and jeopardizing American interests in the emerging nations of Africa and Asia.

The Eisenhower administration's dilemma presented an opportunity to Democratic presidential hopeful, Senator John F. Kennedy, chair of the Senate Foreign Relations Committee's Subcommittee on United Nations Affairs. Unconstrained by presidential office, Kennedy provoked an international firestorm on July 2, when, from the Senate floor, he decried French actions in Algeria and declared his support for Algerian independence. Distinguishing himself as a proponent of nationalism and human rights, Kennedy asserted that French territories would one day "break free and look with suspicion on the Western nations who impeded their steps to independence."[6] Criticized by both Democrats and Republicans in the American foreign policy establishment for jeopardizing American relations with France, Kennedy retorted that if the United States failed to respond to the nationalist impulse, the Soviet Union surely would. African nationalists from across the continent took notice of the young Democrat from Massachusetts.

When Kennedy made his highly publicized speech, the Eisenhower administration was quietly reevaluating its North Africa policy. Since June 1957, the French armed forces had engaged in scores of incursions across the Tunisian border in pursuit of FLN fighters. In February 1958, French forces piloting more than a dozen American planes supplied through NATO bombed the Tunisian village of Sakiet Sidi Youssef, hitting Red Cross vehicles and a school and killing nearly seventy civilians. Concerned that French actions were tarnishing America's reputation in the region and creating an opportunity for Soviet and Nasserite infiltration, the Eisenhower administration condemned the Sakiet bombing and urged France to begin negotiations that would result in Algerian self-determination.

Just as dissension over the Algerian war threatened to fracture the Franco-American alliance, it also challenged France internally. Deep

---

[6] Quoted in Richard D. Mahoney, *JFK: Ordeal in Africa* (New York: Oxford University Press, 1983), 20.

divisions over the Algerian question resulted in tremendous political and economic instability. During the spring of 1958, governments rose and fell in quick succession. Worried that Paris would cave under international pressure, disgruntled French army units prepared to seize power to keep Algeria French. In May, a coup d'état was narrowly averted. In the hope of averting civil war – and retaining a French hold on Algeria – General Charles de Gaulle, the acclaimed Free French leader of World War II, was installed as prime minister in June 1958. He immediately initiated the drafting of a new constitution that would offer French overseas territories more leeway in local self-government but would bind them securely to France in the form of a new Paris-dominated French Community. Citizens of France and its empire were scheduled to vote yea or nay in a constitutional referendum on September 28, 1958.

Nine days before the historic vote, the FLN announced the establishment of a provisional government in exile. Although the government was not recognized by the United States or the Soviet Union, neither of which intended to lose privileged access to France over Algeria, it quickly established diplomatic relations with China, North Vietnam, North Korea, Indonesia, and all the Arab states except Lebanon, which had recently welcomed thousands of American Marines. In October, the Egypt-based Arab League offered the FLN government $34 million in financial assistance.[7] In December, while Algerian leaders toured China, North Vietnam, and North Korea, requesting volunteers and military and economic aid, the American delegation to the UN abstained on an Afro-Asian resolution that recognized the Algerian people's right to independence. Having pried Washington away from its earlier stance of open support for France, the FLN considered the abstention a victory. Paris considered it a slap in the face. In retaliation, France withdrew its Mediterranean fleet from the NATO command and refused to allow American planes armed with nuclear warheads to remain on French soil. Despite the Eisenhower administration's concern about the escalating crisis in Berlin and the need to safeguard Western Europe, it could no longer

---

[7] The Arab League was established in Cairo in 1945 by Egypt, Iraq, Lebanon, Saudi Arabia, Syria, Transjordan (Jordan), and Yemen. The organization's purpose was to promote collaboration among the member states, to protect their independence and sovereignty, and to advance Arab interests more generally. By 1958, the league had been joined by four newly independent North African nations – Libya, Sudan, Morocco, and Tunisia.

afford to be associated with France's Algeria policy. While Washington worried about its reputation in the Third World, the Soviet Union encouraged continued French presence in Algeria to thwart American encroachment.

By 1959, the die had been cast. As FLN spokesman and revolutionary theorist Frantz Fanon observed, "The crushing of the Algerian Revolution, its isolation, its asphyxiation, its death through exhaustion – these are mad dreams."[8] In September, under enormous pressure internally and externally, de Gaulle's government announced a major policy shift. Algerians would be permitted to determine their own future in a referendum. They could choose to remain an integral part of France, to transition to self-government under French authority, or to accede to full independence. Anxious to avert a U.S.-led settlement, the Soviet Union endorsed de Gaulle's initiative. The PCF, which had initially rejected de Gaulle's proposal as an untrustworthy maneuver, quickly followed suit. By October 1960, however, events had taken another turn. Soured by French support for West German designs on Berlin and now certain that it could not entice France from the Western alliance, Moscow saw no point in continuing its unpopular backing of France on the Algerian question. In an about-face, the Soviet Union granted de facto recognition to the FLN government. The PCF, long castigated by other forces on the French Left for its failure to support Algerian independence, was now free to endorse the independence struggle as well.

The election of John F. Kennedy to the American presidency the following month caused great consternation in Paris. Although the Eisenhower administration had begun to apply pressure on the Algerian question, a Kennedy administration was certain to be worse. (In fact, the new president's changes were modest, limited to abstaining on UN resolutions rather than supporting or criticizing French positions.) Shortly after the November 1960 elections, Paris announced that a referendum on Algerian self-determination would be held in January 1961. French citizens voted overwhelmingly to support the notion of Algerian self-determination, which would inevitably lead to full independence. Shortly thereafter, France began negotiating with the FLN. The final accords, signed at Evian in March 1962, permitted France to retain control over military bases, airfields, and nuclear testing sites for many years and to have preferential access to Algerian oil – should the

---

[8] Frantz Fanon, *A Dying Colonialism*, trans. Haakon Chevalier (New York: Grove Press, 1967), 180–81 (first published in 1959 as *L'An Cinq de la Révolution Algérienne*).

PHOTO 2.4. French men fighting to keep Algeria French receive supplies from French women, January 31, 1960 (Bettmann/Corbis).

Algerian people vote for independence. Meanwhile, in 1961–62, as France and West Germany mended fences, Moscow lost hope of rending the Western alliance. After the Evian Accords were signed, the Soviet Union finally gave de jure recognition to the FLN government, three months before Algeria was officially granted independence.

On July 1, 1962, of a total of six million Algerian voters, 99.7 percent cast their ballots for independence. Two days later, after more than 130 years of French rule and seven years of war, Algeria became a sovereign nation. Nearly one million Algerians had been killed, and twice that many had been driven from their homes. Grateful for African and Arab support during the independence struggle, Algeria's new prime minister, Ahmed Ben Bella, joined Egypt's Gamal Abdel Nasser, Ghana's Kwame Nkrumah, and Guinea's Sékou Touré in promoting aid for liberation movements in African territories still under colonial domination. Algeria, like Egypt, quickly became a hub for liberation movements from South Africa, Angola, Portuguese Guinea, and Palestine. American support for France during the war and the Algerian government's embrace of radical liberation movements and hostility toward Israel resulted in decades of mutual antagonism between Algeria and the United States. Although Soviet aid to the FLN had arrived only in the eleventh hour – once it became clear that Algeria would indeed become independent – even belated support allowed the Soviet Union to cultivate a close relationship with the new government, despite the strong anticommunist bias of the ruling party.

Suggested Reading

For a discussion of the Bandung Conference, nonalignment, and the impact of African and Asian actors in shaping the postwar world, see Christopher J. Lee, ed., *Making a World after Empire: The Bandung Moment and Its Political Afterlives* (Athens: Ohio University Press, 2010). For the Bandung Conference and the role of race in U.S. international relations, see Jason Parker, "Cold War II: The Eisenhower Administration, the Bandung Conference, and the Reperiodization of the Postwar Era," *Diplomatic History* 30, no. 5 (November 2006): 867–92, and Cary Fraser, "An American Dilemma: Race and Realpolitik in the American Response to the Bandung Conference, 1955," in *Window on Freedom: Race, Civil Rights, and Foreign Affairs, 1945–1988*, ed. Brenda Gayle Plummer (Chapel Hill: University of North Carolina Press, 2003), 115–40.

A solid, accessible general history of Egypt is Afaf Lutfi Al-Sayyid Marsot's *A History of Egypt: From the Arab Conquest to the Present*, 2nd ed. (New York: Cambridge University Press, 2007).

For Egyptian, British, and American relations in the age of Arab nationalism, see Nigel John Ashton, *Eisenhower, Macmillan, and the Problem of Nasser: Anglo-American Relations and Arab Nationalism, 1955–59* (New York: St. Martin's Press, 1996); Peter L. Hahn, *The United States, Great Britain, and Egypt, 1945–1956: Strategy and Diplomacy in the Early Cold War* (Chapel Hill: University of North Carolina Press, 1992); Salim Yaqub, *Containing Arab Nationalism: The Eisenhower Doctrine and the Middle East* (Chapel Hill: University of North Carolina Press, 2004); Barry Rubin, "America and the Egyptian Revolution, 1950–1957," *Political Science Quarterly* 97, no. 1 (Spring 1982): 73–90; and Douglas Little, "The New Frontier on the Nile: JFK, Nasser, and Arab Nationalism," *Journal of American History* 75, no. 2 (September 1988): 501–27.

For Egyptian-Soviet relations, see Karen Dawisha, *Soviet Foreign Policy towards Egypt* (New York: Macmillan, 1979); O. M. Smolansky, "Moscow and the Suez Crisis, 1956: A Reappraisal," *Political Science Quarterly* 80, no. 4 (December 1965): 581–605; and Aleksandr Fursenko and Timothy Naftali, *Khrushchev's Cold War: The Inside Story of an American Adversary* (New York: W. W. Norton, 2006).

For the historical ramifications of the Suez Crisis, see Wm. Roger Louis and Roger Owen, eds., *Suez 1956: The Crisis and Its Consequences* (New York: Oxford University Press, 1989), which includes many firsthand accounts; and Percy Cradock, *Know Your Enemy: How the Joint Intelligence Committee Saw the World* (London: John Murray, 2002), which was written by the chair of the government committee that analyzed British intelligence during the crisis.

Important works about the Algerian independence war include Alistair Horne, *A Savage War of Peace: Algeria, 1954–1962* (New York: New York Review Books, 2006) and Frantz Fanon, *The Wretched of the Earth*, trans. Richard Philcox (New York: Grove Press, 2004), which explores the psychological impact of colonialism and liberation. Matthew Connelly's *A Diplomatic Revolution: Algeria's Fight for Independence and the Origins of the Post–Cold War Era* (New York: Oxford University Press, 2002) explores Algerian decolonization in the context of the Cold War and examines the ways in which Algerian nationalists played on divisions between the French colonial power and its allies. Similar themes are pursued in Martin Thomas's "France's North African Crisis: Cold War and Colonial Imperatives, 1945–1955," *History* 92, no. 306 (April 2007): 207–34. Irwin M. Wall's *France, the United States, and the Algerian War* (Berkeley: University of California Press, 2001) investigates the role of the United States in shaping the final settlement. John F. Kennedy's reevaluation of American policy is assessed in Theresa Romahn, "Colonialism and the Campaign Trail: On Kennedy's Algerian Speech and His Bid for the 1960 Democratic Nomination," *Journal of Colonialism and Colonial History* 10, no. 2 (Fall 2009) and Richard D. Mahoney, *JFK: Ordeal in Africa* (New York: Oxford University Press, 1983). For the broader impact of the Algerian revolution, see Robert Malley, *The Call from Algeria: Third Worldism, Revolution, and the Turn to Islam* (Berkeley: University of California Press, 1996).

Besides Thomas (mentioned above), two recommended articles examine the Cold War and decolonization in Tunisia and Morocco: Egya Sangmuah's "Eisenhower and Containment in North Africa, 1956–1960," *Middle East Journal* 44, no. 1 (1990): 76–91, explores American attempts to contain Soviet and Egyptian influence, while Yahia H. Zoubir analyzes the dynamics of American, French, and Soviet policies in "The United States, the Soviet Union and Decolonization of the Maghreb, 1945–62," *Middle Eastern Studies* 31, no. 1 (1995): 58–84.

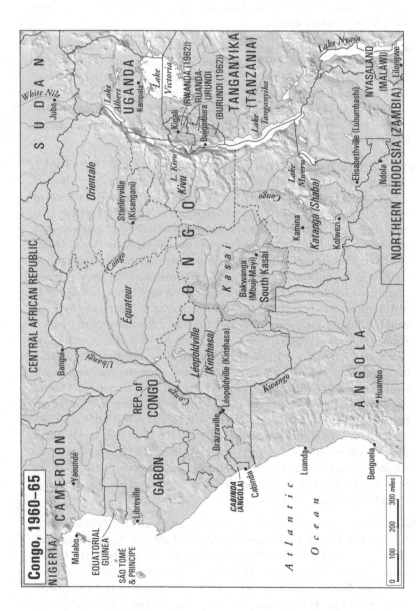

MAP 3.1. Congo, 1960–65. (Map by Philip Schwartzberg, Meridian Mapping, Minneapolis.)

CHAPTER 3

The Congo Crisis, 1960–1965

As the superpowers vied for influence in North Africa and the Middle East, the Belgian Congo became the next African battleground. Bordered by nine other territories in Central, Southern, and East Africa, the Congo was of fundamental political and economic concern to colonial and Cold War powers, the white-minority regimes of Southern Africa, and African and Asian countries in the UN. It was extremely rich in strategic minerals, containing some of the world's most significant deposits of copper, cobalt, and uranium (Katanga Province) and industrial diamonds (South Kasai Province), as well as important sources of tantalum, tin, and zinc. Belgium's most powerful financial group, Société Générale de Belgique, and its affiliates controlled approximately 70 percent of the Congolese national economy, including the Katanga mines, which were dominated by the Belgian-British joint venture Union Minière du Haut Katanga.

During the period 1960–65, the Congo was the target of significant intervention by external actors, some of it under UN auspices. Belgium, the former colonial power, and the United States, the preeminent Cold War player, had especially critical roles, while African nations contributed troops and material aid, primarily through the UN. Although the Soviet Union and Cuba were also involved, compared to that of the West, their role was marginal and their actions ineffective. Foreign commercial interests from Belgium, Britain, the United States, South Africa, and the Central African Federation were deeply embroiled in the conflict, largely in support of the secessionist movement in Katanga.[1] Regional political interests also came into play as the white-ruled regimes of the Central African Federation and South Africa, along with Portugal as the dominant neighboring colonial power, attempted to contain the spread of radical nationalism by undermining the Congo's central government.

This chapter examines the role of external powers in the Congo during two separate phases of the crisis. The first phase encompasses the years 1960–61, when the Congo attained independence and experienced secession, assassination, and a rupture in governmental legitimacy. An array of external forces supported the secession, plotted to assassinate the Congolese prime minister, and helped to orchestrate a coup d'état, while others supported the elected central government. The second phase focuses on the period 1964–65, when rebellion in the east resulted in armed intervention by Western powers on the side of the central government and Cuba on the side of the rebels.

The Crisis of 1960–61

Following a series of political disturbances in 1959 that targeted colonial authorities and rendered parts of the Congo ungovernable, Brussels agreed to grant the colony independence on June 30, 1960. However, Belgium was determined to retain control of the rich Congolese economy. To do this, it needed to ensure that political control passed to a pro-Western government that would not fundamentally alter economic structures. Strategically placed Belgian administrators would remain in the Congo after independence, along with 1,000 Belgian officers commanding the 25,000-man Congolese army. Although the new political officeholders would be Congolese, power would remain in Belgian hands. The interests of the United States, the dominant Cold War power, were largely compatible with these objectives. The Eisenhower administration supported the installation of a government friendly to its NATO ally and one that

---

[1] The settler-dominated Central African Federation, which comprised Northern and Southern Rhodesia and Nyasaland, existed from 1953 to 1963, when it collapsed as a result of African nationalist demands for a greater share of political power and an end to colonial rule.

would guarantee the continued exploitation of Katanga minerals for Western benefit. It was particularly concerned that Katanga's rich uranium deposits not fall into Soviet hands.

The government of Patrice Lumumba, who became prime minister after the May 1960 parliamentary elections, did not fit this bill. His party, the Congolese National Movement (MNC), was the only Congolese party that could claim a national, as opposed to a merely regional or ethnic, base. The MNC envisioned economic transformations that would benefit ordinary Africans – but threaten the unfettered profits of Western mining interests. Favoring a nonaligned foreign policy along the lines articulated at Bandung, the MNC was associated with the pan-Arab and pan-African movements of Egypt's Gamal Abdel Nasser, Ghana's Kwame Nkrumah, and Guinea's Sékou Touré, which alarmed Western powers and regional settler regimes. Their concerns were intensified on Independence Day when Belgian King Baudouin praised his country's colonial mission in the Congo. Lumumba responded with a vehement denunciation of Belgian atrocities, characterizing colonial rule as "the humiliating slavery which was imposed upon us by force" and proclaiming that "the Congo's independence marks a decisive step towards the liberation of the entire African continent."[2] Belgium was convinced that Lumumba was hostile to whites and to their interests, while the United States worried about the spread of radical nationalism and international communism.

Five days after independence, Congolese soldiers mutinied, having been informed by the Belgian army commander that "before Independence = after Independence."[3] There would be no wage increases, promotions, or African officers in the postcolonial army. Calling for the Africanization of government, commerce, and the armed forces, Lumumba dismissed the Belgian officers and promoted Joseph-Désiré Mobutu to army chief of staff. On July 10, responding to appeals from the American, British, and French consuls in Katanga, the Belgian army intervened, purportedly to protect Belgian lives and property. Brussels's assertion of the imperial prerogative was reminiscent of

---

[2] "Patrice Lumumba, the First Prime Minister of the Congo (Zaire), on June 30, 1960, Independence Day," http://www.mtholyoke.edu/~ajavoryi/speech.html.

[3] Quoted in Stephen R. Weissman, *American Foreign Policy in the Congo, 1960–1964* (Ithaca, NY: Cornell University Press, 1974), 56.

French and British actions in Egypt during the Suez Crisis four years earlier. The following day, Moïse Tshombe, who was closely associated with Belgian settler and international mining interests, instigated the secession of Katanga Province, warning that Katanga was threatened by a communist insurgency. The secession deprived the new government of more than half of its annual revenue and most of its foreign exchange earnings.

The Belgian government, along with powerful international business and political interests, actively backed the secessionists. Belgian, British, American, South African, and Rhodesian mining companies and their political supporters were prominent among the pro-Katanga forces. While Brussels provided military and financial assistance, intelligence, and training for the Katanga army, as well as a new officer corps, foreign companies financed the secession by paying taxes to the breakaway Katanga regime rather than to the elected Lumumba government. Concerned about the spread of radical nationalism into other Central and Southern African territories, Britain, Portugal, and the settler regimes of South Africa and the Central African Federation lent both tacit and open support to Tshombe's forces. The Katanga army was bolstered by white mercenaries recruited from Belgium, South Africa, Southern Rhodesia, and France, the latter group including veterans of the Indochinese and Algerian wars. In August, the Katanga secession was followed by that of the diamond-rich South Kasai Province. This move was also backed by the Belgian government and international mining interests.

Convinced that Belgium was attempting to recolonize the country, Lumumba appealed for UN intervention. This solution suited both Cold War superpowers, at least initially. Unwilling to provoke a war with the United States over the Congo, where entrenched Western interests made the odds of Soviet success minimal, Khrushchev was anxious for an international solution that would minimize American gains. From the Soviet perspective, a UN action that would replace the troops of a NATO member with those of the international body was welcome. Such an action would support the Congo's elected government, which was favored by Moscow. Moreover, a UN operation offered the Soviet Union an opportunity to demonstrate its opposition to colonialism and imperialism without the risks of unilateral military intervention. The United States, like other Western powers, was interested in the restoration of law and order, which would protect Western lives and property and undermine opportunities for communist infiltration. In backing UN intervention, the United States could preempt Soviet influence without lending support to a retrograde colonial power – a concern of the American government, if not of the business community. Therefore, both Washington and Moscow approved the July 14 Security Council resolution providing for a UN force in the Congo and calling on Belgian forces to withdraw. Tacitly supporting their fellow colonial power, Britain and France abstained.

In the summer of 1960, the United States dominated UN structures and the American agenda generally prevailed. Americans held key positions in the UN hierarchy – in both New York and the Congo – and Washington paid a disproportionate share of the organization's operating expenses. Many African nations had not yet achieved independence or had done so only recently. As a result, the UN General Assembly included only nine African members. Western European and Latin American nations, in need of American military and economic assistance, were reluctant to rock the boat. Moreover, their own interests frequently coincided with the American campaign against radical nationalism. As a result, the UN generally promoted U.S. policies in the name of international cooperation, thus providing American interests with a mask of multilateralism. Although both the United States and the Soviet Union provided weapons, food, and transport to the UN Congo operation, it was largely an American affair. The Soviet Union contributed twenty-six planes and six helicopters – as well as indirect air support through Ghana and Guinea. The United States, in contrast, provided ninety planes, a number of helicopters, and most of the funding. The majority of UN troops were brought to the Congo in American planes and were transported in the Congo by American vehicles. Americans dominated the UN's civilian operation and controlled communications between UN units in the Congo and with the world outside.

On July 15, the first of some 19,825 UN troops began to arrive in the Congo. The understanding between the superpowers – and between Lumumba and the UN – broke down almost immediately. Although they had come at the request of the Congolese government, the UN forces were under Western authority. Western priorities included first and foremost the protection of white lives and property and the resolution of the crisis to the benefit of Western political and economic interests. The Congolese government, in contrast, gave precedence to the expulsion of Belgian troops and the reunification of the country.

Relations between Lumumba and UN Secretary-General Dag Hammarskjöld strained to the breaking point when Hammarskjöld refused to accede to either of the prime minister's fundamental demands and Lumumba accused the international body of doing the bidding of the West. In late July, Lumumba flew to the United States to appeal directly to the Eisenhower administration. His requests for American aid were rebuffed when the Eisenhower administration claimed that it would work only through the UN. Lumumba had no better luck in Canada and Western Europe.

Although its aims differed, Moscow also responded cautiously to the Congo Crisis. Unwilling to challenge the Western powers militarily in a capitalist stronghold far from Soviet territory, Moscow engaged in a delicate balancing act. It hoped to appeal to Afro-Asian nations by supporting pro-Lumumba efforts in the UN General Assembly and Security Council, by providing material assistance to the UN operation, and by simultaneously criticizing the inaction of the UN hierarchy. However, the Soviet agenda was derailed by events beyond its control. On August 9, the Soviet UN representative voted for an Afro-Asian Security Council resolution calling for an immediate withdrawal of Belgian troops from Katanga and the entry of UN forces to implement the resolution. The same day, South Kasai Province seceded from the Congo and allied itself with Katanga. Having dubbed the Katanga secession an internal affair, and thus outside the UN purview, the international body had opened the door for the second secessionist movement. On August 15, Lumumba formally requested Soviet assistance in quelling the Katanga and Kasai secessions and in restoring the country's territorial integrity. Frustrated by Western control of the UN operation but unwilling to risk war over the Congo, Moscow responded with only limited material support – primarily trucks, transport planes, and technicians, including equipment originally destined for the UN operation. Although Soviet assistance had already been provided under UN auspices, some American officials were adamant that the solicitation of bilateral aid meant that Lumumba was a Soviet stooge who threatened American interests not only in the Congo but also throughout Africa. A local conflict with colonial-era roots had been transformed into a sideshow in the broader geopolitical struggle.

In August and September, Brussels and Washington, now convinced of a clear and present danger, formulated a number of plans to assassinate Lumumba. Wary of his strong popular support and certain that he would win any future elections, they believed that he would remain a threat if simply removed from power. Both governments urged Joseph Kasavubu, who held the largely ceremonial position of Congolese president, to stage a coup d'état. On September 5, Kasavubu fired Lumumba, a move that was rejected by the Congolese parliament as being without legal foundation. American diplomat Andrew Cordier, who headed the UN operation in the Congo, ordered the closure of the national radio station and the Léopoldville airport, thus obstructing Lumumba's ability to rally his forces. On September 14, when the parliament continued to back Lumumba, Kasavubu adjourned it. With CIA and Belgian military support and bolstered by UN passivity, army chief of staff Joseph-Désiré Mobutu staged a second coup d'état. Although Kasavubu remained president and Mobutu established the facade of a civilian government, the military strongman was the real power behind the throne. Lumumba was placed under house arrest, guarded by Congolese troops who in turn were monitored by UN forces from Ghana, Morocco, and Tunisia. The Soviet and Czech embassies were closed and their diplomats and technicians expelled, along with a Chinese delegation that had hoped to establish diplomatic relations. Soviet pilots and planes, which had been helping to put down the Katanga and Kasai secessions, were recalled, while Soviet trucks were confiscated by Mobutu's army and police.

As the legally elected government of the Congo crumbled, the UN took sides. Although it termed the Katanga and Kasai secessions internal matters over which it had no authority, the UN intervened in the Congo's domestic affairs in other instances. Days before Mobutu's coup d'état, the UN used American funds to pay Mobutu's restless troops, thus ensuring their loyalty. It intervened again when UN soldiers prevented Lumumba from using the national radio to rally support for the central government or the Léopoldville airport to ferry troops from his loyalist stronghold in Stanleyville (eastern Congo) to the capital. At the Secretariat in New York, the UN adhered to Washington's position and refused to recognize Lumumba's delegation, seating Kasavubu's contingent instead. Protests by the Soviet Union and African and Asian nations were to no avail.

Although the UN's role as a neutral arbiter had been damaged irreparably by the fall of 1960, the institution had not been rendered irrelevant. When Moscow called for Hammarskjöld's resignation and for the restructuring of the Secretariat to give more power to socialist and nonaligned countries, African and Asian countries withheld their support. Ghana, Guinea, and the United Arab Republic, the most radical African UN members, were outspoken in their condemnation of UN actions in the Congo and vociferous in their support of Lumumba. However, they were not willing to court Western opprobrium by siding with the Soviet Union on a highly inflammatory tangential issue. Whatever its failings, the UN remained the last best chance of keeping the Cold War at bay in the Congo. If the Congo became "a battlefield between East and West," Nkrumah warned Lumumba in August, "this would be a disaster for all of us in Africa."[4] Increasingly wary of any superpower influence in the Congo, the Ghanaian president urged the Congolese leader not to accept further Soviet aid, unless offered through the UN.

Divisions within the UN were not only between East and West but also between the Northern and Southern Hemispheres. In the fall of 1960, sixteen new African nations joined the UN, bringing African membership to twenty-five. While the West still dominated the Security Council and Secretariat, African, Asian, and Latin American nations became the dominant voices in the General Assembly. Approximately 80 percent of the UN troops in the Congo had been provided by African and Asian nations, most of which supported Lumumba. Thus, when Mobutu's soldiers attempted to remove Lumumba from his home in September, UN troops from Ghana prevented them from doing so. In late November, Western fortunes rose when Lumumba escaped from house arrest. Mobutu's army, with CIA and Belgian assistance, conducted an all-out search and captured him on December 1. Despite Soviet protests, UN forces, under instructions from headquarters, failed to intervene. The official position, supported by the United States, was that Lumumba had been legitimately arrested on the orders of the Congolese head of state, Joseph Kasavubu.

To implement the final assassination plan, high-level Belgian officials ordered Lumumba's transfer to Katanga, where he would be turned over to his enemies. Brussels was concerned that the incoming

4 Kwame Nkrumah, *Challenge of the Congo* (New York: International Publishers, 1967), 33.

PHOTO 3.1. Congolese troops loyal to Mobutu manhandle Lumumba after his capture, December 6, 1960 (Bettmann/Corbis).

Kennedy administration might be more sympathetic to Lumumba than the Eisenhower administration, which had instigated plans for his assassination. Hence, Belgian military and intelligence advisors, with CIA connivance, pressed Mobutu to surrender Lumumba to Moïse Tshombe's secessionist forces, who had vowed to kill him. On January 17, 1961, three days before Kennedy's inauguration, Lumumba was brutally tortured and executed at the hands of Tshombe's men – in the presence of Belgian officers who commanded the secessionist army and were under the authority of the Belgian Defense Ministry.

Lumumba's assassination was a blow to the Soviet Union. However, it did not harm Soviet prestige in Africa and Asia. On the contrary, having supported Lumumba and his cause more than any other non-African power, the Soviet Union emerged from the 1960 Congo Crisis with the respect of many nonaligned nations. The United States, in contrast, found its reputation badly damaged. Complicit with the

PHOTO 3.2. Secessionist leader Moïse Tshombe with Belgian commander of the Katanga Army, Lieutenant Colonel Jean-Marie Crèvecoeur, February 1, 1961 (Terrence Spencer/Time Life Pictures/Getty Images).

old colonial order, the United States and Belgium were held responsible for Lumumba's murder. In a radio broadcast to the Ghanaian people, Nkrumah decried "the colonialists and imperialists" who had killed Lumumba, while proclaiming that "African freedom, the unity and independence of Africa and the final complete destruction of colonialism and imperialism," for which Lumumba had sacrificed his life, would endure.[5] Worried that the Soviet Union was winning the battle for hearts and minds, the incoming Kennedy administration was determined to burnish America's image in the developing world.

The arrival of the Kennedy administration resulted in a shift in America's Africa policy. In contrast to his predecessors, Kennedy realized that African nationalism would play an important role in the continent's future and that it was in American interests to befriend emerging nations. In his view, selective accommodation of noncommunist

[5] Nkrumah, *Challenge of the Congo*, 133.

PHOTO 3.3. Picketers protesting UN and Belgian actions in the Congo demonstrate in front of the United Nations, February 1, 1961 (Yale Joel/Time Life Pictures/Getty Images).

independence movements, rather than stubborn support of a doomed imperial order, was the best way to prevent the spread of communism and to protect American economic concerns. Kennedy immediately challenged the Eisenhower legacy in this regard. In December 1960, shortly before Eisenhower left office, the United States had joined France, Britain, Belgium, Portugal, and South Africa in abstaining on a UN General Assembly resolution that supported the right of all peoples to self-determination and independence and called for an end to all forms of colonialism. Rejecting Eisenhower's policies as retrograde and certain to inspire African resistance, the Kennedy administration retroactively endorsed the UN resolution opposing colonialism.

In the Congo, Kennedy pursued a similar tack. Convinced that both radical nationalism and Belgian recolonization would play into Soviet hands, Kennedy sought a third way. During his administration, Washington became the Congo's primary source of military and economic assistance. The United States trained Congolese soldiers in America and provided airplanes equipped with anti-Castro Cuban pilots to quell rebellions and unrest. The CIA attempted to garner support for American interests by disbursing funds to trade union and youth organizations. To win legitimacy for the new Congolese government, Kennedy favored the reopening of parliament – as long as Lumumba's supporters were kept to a minimum.

The Kennedy administration's choice for prime minister was Cyrille Adoula, an anticommunist trade unionist with CIA connections, who, it transpired, had little popular backing. At the July 1961 parliamentary conference, Antoine Gizenga, Lumumba's deputy prime minister, emerged as a clear favorite. The prospects of a Gizenga premiership set off alarm bells in Washington. In December 1960, Gizenga had established a rebel regime in Stanleyville, which he claimed was the true heir to the Lumumba government. The Soviet Union and a number of African and Asian states had recognized his regime as the Congo's sole legitimate government. Moscow, however, was wary of the logistical obstacles involved in moving supplies through African countries with entrenched Western interests and had balked at providing material aid. Washington was determined to prevent Gizenga's rise to power in the capital. The CIA planted pro-Adoula newspaper articles and distributed money to those willing to support his candidacy. The Kennedy administration concluded that if Gizenga prevailed, Mobutu and his colleagues should be prompted to instigate another coup d'état. However, in August 1961, the American candidate, Cyrille Adoula, was duly installed as the Congo's prime minister. As a result of Lumumba's continued popularity, Adoula's shaky coalition government was forced to include a large number of Lumumbist ministers, including Gizenga, who once again became deputy prime minister.

In this precarious situation, Adoula's survival required political stability. This meant, first and foremost, an end to the secessionist movement in Katanga. By September 1961, Kennedy had become convinced that if the West refused to support reunification, Adoula, under pressure from government leftists, might follow Lumumba's lead and turn to the Soviet Union. The move to support the central government divided the U.S. State Department, with the African and International Organization Affairs bureaus on one side and the European bureau on the other, while the Pentagon aligned itself with the Europeanists. The proposed policy shift was vehemently opposed by the American Katanga lobby, which brought together a group of anticommunist, anti-UN politicians, industrialists, and missionaries. This prosecessionist lobby included a vocal contingent of prosegregation Southern whites and Americans with business interests in Katanga, South Africa, and Southern Rhodesia. Despite pressure from the Katanga lobby and Europeanists in the administration, the United States eventually broke with the regional colonial powers of Belgium, Britain, France, and Portugal, as well as white-minority-ruled South Africa and the settler-dominated Central African Federation. In November 1961, Washington joined Moscow in supporting an Afro-Asian Security Council resolution authorizing the UN to use its troops to expel foreign mercenaries from Katanga. The United States also provided the planes, trucks, and weapons necessary to conduct the operation. It was understood that the expulsion of the mercenaries would effectively end the Katanga rebellion.

Meanwhile, politics in the Congo had disintegrated into rivalry between local leaders who manipulated regional and ethnic loyalties to promote personal interests and between competing groups in the Congolese army. Although Lumumba's MNC had laid the foundations for a national political party, after Lumumba no other leader had the strength or vision to unite the opposing factions. As the year drew to a close, a number of Lumumbists resigned from Adoula's fragile coalition government, and Gizenga again rallied resistance in eastern Congo. In January 1962, with American and UN support, Adoula arrested his antagonist and purged the remaining Lumumbists from his regime, excluding from power the largest, single most important political force in the Congo.

Although the South Kasai secession was finally quelled in September 1962 and that in Katanga the following January, peace did not come to the Congo. Government corruption and economic decline had led to widespread discontent in the civilian population. Convinced that disorder was a breeding ground for communism, Kennedy supported General Mobutu's strong-arm tactics. During Mobutu's visit to Washington in May 1963, Kennedy told him that "there was nobody in the world that had done more than the General to maintain freedom against the Communists."[6] In October 1963, with a green light from Washington, Mobutu declared martial law and took effective control of the Congolese government. In June 1964, Adoula resigned from his now powerless position as prime minister. Nine days later, UN troops left the country.

The Crisis of 1964–65

Kennedy had finally broken with Belgium and the other colonial powers over Katanga; his successor returned to the colonial fold. The Johnson administration, which took office after Kennedy's November 1963 assassination, had important links to the Katanga lobby, especially to its Southern advocates in the U.S. Senate. Moreover, Johnson was much less concerned about African opinion than his predecessor. He was personally charmed by Moïse Tshombe, who had ordered Lumumba's murder and whose name in Africa was synonymous with treachery. In July 1964, Tshombe maneuvered his way through a minefield of Congolese politics and was installed as prime minister of the Congo. Brussels and Washington quickly endorsed the new leader, while Belgian advisors and South African mercenaries assumed prominent roles in his government. Despite his past as a secessionist leader who was reviled as a sellout across the continent,

---

[6] Quoted in Odd Arne Westad, *The Global Cold War: Third World Interventions and the Making of Our Times* (New York: Cambridge University Press, 2005), 36.

PHOTO 3.4. President Kennedy with General Mobutu after their White House meeting, May 31, 1963 (Bettmann/Corbis).

Tshombe was perceived by the West to be the strongman needed to restore order and stem the radical tide.

Tshombe was faced with an enormous task. By the time UN troops left the Congo in June 1964, the country was in chaos, with several focal points of rebellion. Lumumbist rebels had gained control of much of the eastern region, as well as some territory in the west. Pierre Mulele led the western Chinese-supported rebellion while rebel forces led by Gaston Soumaliot, Christophe Gbenye, and Laurent Kabila coalesced as the Simbas (lions) in the east. Although Kabila's rebels were briefly supported by a Cuban contingent led by Che Guevara, the eastern rebels were not communists, and they had little external support. Nonetheless, the Johnson administration warned American allies that the Congo was threatened by a communist insurgency. In a reversal of the Suez Crisis, when the colonial powers instigated an armed intervention and the United States called for diplomacy, Washington urged Belgium, France, and Britain to intervene militarily in the Congo, claiming that the maintenance of law and order in Africa was their responsibility. None of the European powers took the bait, believing the threat to be neither communist nor significant. Even if the rebels won, which they deemed unlikely, the Congolese would still be reliant on Belgian technical and economic assistance, and hence would continue to do business with the West.

Unable to convince other countries to supply troops, Washington was forced to devise a two-pronged strategy: it would provide overt military aid to the Tshombe government while covertly training a mercenary army. Under duress, Brussels agreed to participate in the American-led mercenary operation. Thus, the United States and Belgium secretly helped Tshombe recruit, train, and finance a 1,000-man mercenary army, composed primarily of white South Africans and Southern Rhodesians but with a share of Belgian, French, British, and Spanish hired guns. Meanwhile, American technicians and counterinsurgency experts openly trained the Congolese army, and fifty-six American parachutists were supplied from Fort Bragg. The United States and Italy provided bombers and transport planes, while military equipment was furnished by South Africa and the United States. Because the Congo had no air force, the donated planes were piloted by South African and European mercenaries, along with anti-Castro Cuban veterans of the Bay of Pigs operation, recruited and paid for by the CIA.

By August 1964, Lumumbist rebels controlled more than one-third of the country. The following month, they established a People's Republic with Stanleyville as its capital. As the combined mercenary and Congolese forces advanced toward Stanleyville, mercenary pilots bombed railroads, bridges, and populated areas without regard for civilian casualties, while mercenary and Congolese soldiers committed untold atrocities – raping, robbing, and killing with abandon. In October, the rebels took some 300 Belgian and American civilians hostage, hoping to negotiate an end to the onslaught. However, Brussels and Washington refused all concessions and opted instead for armed intervention. In late November, 545 Belgian paratroopers transported by a dozen American planes were dropped into Stanleyville in an operation financed by the United States, Belgium, and Israel. Coordinating with Congolese soldiers and mercenaries on the ground, the paratroopers recaptured the city. As the combined forces approached, the rebels killed some two dozen hostages. By the end of the raid, sixty hostages were dead. In the days that followed, the mercenary and Congolese armies conducted a ruthless campaign of retaliation against the civilian population, killing more than 1,000 people. The rebels counterattacked, indiscriminately killing local government officials and their supporters and any European who crossed their path. The short-lived People's Republic fell, and between 1964 and 1967, when the last white mercenaries left, eastern Congo was embroiled in a bloody civil war.

As would be true throughout the Congo's troubled future, the rebels were by no means liberators. Like the government and mercenary armies they opposed, many took advantage of the lawlessness to promote their own interests and to settle personal scores. They executed civilians because they were wealthy, educated, or powerful; because they worked for the government; or because they were members of a particular ethnic group. In an assessment that would bode ill for the Congo's future, Che Guevara wrote despairingly of rebel forces that were wracked by ethnic divisions, indiscipline, and leadership rivalries and who mistreated local populations. He worried that Cuba's indiscriminate support would allow unfit leaders "to replace colonialism with neo-colonialism." His disparaging characterization of Kabila, whom he claimed lacked "revolutionary seriousness, an ideology that can guide action, a spirit of sacrifice that accompanies one's actions," would return to haunt the Congo more than three decades later.[7]

The Stanleyville raid and its bloody aftermath caused an outcry in Africa, where mercenary atrocities were condemned and rebel abuses largely ignored. Ghana, Guinea, Algeria, the United Arab Republic, Congo-Brazzaville (Republic of Congo), Tanzania, Sudan, Kenya, Uganda, and Burundi responded with money, weapons, and permission for rebels to use their territories for transit. Communist nations, which had provided little aid prior to this time, intensified their support for the rebel cause. The Soviet Union and East Germany joined China in providing military assistance. Cuba sent some 120 soldiers and military instructors under the leadership of Che Guevara. The Havana contingent eventually fought the CIA-sponsored Cuban exiles on Lake Tanganyika. However, none of these initiatives approached the magnitude of Western support for Léopoldville. In Stanleyville's aftermath, the United States stepped up its aid to the Congolese government, helping Mobutu to establish a sophisticated, well-equipped army that would eventually transform his country into a regional powerhouse.

---

[7] Ernesto "Che" Guevara, *The African Dream: The Diaries of the Revolutionary War in the Congo*, trans. Patrick Camiller (New York: Grove Press, 2000), 244.

Under pressure from the United States, Belgium, France, and
Britain, a number of African countries withdrew their support for
the rebel cause. Without funding, weapons, or transit areas, the Simbas were forced to capitulate. On November 18, 1965, they agreed to
end the war – even as mercenaries continued their depredations in the
east. Three days later, Che Guevara's Cuban contingent left the country. On November 24, Mobutu, with tacit American approval, staged
another coup d'état. This time, he did not bother with the facade
of a civilian government but retained the reins of power for himself.
His brutal dictatorship lasted until 1997, when Laurent Kabila's rebel
army overthrew him.

Suggested Reading

For an overview of the Congo Crisis, three books are especially recommended.
Stephen R. Weissman's *American Foreign Policy in the Congo, 1960–1964*
(Ithaca, NY: Cornell University Press, 1974) remains one of the best in-
depth scholarly analyses of the crisis. Chapter 5 of William Minter's *King
Solomon's Mines Revisited: Western Interests and the Burdened History of Southern Africa* (New York: Basic Books, 1986) offers a concise and accessible overview, examining the key actors and their political and economic
interests. Piero Gleijeses's *Conflicting Missions: Havana, Washington, and
Africa, 1959–1976* (Chapel Hill: University of North Carolina Press, 2002)
explores the 1964–65 rebellion and its aftermath, examining the roles of the
UN, Western powers, and Cuba.

For general historical background, two books are recommended. Adam
Hochschild's *King Leopold's Ghost: A Story of Greed, Terror, and Heroism
in Colonial Africa* (New York: Houghton Mifflin, 1998) tells the story of
colonial conquest, exploitation, and contemporary human rights protests
that altered the course of the Congo's history. Georges Nzongola-Ntalaja's
The Congo from Leopold to Kabila (London: Zed Books, 2002) is a highly
readable historical overview by a leading Congolese scholar.

For Lumumba's political thought, see Patrice Lumumba, *Congo, My Country*
(New York: Praeger, 1962).

Several important scholarly accounts written immediately after the crisis provide insight into the interests and objectives of Congolese political actors,
Western powers, the Soviet Union, African nations, and the UN. See
Catherine Hoskyns, *The Congo since Independence, January 1960–December
1961* (New York: Oxford University Press, 1965); René Lemarchand, *Political Awakening in the Belgian Congo*, 2nd ed. (Westport, CT: Greenwood

Press, 1982; first published, 1964); Crawford Young, *Politics in the Congo: Decolonization and Independence* (Princeton, NJ: Princeton University Press, 1965).

The role of the UN has been explored by both scholars and participants. John Kent's *America, the UN and Decolonisation: Cold War Conflict in the Congo* (New York: Routledge, 2010) shows how the UN helped to preserve the existing social and economic order. Carole Collins's article "Fatally Flawed Mediation: Cordier and the Congo Crisis of 1960," *Africa Today* 39, no. 3 (1992): 5–22, focuses on Andrew Cordier, the American diplomat who served as the first head of the UN operation. Rajeshwar Dayal, the Indian diplomat who replaced Cordier and was less sympathetic to Belgian and American interests, produced an insightful memoir, *Mission for Hammarskjöld* (London: Oxford University Press, 1976). Critical assessments of the UN operation are offered by political scientist David N. Gibbs and by Irish diplomat Conor Cruise O'Brien, who represented the UN in Katanga. See David N. Gibbs, "Dag Hammarskjöld, the United Nations, and the Congo Crisis of 1960–1: A Reinterpretation," *Journal of Modern African Studies* 31, no. 1 (March 1993): 163–74, and Conor Cruise O'Brien, *To Katanga and Back: A UN Case History* (New York: Simon & Schuster, 1962).

Interpretations of the U.S. role are offered in a number of studies based on declassified government documents, interviews, and other primary sources. In addition to Weissman (mentioned above), the most useful include Madeleine G. Kalb, *The Congo Cables: The Cold War in Africa – From Eisenhower to Kennedy* (New York: Macmillan, 1982); William Minter, "Candid Cables: Some Reflections on U.S. Response to the Congo Rebellions, 1964," in *The Crisis in Zaire: Myths and Realities*, ed. Georges Nzongola-Ntalaja (Trenton, NJ: Africa World Press, 1986), 265–87; and Richard D. Mahoney, *JFK: Ordeal in Africa* (New York: Oxford University Press, 1983). The influence of American business interests on the making of U.S.-Congo policy is explored in David N. Gibbs, *The Political Economy of Third World Intervention: Mines, Money, and U.S. Policy in the Congo Crisis* (Chicago: University of Chicago Press, 1991) and Jonathan Kwitny, *Endless Enemies: The Making of an Unfriendly World* (New York: Congdon and Weed, 1984).

In addition to Kalb (mentioned above), a number of works examine American and Belgian plots to assassinate Lumumba. The results of a U.S. congressional investigation are included in the "Church Committee Report": U.S. Senate, *Alleged Assassination Plots Involving Foreign Leaders: An Interim Report of the Select Committee to Study Governmental Operations with Respect to Intelligence Activities* (Washington, DC: U.S. Government Printing Office, 1975). The CIA station chief, Lawrence Devlin, produced a memoir that provides new insights into the American covert operations: *Chief of Station, Congo: Fighting the Cold War in a Hot Zone* (New York: Public Affairs, 2007). Stephen R. Weissman's "An Extraordinary Rendition," *Intelligence and National Security* 25, no. 2 (April 2010): 198–222, uses declassified U.S. government documents, memoirs of Belgian and American covert operatives, and interviews to provide a new interpretation of the American role in Lumumba's death. Ludo De Witte's *The Assassination of Lumumba*, trans. Ann Wright and Renée Fenby (New York: Verso, 2001) uses declassified Belgian government documents and interviews to expose the Belgian government's role in Lumumba's death. De Witte's book sparked a Belgian parliamentary inquiry (2000–1) and a formal apology to the Congolese people.

Several works explore the involvement of other colonial and regional powers. Alan James's *Britain and the Congo Crisis, 1960–63* (New York: St. Martin's Press, 1996) examines British economic interests in Katanga and political concerns about the region's future. Rosalynde Ainslie's *The Unholy Alliance: Salazar-Verwoerd-Welensky* (London: Columbia Printers, 1962) and Matthew Hughes's "Fighting for White Rule in Africa: The Central African Federation, Katanga, and the Congo Crisis, 1958–1965," *International History Review* 25, no. 3 (September 2003): 592–615, investigate the role of regional powers such as South Africa and the Central African Federation in the Congo Crisis.

Memoirs by white mercenaries include Mike Hoare's *Congo Warriors* (London: Hale, 1991), which describes his experiences in Katanga in 1961–62 and *Congo Mercenary* (London: Hale, 1967; reprinted as *The Road to Kalamata: A Congo Mercenary's Personal Memoir*, Lexington, MA: Lexington Books, 1989), which discusses his role in suppressing the Congo rebellion in 1964–65. Another account of the 1964–65 operations is Jerry Puren's *Mercenary Commander* (Alberton, South Africa: Galago, 1986).

Several works examine Soviet involvement, drawing on newly available Soviet-era archives. See Aleksandr Fursenko and Timothy Naftali, *Khrushchev's Cold War: The Inside Story of an American Adversary* (New York: W. W. Norton, 2006) and Sergey Mazov, *A Distant Front in the Cold War: The USSR in West Africa and the Congo, 1956–1964* (Washington, DC: Woodrow Wilson Center Press; Stanford, CA: Stanford University Press, 2010).

Cuba's role is explored in Gleijeses's book (mentioned above) and two others with opposing perspectives. Ernesto "Che" Guevara's memoir, *The Africa Dream: The Diaries of the Revolutionary War in the Congo*, trans. Patrick Camiller (New York: Grove Press, 2000), describes his experiences as the leader of Cuban troops supporting the Lumumbist rebellion in eastern Congo in 1965. Frank Villafaña's book, *Cold War in the Congo:*

The Confrontation of Cuban Military Forces, 1960–1967 (New Brunswick, NJ: Transaction Publishers, 2009), explores the conflict in eastern Congo from the perspective of anti-Castro Cuban pilots provided to the central government by the CIA.

For the role of African and nonaligned countries see Kwame Nkrumah, *Challenge of the Congo* (New York: International Publishers, 1970) and Eberi Nwaubani, "Eisenhower, Nkrumah and the Congo Crisis," *Journal of Contemporary History* 36, no. 4 (October 2001): 599–622.

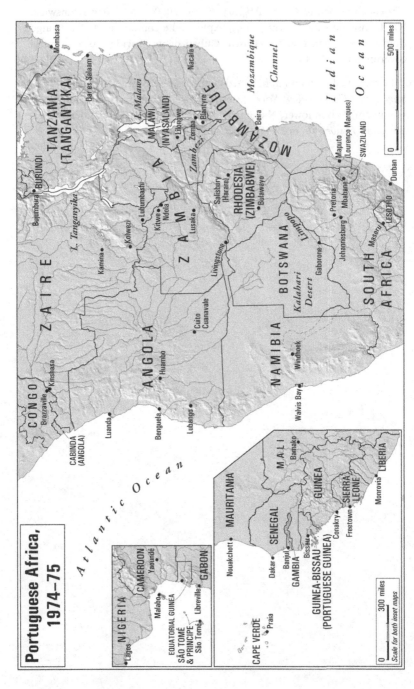

MAP 4.1. Portuguese Africa, 1974–75. (Map by Philip Schwartzberg, Meridian Mapping, Minneapolis.)

CHAPTER 4

War and Decolonization in Portugal's African Empire, 1961–1975

While its NATO allies focused on the Congo, Portugal had its own African concerns. By the early 1960s, it was clear that France, Britain, and Belgium could maintain neocolonial economic relationships with their African colonies without the hassles of political control. With growing demands for economic development and burgeoning political unrest, independence had become an attractive option for both colonizer and colonized. For Portugal, ruled by the fascist dictatorship of António Salazar since 1932, African independence was out of the question. In contrast to its northern European counterparts, Portugal was an impoverished country with an underdeveloped economy. However, it maintained the illusion of grandeur with significant African possessions: Portuguese Guinea and the strategically important island of Cape Verde in West Africa and its environs; the islands of São Tomé and Príncipe off the coast of Central Africa; and Mozambique and Angola in Southern Africa. Without the cheap labor and raw materials that resulted from a harsh forced labor regime, Portugal's industries would not be profitable. Unable to compete in an unprotected market, Portugal was determined to retain political control of its colonies. With the exception of their settler colonies, France, Britain, and Belgium generally acquiesced to political independence without armed struggle. Portugal, in contrast, considered its colonial possessions to be overseas provinces akin to French Algeria and waged devastating colonial wars to retain them. This chapter examines the national liberation movements and external actors in Portugal's three mainland colonies; the transformations in American policy toward its

NATO ally; and the contours of the struggles in Portuguese Guinea, Mozambique, and Angola.

The National Liberation Movements

By the early 1960s, armed resistance had begun in all three of Portugal's mainland African colonies. The nationalist movement in Portuguese Guinea, which embraced the adjacent Cape Verde islands, was launched in September 1956, with the establishment of the African Party for the Independence of Guinea and Cape Verde (PAIGC). Although other nationalist organizations jockeyed for position, the PAIGC was by far the strongest and most effective. Led by Amílcar Cabral, a Portuguese-educated agronomist from Cape Verde, the PAIGC included Western-educated intellectuals, urban workers, city dwellers whose informal sector activities subjected them to continuous police harassment, and deserters from the Portuguese colonial army. Although not a communist himself, Cabral was convinced that Marxism provided useful tools for analyzing colonial problems. He sought support from diverse actors in the international community. These included the UN, which Cabral claimed "had demanded the elimination of the system of colonial domination," as well as African, Nordic, and socialist countries; the World Council of Churches; and other nongovernmental organizations.[1]

In Mozambique, the nationalist movement emerged from Western-educated and working-class populations in the south and from emigrants in neighboring countries who had originally hailed from central and northern Mozambique. In 1962, three ethnically and regionally based organizations established by Mozambicans working in Southern Rhodesia, Nyasaland, and Tanganyika merged to form FRELIMO. Led by Eduardo Mondlane, who had studied in South Africa, Portugal, and the United States and earned a Ph.D. from Northwestern University, FRELIMO's goal was to unite in a single nationalist movement people of all races, regions, ethnic groups, and socioeconomic classes.

[1] Amilcar Cabral, "Second Address before the United Nations," in *Return to the Source: Selected Speeches by Amilcar Cabral*, ed. Africa Information Service (New York: Monthly Review Press, 1973), 19.

In Angola, three nationalist organizations strove for dominance. The MPLA, founded in 1956, was led by Agostinho Neto, a Portuguese-educated medical doctor. The FNLA, established in 1962 as a merger of two regional parties, was led by Holden Roberto, a brother-in-law and protégé of Joseph-Désiré Mobutu, who seized power in the Congo in 1965. UNITA, which broke from the FNLA in 1966, was led by Jonas Savimbi, a Swiss-educated political scientist with a master's degree from the University of Lausanne. Each of the movements was roughly associated with one of Angola's three main ethnic groups, although each had members of different ethnic origins, and the MPLA in particular stressed its inclusive national appeal. The MPLA's stronghold was among the Mbundu in north-central Angola, which included the capital city of Luanda. It also found strong support among Western-educated intellectuals (*assimilados*), urban workers and the petit bourgeoisie, people of mixed race (*mestiços*), and a small number of Angola's 200,000 Portuguese settlers. The FNLA evolved from earlier ethnically based movements in the northwest and was dominated by the Bakongo, who had ties to similar populations in the Congo. UNITA was based primarily among the Ovimbundu in the central highlands.

The three Angolan movements were also distinguished by ideology. The MPLA was avowedly Marxist. Leading members had ties to the Portuguese Communist Party dating to the 1950s. The FNLA and UNITA used anticommunist rhetoric to win international backing but accepted support from China, which was intent on countering Soviet patronage of the MPLA. Internally, UNITA adopted a hard-line Maoist ideology, at least initially. Both the FNLA and UNITA criticized the prominence of whites, *mestiços*, and Western-educated Africans in the MPLA and presented themselves as the only representatives of authentic African nationalism. Both organizations spurned the MPLA's offer to establish a common front and systematically attacked MPLA cadres. While the MPLA, and to a lesser extent the FNLA, bore the brunt of the fighting against the Portuguese, UNITA concentrated its efforts on ousting the MPLA from the eastern part of the country, where both movements were recruiting among the smaller ethnic groups. By 1971, Savimbi had signed secret deals with Lisbon in which UNITA agreed to suspend military operations and to collaborate with Portugal against its rivals.

In 1961, the PAIGC, FRELIMO, and the MPLA established the Conference of Nationalist Organizations of the Portuguese Colonies (CONCP), with the goal of coordinating the liberation struggle in all three territories. The three organizations also participated in the 1966 Tricontinental Conference in Havana, where the Organization of Solidarity with the Peoples of Asia, Africa, and Latin America was founded with the pledge to support national liberation and economic development on all three continents.

External Actors

Although Soviet involvement in the Portuguese territories was minimal in the 1960s, Lisbon claimed that it faced a Soviet-backed communist insurgency and sought support from its NATO allies. The NATO countries responded by providing hundreds of millions of dollars in military and economic aid that enabled Portugal to finance three simultaneous wars and bolster its failing economy. By far the largest military supplier, France contributed armored cars, helicopters, planes, warships, submarines, and ammunition. In addition to ships and planes, West Germany furnished weapons and napalm and collaborated with the Portuguese secret police against the liberation movements. As part of the NATO defense pact, the United States provided military equipment to Portugal for European defense. Although Washington stipulated that American equipment could not be used in Portugal's African wars, Lisbon openly violated the agreement, and Washington did nothing to enforce it. From the Kennedy through the Nixon administrations, American weapons, tanks, planes, ships, helicopters, napalm, and chemical defoliants were used against Africans in the Portuguese colonies, while American military personnel trained thousands of Portuguese soldiers in counterinsurgency techniques.

NATO's official support for Portugal was countered by a disparate group of nations and nongovernmental organizations that sustained the anticolonial movements. The most significant liberation supporters were the Nordic countries, which included neutral Sweden and Finland as well as NATO members Norway and Denmark. The Nordics established close relationships with the liberation movements and were their main source of humanitarian assistance. The World Council of Churches, whose Programme to Combat Racism established a special fund to provide humanitarian aid to the liberation movements, was another important source of moral backing and material aid. The OAU, established by thirty-two independent African countries in 1963 to unite the continent and eradicate colonialism, mobilized military, economic, and diplomatic support through its Tanzania-based Liberation Committee. Finally, communist countries – most importantly, the Soviet Union, Cuba, and China – responded to the Portuguese onslaught with military assistance to the various liberation organizations.

The United States and Portugal: The Shifting Alliance

American policy toward Portugal and its colonies underwent many transformations between 1961 and 1975. The Eisenhower administration had joined the European imperial powers in abstaining on the December 1960 UN General Assembly resolution calling for self-determination and independence for all colonized peoples. The Kennedy administration retroactively endorsed the resolution and used it repeatedly to challenge Portuguese rule in Africa. Convinced that unwavering support for imperialism strengthened the hand of international communism, Kennedy was determined, first and foremost, to prevent communist success. In Portugal's African colonies, as in the Congo, he hoped to outflank radicalism through reforms that catered to Africans' rising expectations without undermining Washington's relationship with its European ally. He sought relationships with "moderate" nationalists who would promote Western interests while mollifying African discontent. This Africa-centered policy sparked significant debate within the Kennedy administration and was effectively sidelined by late 1962, as the United States sought a closer relationship with Portugal due to Cold War and strategic concerns. Preoccupied by Vietnam, Johnson took little interest in Africa, whereas Nixon and Ford tilted increasingly toward Portugal and its colonial regimes. By 1975, American policy toward Portugal had come full circle.

Kennedy's balancing act was tested shortly after he took office. In February 1961, MPLA partisans and other government opponents attacked the prisons in the Angolan capital of Luanda in a futile attempt to free political prisoners. Several Portuguese soldiers and police were killed, and hundreds of Angolan civilians were massacred in retaliation. In March, conscript workers and activists loosely linked to the Union of Peoples of Angola (later absorbed into the FNLA) killed some 250 Portuguese settlers in the coffee-producing areas north of the capital. They also targeted *mestiços* and Ovimbundu migrant laborers. Portugal hit back, using American weapons, tanks, planes, and napalm – as well as 25,000 Portuguese NATO troops – in a brutal campaign that killed thousands of Angolans and caused an outcry from African states.

Anxious to win favor with African countries and to pressure Portugal to implement reforms that would undermine the appeal of radical nationalism, the Kennedy administration broke a longstanding tradition of support for Portugal in the UN. In March it supported an Afro-Asian Security Council resolution calling for an investigation into Portuguese repression. In June, it voted for another that "deeply deplor[ed] the large-scale killings and the severely repressive measures in Angola" and urged a speedy end to colonial rule.[2] In a pattern reminiscent of those that emerged during the Suez Crisis in 1956 and the Katanga secession in 1961, the Cold War superpowers and the European colonial powers stood on opposing sides. While the Soviet Union joined the United States in supporting both resolutions, France and Britain abstained. Cognizant of the Algerian parallel, France argued that Portuguese involvement in Angola – which it claimed as an "overseas province" – was a domestic matter and thus outside the UN's purview. Britain actually increased weapons sales to Portugal so that it could respond more effectively to the rebellion. Accusing the United States of supporting communist subversion, Prime Minister Salazar denounced the American stance and declared his intention to continue the counterinsurgency campaign.

As tensions threatened the Western alliance, fractures surfaced in the Kennedy administration. The secretaries of Defense and State, supported by the State Department's European division, emphasized Portugal's importance to NATO. During the Kennedy years, three-quarters of American military traffic to Europe and the Middle East passed through Portugal's Azores islands air base. American carriers had used the base during the 1958 intervention in Lebanon and the 1961 Berlin Crisis. The administration's Europeanists argued that

---

[2] UN Security Council Resolution 163 (1961), June 9, 1961, http://www.un.org/ga/search/view_doc.asp?symbol=S/RES/163(1961).

American access to the base had to be protected at all costs. The administration's Africanists – led by the State Department's number-two man, Under Secretary of State Chester Bowles, along with Assistant Secretary of State for African Affairs G. Mennen Williams, and UN Ambassador Adlai Stevenson – vehemently disagreed. Convinced that Salazar's intransigence could lead to a full-scale war with Soviet involvement, Kennedy sought a middle ground. His administration quietly reduced military aid to Portugal and in 1961, over the protests of the U.S. ambassador to Lisbon, banned Portugal's use of American weapons and military equipment in Africa. Henceforth, American military aid could be used only for NATO purposes within the area prescribed in the NATO treaty. No part of Africa fell within these boundaries.

As Salazar rejected plea after plea for self-determination in Angola, the Kennedy administration began to court the Portuguese political opposition, young middle-level army officers, and even African nationalists, hoping to turn the latter away from communism and armed struggle. Funneling covert aid through the Adoula administration in neighboring Congo, the CIA provided Holden Roberto with a $6,000 annual retainer fee, in exchange for intelligence and to strengthen the Union of Peoples of Angola/FNLA against the more radical MPLA. The Kennedy administration also assisted some 150,000 Angolan refugees in the Congo and provided scholarships to Portuguese African students living in exile – but rebuffed MPLA requests for assistance.

The Africanist leanings of the Kennedy White House sparked an immediate backlash. In Congress, an eclectic group bearing a striking resemblance to the Katanga lobby supported the Portuguese government's position. Composed of anticommunists and Southern segregationists, and fueled by a New York public relations firm hired by Lisbon, the congressional coalition teamed up with Europeanists in the State and Defense Departments to champion America's access to the Azores and its special relationship with Portugal. Liberals cautioned that a pro-Portugal stance threatened to overturn policies that had successfully outmaneuvered the Soviets in Africa. In the wake of the Berlin Crisis, which lasted from June to November 1961, Europeanists gained the upper hand. Chester Bowles was forced from office in November, and the State Department's second-ranked position was assumed by George Ball, a staunch Europeanist.

In the end, it was the ongoing tension over Berlin and the Cuban Missile Crisis in October 1962 that sidelined the Africanists and pushed the president to Lisbon's side. By the fall of 1962, the Kennedy administration no longer protested when Portugal used American-supplied NATO equipment in Africa. It no longer called for self-determination in Portugal's African colonies but instead for programs of political and economic reform. From that time forward, Kennedy's UN delegation abstained on virtually all Security Council resolutions critical of Portugal. Administration contacts with Holden Roberto and other nationalists were severed. When the Azores base lease expired in December 1962, Lisbon augmented its political leverage by acceding only to temporary arrangements to be renewed at Portugal's pleasure. American pressure on Portugal effectively ceased, and American tanks, planes, and weapons continued to be diverted for use in Portugal's African wars. In July 1963, Kennedy ordered Stevenson to join France and Britain in abstaining on a Security Council resolution imposing a voluntary arms embargo on Portugal – even though Stevenson had helped to water down the resolution in an attempt to make it acceptable.

President Lyndon Johnson, in contrast to Kennedy, took little interest in Africa. His focus in 1964–65 was domestic civil rights and antipoverty legislation. As his presidency drew to a close, the Vietnam War overshadowed all else. Anxious not to antagonize the former colonial powers, whose support he needed for the war effort, and determined to maintain access to the Azores air base, Johnson avoided the issue of self-determination in Portugal's African colonies. Europeanists in the State Department became even more prominent in the shaping of U.S.-Africa policy. The shift was evident in November 1964, when American planes flew Belgian paratroopers to Stanleyville, Congo, via the Azores. Six months later, in a State Department–approved operation, the CIA arranged to sell Portugal seven B-26 bombers for use against rebels in Angola and Mozambique. While the Johnson administration provided a small amount of covert nonmilitary aid to the FNLA and FRELIMO between 1964 and 1968, by the end of his term Johnson deemed Mondlane too radical and cut off all FRELIMO support. Although American ties to the FNLA were not severed, the organization had only a weak presence in Angola.

Like Johnson, Richard Nixon had little interest in Africa, which he continued to view as a European imperial domain. Henry Kissinger, who served Nixon as both national security advisor and secretary of state, regarded Africa with open disdain. He consistently rejected the advice of his Africa experts, whom he considered too sympathetic to African nations and liberation movements. Forcing out those who rejected his positions, Kissinger ran through four assistant secretaries of state for African affairs between 1973 and 1975.

Convinced that his predecessors had jeopardized relations with important allies, Nixon ordered a thorough review of American policies and objectives in Southern Africa, focusing on the Portuguese colonies and white-settler regimes. The resulting "Study in Response to National Security Study Memorandum 39," completed in December 1969, signaled the eclipse of the State Department by the Pentagon and National Security Council in the formulation of U.S.-Africa policy. According to the classified study, central American objectives in the region included the protection of economic and strategic interests and the minimization of "opportunities for the USSR and Communist China . . . to gain political influence with black governments and liberation movements." Disavowing the Kennedy administration's courtship of African nationalists, the Nixon policy would be premised on the notion that "the whites are here to stay and the only way that constructive change can come about is through them. There is no hope for the blacks to gain the political rights they seek through violence, which will only lead to chaos and increased opportunities for the communists." Moreover, in keeping with the study's prescriptions, the United States would adopt an attitude of consultation, rather than confrontation, with the white regimes, maintaining "public opposition to racial repression but relax[ing] political isolation and economic restrictions on the white states."[3]

The new approach was readily apparent in Nixon's public attitude toward Portugal. Rejecting Kennedy's pressure tactics and Johnson's benign neglect, Nixon embraced the regime of Marcello Caetano, which had replaced that of Salazar in September 1968. Viewing Portugal as a bulwark against communism and a force for stability in Southern Africa, Nixon emphasized Portugal's role as a regional policeman.

[3] National Security Council Interdepartmental Group for Africa, "Study in Response to National Security Study Memorandum 39: Southern Africa," December 9, 1969, in *South Africa and the United States: The Declassified History*, ed. Kenneth Mokoena (New York: New Press, 1993), 209, 211.

American foreign service officials were ordered to cease all contacts with Angolan and Mozambican nationalists, and Roberto's retainer fee was eliminated. In August 1970, Washington officially relaxed the nine-year-old prohibition on the use of American arms and military equipment in Portuguese Africa, exempting certain dual-use items that could be used for either civilian or military purposes. Lisbon immediately bought Boeing planes to transport troops to Africa and Bell helicopters to defoliate rebellious areas. Meanwhile, American investments grew. Gulf Oil, with a huge stake in the Cabinda Enclave, became the largest single investor in the Portuguese colonies. By the early 1970s, Gulf Oil revenues provided Portugal with approximately 60 percent of its Angola war budget.

The United States also bolstered Portugal's war-weakened economy. In December 1971, Washington granted Lisbon credits worth $436 million in exchange for rights to the Azores air base through February 1974. Despite these victories, Portugal continued to up the ante. During the course of the 1973 Arab-Israeli War, the United States sent 20,000 tons of weapons to Israel. With the exception of Portugal, NATO countries, dependent on Middle Eastern oil, refused to allow the American supply planes to refuel on their soil. In return for use of the Azores base, Portugal successfully negotiated another relaxation of the arms embargo. In January 1974, one month before the Azores agreement expired, Lisbon offered to extend it again – in exchange for sophisticated weapons and the lifting of the prohibition against the use of American weapons in Africa. Because the prohibition was riddled with loopholes and had been regularly circumvented, Lisbon's motivations were largely symbolic; Portugal hoped to end its pariah status in the international community. Kissinger favored accommodating Portugal – against the better judgment of his Africa advisors, who warned of negative consequences in Africa and the UN. A military coup in Portugal rendered the question moot.

By 1974, some 200,000 Portuguese troops were engaged in the African wars, which had drained the Portuguese economy and taken a heavy toll on the lower classes, whose conscripted sons bore the brunt of the fighting. In April, young army officers, disenchanted by the grueling colonial wars and poverty and oppression at home, staged a coup d'état. The new government of national unity, which included leaders of the Portuguese Socialist and Communist Parties, rapidly ended the wars. Portuguese Guinea was granted independence in September 1974, followed by Mozambique in June 1975, Cape Verde in July, and Angola in November of the same year. Worried about the prominence of the Portuguese Communist Party in the coalition government, Kissinger and Defense Secretary James Schlesinger devised a plan for an American takeover of the Azores islands. The Socialist Party's victory at the polls in April 1976, bolstered by covert British and West German aid, made the U.S. contingency plan irrelevant.

African Battlegrounds: Portuguese Guinea, Mozambique, and Angola

Portuguese Guinea

As relations between Washington and Lisbon sweetened and soured, armed struggle began in Portuguese Guinea, Mozambique, and Angola. Although external actors provided weapons, military equipment, and training to movements in all three territories, only in Angola were foreign troops a critical factor.

In Portuguese Guinea the most significant nationalist forces coalesced behind a single liberation movement, the PAIGC. Influenced by the Portuguese Communist Party, the PAIGC first mobilized among Guinea's small urban working class. After a calamitous dockworkers' strike in 1959, during which some fifty workers were killed, the party shifted its attention to the countryside. Inspired by the Chinese and Cuban revolutions and the Algerian independence war, the PAICG carried out mass politicization in Guinea's rural areas, preparing the population for a protracted war, which was launched in late 1962. Operating under Cabral's directive, "Tell no lies. . . . Claim no easy victories," the party was enormously successful in winning hearts and minds.[4] Despite the presence of 20,000 Portuguese troops, the PAIGC controlled one-third of Guinea by 1965. Although they agreed on little else, Washington and Havana judged the PAIGC the strongest liberation movement in Portugal's African colonies. It was

---

[4] Amilcar Cabral, "Tell No Lies, Claim No Easy Victories," in Amilcar Cabral, *Revolution in Guinea: Selected Texts*, trans. and ed. Richard Handyside (New York: Monthly Review Press, 1969), 89.

superior in terms of leadership, political mobilization, the establishment of alternative governing structures and social services in liberated areas, and the promotion of national unity.

From the outset, the PAICG cast a wide net for diplomatic and material support. In the fall of 1962, Cabral sent feelers to Washington, but the Kennedy administration, in the midst of renegotiating the Azores base lease, ignored him. Western countries snubbed the PAIGC until 1969, when Sweden initiated a program of humanitarian assistance that quickly became the movement's largest source of non-military aid. By the early 1970s, Norway, Denmark, Finland, and the Netherlands had followed Sweden's lead, and nongovernmental organizations such as the World Council of Churches began to provide grants for educational, medical, and economic projects. The PAIGC also garnered the support of neighboring African states. From 1960, the movement maintained its headquarters in Conakry, the capital of former French Guinea, as well as safe havens in Guinea (Conakry) and Senegal. As the decade progressed, PAIGC recruits were sent for military training in Guinea (Conakry), Ghana, Algeria, and Morocco – as well as Cuba, China, and Czechoslovakia. Morocco was the first of several African and Asian countries to provide the movement with weapons, while the OAU Liberation Committee supplied arms and military training. The Soviet Union, which had initially withheld support because of the PAIGC's suspected pro-China sentiments, began furnishing military aid in 1962 – eventually providing nearly all of the movement's armaments. Cuban support was initiated three years later, when Havana began to ship food, medicine, doctors, and weapons to the guerrilla and civilian populations and to instruct PAIGC cadres in the use of sophisticated Soviet weaponry.

By 1969, the PAIGC had gained control of 60 percent of Guinea's territory, where it provided social services and economic infrastructure that were virtually unknown under colonial rule. Portugal augmented its troop strength to 40,000 and systematically destroyed schools, clinics, crops, barter shops, and villages in the liberated areas. Airpower was the cornerstone of Portugal's counterinsurgency strategy. While bombarding the fruits of liberation, Portugal also focused on the PAIGC's civilian leadership. In November 1970, the Portuguese army invaded Conakry in a failed attempt to assassinate Cabral and overthrow Sékou Touré's government, thereby depriving the PAIGC of its primary pillar of support. While Nixon refused Conakry's appeals for assistance, the Soviet Union responded by deploying a destroyer, an oil tanker, and a tank landing ship. The next Portuguese attempt was successful. In January 1973, Cabral was assassinated in Conakry by a disgruntled PAIGC member in a plot orchestrated by the Portuguese secret police.

Despite its loss, the PAIGC continued to grow stronger as Soviet weapons and Cuban training permitted the movement to challenge Portuguese air superiority. Shortly after Cabral's assassination, a shipment of Soviet surface-to-air missiles arrived in the liberated areas. In four months' time, PAIGC guerrillas shot down eighteen Italian-, American-, and German-made planes. By May 1973, an estimated 8,000 PAIGC soldiers controlled nearly two-thirds of Guinea's territory and half of its population. The CIA concluded that Portugal could no longer win the war. On September 24, the elected government in the liberated areas proclaimed the country's independence and renamed it the Republic of Guinea-Bissau. In early November, the UN General Assembly effectively recognized the new republic by condemning its "illegal occupation by Portuguese military forces" and Portugal's acts of aggression "against the people of the Republic."[5] The United States, Britain, Portugal, and South Africa were among the seven nations that opposed the resolution. Under pressure from the PAIGC and independent African states, the Portuguese government that took power after the April 1974 coup recognized the Republic of Guinea-Bissau on September 10, 1974.

Mozambique

Mozambique, like Portuguese Guinea, was an agrarian society with a small urban working class. The leaders of FRELIMO, like those of the PAIGC, were influenced by the Chinese practice of mobilizing the rural population for a protracted war. Armed struggle began in September 1964, with Tanzania (formerly Tanganyika) serving as a rear base. In the contested areas, the local population fed, clothed, and hid FRELIMO fighters and gathered intelligence about enemy operations. By 1967, FRELIMO controlled extensive liberated zones

---

[5] UN General Assembly Resolution 3061, "Illegal Occupation by Portuguese Military Forces of Certain Sectors of the Republic of Guinea-Bissau and Acts of Aggression Committed by Them against the People of the Republic," November 2, 1973, http://www.un.org/ga/search/view_doc.asp?symbol=A/RES/3061(XXVIII)&Lang= E&Area=RESOLUTION.

where alternative political and economic structures served as models for a new postcolonial society.

Like the PAIGC, FRELIMO sought to balance its external support, seeking aid from both East and West, nonaligned countries, and the OAU Liberation Committee. In early 1963, Mondlane met with high-level Kennedy administration officials, and by late spring, he had obtained a $60,000 CIA subsidy. However, the Kennedy administration ignored his request for military aid, and Johnson severed financial ties in late 1968. In February 1969, Mondlane was assassinated by disenchanted FRELIMO cadres in a plot organized by the Portuguese secret police – prefiguring the later assassination of the PAIGC's Cabral. The Ford administration rebuffed Mondlane's successor, Samora Machel, when he expressed interest in developing trade, aid, and investment relations with the United States – effectively pushing FRELIMO toward the Eastern Bloc. While the most powerful NATO countries supported Portugal up to the 1974 coup, other members, including Denmark, Norway, and the Netherlands, furnished FRELIMO with humanitarian assistance, as did neutral Sweden and the nongovernmental World Council of Churches. Among the communist countries, the Soviet Union, China, and Cuba provided weapons and military training.

Angola

The richest and most strategic of the Portuguese colonies, Angola attracted the most outside interest during the periods of decolonization and the Cold War. A major producer of oil, industrial diamonds, and coffee, Angola was the site of significant investments by American, British, Belgian, French, and West German firms. The colony bordered Mobutu's Congo (renamed Zaire in 1971) and South African–occupied Namibia. Zaire and South Africa were determined to install a compliant regime on their perimeters. Angola became a Cold War battleground when the United States, the Soviet Union, China, and Cuba embroiled themselves in the conflict on the eve of Angolan independence.

From the outset, Angola's three liberation movements aroused interest among the Cold War players. In the 1960s, the United States supported Portugal but hedged its bets by giving token financial and military support to the FNLA. Although American aid was not substantial enough to threaten Portugal's hold, it did strengthen the FNLA vis-à-vis the better-educated, better-organized MPLA. Indirect support for the FNLA through the American client regime in Zaire proved to be far more significant. Mobutu hoped to use the FNLA and the French-backed separatist movement, Front for the Liberation of the Enclave of Cabinda, to annex Angola's Bakongo areas and the oil-rich Cabinda Enclave, thus forming a wealthier, more powerful Greater Zaire. In the early 1970s, China, North Korea, and Romania also supplied the FNLA with weapons and advisors, while China gave further aid to UNITA. Initially the recipient of both Chinese and Soviet aid, the MPLA became entangled in the Sino-Soviet conflict, and opposing sympathies fractured its leadership. The MPLA-Soviet relationship survived but remained tense due to Soviet distrust of the independent-minded Neto. In 1965, a small number of Cubans helped the MPLA in its battles against the Portuguese. In subsequent years, MPLA soldiers received material assistance and military training from China, Cuba, North Korea, and Eastern Europe, as well as the Soviet Union. Soviet disenchantment with the MPLA – due primarily to its internal leadership struggles – led to the cessation of Soviet aid for several months in 1974. Yugoslavia, which prized its independence from the Soviet Union, stepped into the breach and became the MPLA's main external source of support during this period. As in the cases of Portuguese Guinea and Mozambique, the Nordic countries, especially Sweden, were a significant source of humanitarian assistance – in this case for the MPLA.

The Portuguese coup in April 1974 dramatically altered the lay of the land. China immediately intensified aid to both the FNLA and UNITA, using Zaire as a conduit to send arms, advisors, and military instructors. The CIA followed suit, funneling support to the FNLA through Mobutu's territory. In August, the Soviet Union announced its moral support for the MPLA but demanded that the movement reconcile factional differences before Moscow would consider providing material aid. By autumn, it was clear that the MPLA would not soon resolve its internal disputes. Concerned by the escalating involvement of China and the United States, the Soviet Union reluctantly threw its weight behind the strongest faction, led by Agostinho Neto.

In fact, Moscow was not anxious to embroil itself in the Angolan conflict. Urging the three movements to resolve their differences through negotiation, the Soviet Union supported an African-led peace initiative. The resulting Alvor Accord, signed by Portugal and the three liberation movements on January 15, 1975, obliged the signatories to form a transitional government that included representatives from all three movements and to hold constituent assembly elections in October. The elected assembly would choose a president, and independence would be granted on November 11, 1975. Twenty-four thousand Portuguese troops would remain in Angola to implement the agreement.

The Alvor Accord was violated almost immediately. The FNLA was the strongest movement militarily, but the MPLA was far better established among the civilian population. It had developed a broader base and achieved greater grassroots mobilization than either the FNLA or UNITA. War would play to the FNLA's strengths, whereas peaceful political activism would benefit the MPLA. Despite Washington's public support for the Alvor Accord and the warning by Africanists in the foreign service against choosing sides, Henry Kissinger considered the MPLA to be a Soviet proxy and was determined to challenge it. In his dual role as Ford's national security advisor and secretary of state, Kissinger showed no interest in reconciliation. The CIA resumed covert support for the FNLA less than a week after the signing of the Alvor Accord, authorizing $300,000 in covert funds on January 22. The money was used to buy vehicles, a newspaper, and a television station – in short, to provide greater means for the politically weaker movement to reach the Angolan people. More significantly, Washington began to provide substantial military and economic support for the FNLA through the Mobutu regime, which had lobbied hard for American involvement. From March through May, the FNLA launched a series of attacks that killed MPLA activists in the capital and elsewhere in northern Angola. Meanwhile, more than 1,000 Zairian soldiers infiltrated into Angola to fight on the FNLA's behalf. Resisting Portuguese requests that it keep Mobutu at bay, Washington refused to intercede, asserting that it was not the United States' business to impose policy positions on the Zairian president.

Lukewarm about the MPLA, Moscow responded reluctantly to the American-led escalation. It was only in March 1975, when it became clear that Zaire and the United States planned to exclude the MPLA from the political arena, that Moscow resumed weapons shipments – the first since 1974. By the end of May, a strengthened MPLA was able to expel the FNLA from Luanda, where the MPLA had enormous popular support. In late June, South African intelligence reported that an MPLA victory could be thwarted only through South African support for its rivals.

July ushered in a new phase of the struggle, during which South African and American intelligence collaborated closely, and the United States pressed South Africa to intervene militarily. Moving in tandem, Pretoria and Washington funneled weapons and vehicles valued at tens of millions of dollars to the FNLA and UNITA. On July 14, South Africa authorized a weapons shipment worth $14.1 million. A few days later, the CIA began to channel another $14 million in weapons, tanks, and armored cars, using Zaire as its base of operations. Nearly $3 million of these funds were allotted to reimburse to Mobutu for his part in the war effort. On August 20, another $10.7 million in covert American funds were authorized. Two days later, South African troops crossed the border into southern Angola in pursuit of Namibian guerrillas from the South West Africa People's Organization (SWAPO), who were fighting South Africa's illegal occupation of their homeland. South African raids would continue through September, as FNLA and UNITA forces assisted South African soldiers in locating and destroying SWAPO guerrillas. The incursions into Angola by soldiers from the apartheid state upped the ante, dramatically altering the political stakes.

As Washington and Pretoria bolstered the FNLA and UNITA, Moscow escalated its support for the MPLA, supplying more arms and military advisors. In September, East Germany followed suit with $2.5 million in military aid, furnishing weapons, instructors, pilots, and doctors. By September 22, the MPLA, with its augmented external support, had halted the advance toward Luanda of FNLA and Zairian troops accompanied by Portuguese mercenaries. By that time, the MPLA was dominant in nine of Angola's sixteen provinces, including the capital, the coastline from Luanda to Namibia, and the coastal hinterland. Angola's five major ports, the oil-rich Cabinda Enclave, and most of the diamond-bearing Lunda district were also under MPLA control.

Although Zairian troops had been involved in the Angolan conflict from the outset, foreign intervention took on a new dimension in mid-October when the South African Defence Force (SADF) launched a massive invasion. By the end of the month, an estimated 1,000 South African soldiers were entrenched in Angola. Another 2,000 troops,

PHOTO 4.1. UNITA leader Jonas Savimbi with his troops in Nova Lisboa, Angola, September 1975 (Patrick Chauvel/Sygma/Corbis).

as well as planes, helicopters, and armored vehicles, were poised on the border. Joined in Angola by FNLA and UNITA soldiers, Zairian troops, and European mercenaries, the South African contingent, with CIA encouragement, began to advance on Luanda, rapidly winning the territory that the FNLA and UNITA had been unable to conquer on their own.

Until this point, Cuba's response to MPLA requests had been relatively modest. During the waning years of Portuguese rule, Cuba trained MPLA cadres in neighboring Congo-Brazzaville; in the spring of 1975 it sent military advisors to assist in MPLA military planning, and in August it provided $100,000 for weapons transportation. It was only after the South African invasion in October that Cuba responded to the MPLA's pleas for troops. Unwilling to upset a tenuous détente with the United States, Moscow had refused to supply Soviet troops – or to airlift Cuban soldiers – until after Independence Day, which according to the Alvor Accord would be on November 11. As the agreement disintegrated, it became clear that whoever controlled the capital on Independence Day would determine the government. Convinced that South Africa would take Luanda before November 11 unless impeded by outside forces, Havana was unwilling to wait. On October 23, Cuban soldiers participated in the fighting for the first

PHOTO 4.2. Cuban military officer in Angola, February 23, 1976 (AFP/Getty Images).

time. A few days later, Chinese military instructors, who had been training FNLA soldiers in Zaire, ceased their support – embarrassed by their now-public association with the apartheid regime. On November 10, MPLA and Cuban forces held Luanda against an onslaught of 2,000 FNLA and 1,200 Zairian soldiers, more than 100 Portuguese mercenaries, and advisors supplied by South Africa and the CIA. The Portuguese high commissioner transferred sovereignty to "the Angolan people," rather than to any of the warring movements, and on November 11 the MPLA announced the establishment of the People's Republic of Angola.[6]

---

[6] Norrie MacQueen, "An Ill Wind? Rethinking the Angolan Crisis and the Portuguese Revolution, 1974–1976," *Itinerario* 26 , no. 2 (July 2002), 22.

After independence, thousands of foreign troops poured into
Angola. Having waited until November 11 to intervene directly, the
Soviet Union embarked on a massive sea- and airlift, transporting
more than 12,000 Cuban soldiers between November 1975 and January 1976. Moscow also sent military instructors and technicians,
along with heavy weapons, tanks, missiles, and fighter planes. Meanwhile, thousands of South Africa troops and hundreds of European
mercenaries, the latter recruited and paid for by the CIA, arrived to
assist the MPLA's rivals. In late November, with a final expenditure
of $7 million for the Angolan operation, the CIA's secret Contingency
Reserve Fund was depleted. By that time, America's once-covert role
had been exposed. Embarrassed by the imbroglio, especially American collaboration with white-ruled South Africa, Congress passed two
bills that banned further funding of covert activities in Angola, and
a reluctant President Ford signed them into law.[7] Abandoned by its
allies, South Africa withdrew from Angola during the first few months
of 1976. Without Pretoria's backing, the FNLA and UNITA rapidly
collapsed. By February 1976, the MPLA, with Cuban assistance, controlled all of northern Angola. Disgusted by the collaboration between
the MPLA's rivals and apartheid South Africa, the OAU and the vast
majority of African nations recognized the MPLA government. By the
early 1980s, only the United States and South Africa continued to
withhold diplomatic recognition.

Suggested Reading

For this chapter, four books are especially recommended. Two offer detailed
histories of Portuguese colonialism in Africa: W. G. Clarence-Smith,
*The Third Portuguese Empire, 1825–1975: A Study in Economic Imperi-
alism* (Dover, NH: Manchester University Press, 1985) and M. D. D.
Newitt, *Portugal in Africa: The Last Hundred Years* (London: Longman,
1981). Two focus on foreign intervention during the decolonization process.
For a comprehensive archive-based assessment of Cuba's role in Angolan

---

[7] The Tunney Amendment to the 1976 Defense Appropriations Bill, which included
the CIA budget, banned the use of fiscal year 1976 funds in Angola, except for the
purpose of intelligence gathering. The Clark Amendment, enacted as part of the International Security Assistance and Arms Export Control Act of 1976, prohibited any
future American aid to organizations involved in military or paramilitary operations
in Angola.

decolonization and shifting U.S. and Soviet policies, see Piero Gleijeses, *Conflicting Missions: Havana, Washington, and Africa, 1959–1976* (Chapel Hill: University of North Carolina Press, 2002). For a firsthand account of American involvement, written by the CIA's Angola Task Force chief, see John Stockwell, *In Search of Enemies: A CIA Story* (New York: W. W. Norton, 1978).

Several important works focus on the United States, Portugal, and African decolonization. William Minter's *Portuguese Africa and the West* (New York: Monthly Review Press, 1972) examines Portuguese colonialism, the liberation movements, and U.S. and Western government policies and business interests. Witney Schneidman's *Engaging Africa: Washington and the Fall of Portugal's Colonial Empire* (Lanham, MD: University Press of American, 2004) focuses on U.S.-Portuguese relations during the decolonization period. Two recommended books pertain to the Kennedy and Johnson administrations' Africa policies, with a significant focus on the Portuguese colonies: Richard D. Mahoney, *JFK: Ordeal in Africa* (New York: Oxford University Press, 1983) and Thomas J. Noer, *Cold War and Black Liberation: The United States and White Rule in Africa, 1948–1968* (Columbia: University of Missouri Press, 1985). For an in-depth assessment of Kennedy's top Africa official, see Noer's *Soapy: A Biography of G. Mennen Williams* (Ann Arbor: University of Michigan Press, 2006). For the Ford administration's policies toward Portugal's African colonies, see Stockwell (mentioned above) and works by two of Ford's top Africa officials: Donald Easum, *Hard Times for the Africa Bureau, 1974–1976: A Diplomatic Adventure Story* (Chapel Hill, NC: American Diplomacy Publishers, June 7, 2010), http://www.unc.edu/depts/diplomat/item/2010/0406/fsl/fsl_hardtimes.html and Nathaniel Davis, "The Angola Decision of 1975: A Personal Memoir," *Foreign Affairs* 57, no. 1 (Fall 1978): 109–24.

The Nordic countries were among the few Western states to support African liberation struggles. For insight into Nordic involvement in the Portuguese colonies, see the Nordic Africa Institute's six-volume series, *National Liberation in Southern Africa: The Role of the Nordic Countries*, http://www.liberationafrica.se/publications.

For Portuguese Guinea (Guinea-Bissau), a number of important works focus on the revolutionary period. For writings by PAIGC Secretary-General Amílcar Cabral, see the Africa Information Service's edited collection, *Return to the Source: Selected Speeches of Amílcar Cabral* (New York: Monthly Review Press, 1973) and Cabral's *Unity and Struggle: Speeches and Writings*, trans. Michael Wolfers (New York: Monthly Review Press, 1979). Patrick Chabal assesses Cabral and the PAIGC in *Amílcar Cabral: Revolutionary Leadership and People's War* (New York: Cambridge University

Press, 1983). For firsthand accounts by scholars who traveled with the PAIGC during the liberation war, see Gérard Chaliand, *Armed Struggle in Africa: With the Guerrillas in "Portuguese" Guinea*, trans. David Rattray and Robert Leonhardt (New York: Monthly Review Press, 1969); Basil Davidson, *The Liberation of Guiné: Aspects of an African Revolution* (Baltimore, MD: Penguin Books, 1969); and Stephanie Urdang, *Fighting Two Colonialisms: Women in Guinea-Bissau* (New York: Monthly Review Press, 1979). Other scholars have produced more recent assessments of the liberation struggle, focusing on political mobilization, life in the liberated areas, and Portuguese counterinsurgency. See especially Lars Rudebeck, *Guinea-Bissau: A Study of Political Mobilization* (Uppsala, Sweden: Scandinavian Institute of African Studies, 1974) and Mustafah Dhada, *Warriors at Work: How Guinea Was Really Set Free* (Niwot: University Press of Colorado, 1993).

For Mozambique, three histories of colonialism and the liberation struggle are especially recommended: M. D. D. Newitt, *A History of Mozambique* (Bloomington: Indiana University Press, 1995); Allen Isaacman and Barbara Isaacman, *Mozambique: From Colonialism to Revolution, 1900–1982* (Boulder, CO: Westview Press, 1983); and Barry Munslow, *Mozambique: The Revolution and Its Origins* (New York: Longman, 1983). For the political writings of FRELIMO's first two presidents, see Eduardo Mondlane's *The Struggle for Mozambique* (Baltimore, MD: Penguin, 1969) and Barry Munslow's *Samora Machel: An African Revolutionary* (London, Zed Books, 1985), which includes selected speeches and writings.

For Angola, a highly readable general history is Basil Davidson's *In the Eye of the Storm: Angola's People* (Garden City, NY: Anchor Books, 1973). The classic history of the independence struggle is John A. Marcum's two-volume work: *The Angolan Revolution*, which includes *The Anatomy of an Explosion (1950–1962)*, vol. 1 (Cambridge, MA: MIT Press, 1969), and *Exile Politics and Guerrilla Warfare (1962–1976)*, vol. 2 (Cambridge, MA: MIT Press, 1978). Two more recent works provide additional understanding of the relationships between the liberation movements and the tensions that were exploited by outside powers: Franz-Wilhelm Heimer, *The Decolonization Conflict in Angola, 1974–76: An Essay in Political Sociology* (Geneva: Institut Universitaire de Hautes Études Internationales, 1979) and Fernando Andresen Guimarães, *The Origins of the Angolan Civil War: Foreign Intervention and Domestic Political Conflict* (New York: St. Martin's Press, 1998). For documents revealing the collaboration of UNITA and the Portuguese military against the MPLA, see William Minter, ed., *Operation Timber: Pages from the Savimbi Dossier* (Trenton, NJ: Africa World Press, 1988). The impact of foreign intervention in the decolonization process is explored in Gleijeses, Stockwell, and Guimarães (mentioned above). Finally, Polish journalist Ryszard Kapuscinski provides a powerful firsthand account of the last months of colonial rule and the onset of civil war in *Another Day of Life*, trans. William R. Brand and Katarzyna Mroczkowska-Brand (San Diego, CA: Harcourt Brace Jovanovich, 1986).

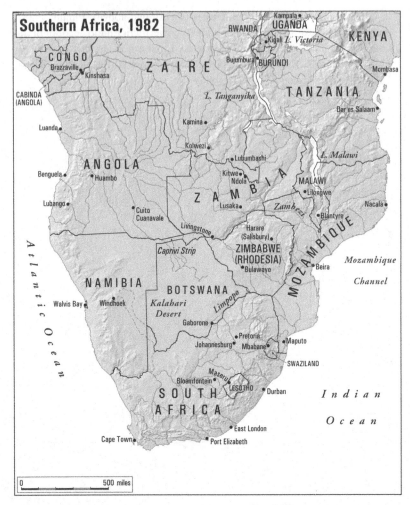

MAP 5.1. Southern Africa, 1982. (Map by Philip Schwartzberg, Meridian Mapping, Minneapolis.)

CHAPTER 5

White-Minority Rule in Southern Africa, 1960–1990

In the white-ruled territories of Southern Africa, as elsewhere on the continent, Cold War concerns were superimposed on local struggles emanating from colonial conditions. Colonies with significant settler populations generally rejected the notion of independence and majority rule. As in Algeria, Angola, and Mozambique, white-run governments in the Anglophone territories of South Africa and Southern Rhodesia fought to retain political power and economic privilege in European hands, while South Africa's apartheid regime sought to maintain its illegal occupation of Namibia. To mask the fundamental issue, which was the transfer of power from a privileged white minority to the majority of the population, the settler regimes of Southern Africa employed Cold War rhetoric to garner Western support. Pretoria, especially, played on the threat of a communist onslaught that would consume the last bastion of white Western Christian civilization in Southern Africa.

Despite their public criticism of a system that entrenched racial privilege, the United States and other Western powers generally supported the embattled South African government and shared its concerns about the increasingly radical liberation movements both inside the country and on its borders. Nordic countries were among the few Western nations to provide the African liberation movements with even humanitarian aid. Opposing their governments' policies, grassroots anti-apartheid and Southern African solidarity movements emerged in the United States and Western Europe. The predominantly African American Council on African Affairs, established in 1937, may have been the first American movement in solidarity with anticolonial and anti-apartheid struggles. The victim of a Cold War era witch hunt, the council dissolved in 1955. Beginning in 1953, the American Committee on Africa brought together civil rights and religious organizations, trade unions, and students to mobilize against colonialism and white-minority rule. A host of other national and local solidarity and anti-apartheid organizations emerged in dozens of countries in the 1960s and 1970s. The African American–inspired Free South Africa Movement, established in 1984, organized demonstrations at the South African Embassy in Washington and at consulates across the United States, resulting in thousands of arrests and much adverse publicity for Pretoria. These grassroots movements in Western countries intensified domestic pressure for arms embargoes and economic sanctions, which culminated in the late 1980s.

Failing to obtain assistance from the Western powers, the Southern African liberation movements turned elsewhere for support. The Soviet Union and Eastern Europe, China, and various African nations provided military aid. Independent African countries bordering those under white rule – the so-called Frontline States – also played a key role, often with severe consequences for their own people.[1] Some provided safe haven for refugees and political activists. Others permitted guerrillas and weapons to transit through their territories. A few allowed the establishment of military camps and training bases inside their borders. All of the Frontline States helped intensify international pressure for negotiated settlements that would result in majority rule. With outside support, Zimbabwe (formerly Southern Rhodesia) attained majority rule in 1980, followed by Namibia in 1990, and South Africa in 1994. In the intervening years, the apartheid state waged costly wars of destabilization against its neighbors in order to protect the last vestiges of white-minority rule.

This chapter is divided into five sections. The first three focus on the white-ruled Southern African regimes that included significant settler populations – South Africa, Southern Rhodesia, and Namibia – while the fourth and fifth examine South Africa's relations with the region and the international community's unique response to the Southern African case. The first section (1960–90) considers South Africa, the region's economic powerhouse, which was governed by

---

[1] The original Frontline States – Mozambique, Zambia, Tanzania, Botswana, and Angola – were joined by Zimbabwe in 1980.

a predominantly Afrikaans-speaking white minority and dominated economically by English-speaking whites. Although Britain, France, West Germany, and Japan also maintained strong ties with South Africa, this section concentrates on Pretoria's relations with the American superpower. The second section (1965–80) focuses on Southern Rhodesia, a renegade British colony that declared independence on the basis of white minority rule. When Britain failed to return the regime to legality and progress toward majority rule, the UN imposed economic sanctions, and African liberation movements initiated armed struggle. The third section (1966–90) explores attempts by the international community to end South Africa's illegal occupation of Namibia. While Western powers tried to shield Pretoria from UN economic sanctions, other countries supported the Namibian liberation struggle. The fourth section (1975–90) examines South African destabilization of the Southern African region in an effort to impose its political and economic hegemony. The white regimes of Southern Africa were atypical African colonies. Foreign response to them was unique in many ways. The final section contrasts the nature of international involvement in Southern Africa with that in other parts of the continent.

South Africa and the United States (1960–90)

South Africa was the economic linchpin of the Southern African region. Built on a system of migratory labor and impoverished ethnic reserves, dubbed African "homelands," South Africa's cheap labor economy and mineral wealth attracted billions of dollars in foreign investments. Although South Africa was a British dominion from 1910 to 1961, the Afrikaner-dominated government maintained an often tense relationship with Britain, especially after the establishment of the racially based apartheid system in 1948.[2] Relations deteriorated further as new African and Asian members of the Commonwealth

---

[2] Apartheid, literally "apartness" in Afrikaans, was a brutal political, economic, and social system in South Africa that allocated rights and privileges on the basis of race. Under the apartheid system, which lasted from 1948 to 1994, native Africans (70 percent of the population) were deprived of their land and citizenship, constricted in their movements and economic opportunities, and subjected to draconian security laws. Colored (mixed-race) and Asian populations were relegated to second-class citizenship, while the white minority controlled the government and the economy.

sharply criticized apartheid and urged Britain to take action against
it. Following a whites-only referendum in 1960, South Africa declared
itself a republic and left the Commonwealth. Britain continued to have
significant investments in South Africa and maintained strong trade
links. However, as the United States became the world's primary economic powerhouse after World War II, its stake in South Africa grew
accordingly.

During the periods of decolonization and the Cold War, white-
ruled South Africa was the cornerstone of U.S. policy toward the
region. Although their methods varied, every presidential administration strove to ward off communist influence and to protect American
trade, investments, and access to South Africa's strategic minerals.
By the early 1980s, the United States had surpassed Britain as South
Africa's largest trading partner. American corporations had expanded
their direct investments to $2.6 billion, accounting for 20 percent of
all direct foreign investment in South Africa. U.S. firms controlled the
most strategic sectors of the South African economy, including 40 percent of the petroleum products market and 75 percent of the computer
market. They were heavily involved in the automobile, chemical, and
machinery manufacturing industries. Even more significant was the
transfer of American technology and expertise, which helped develop
South Africa's nuclear and military programs, as well as other sectors
of the economy. Billions of dollars in American bank loans allowed
South Africa to build its military, stockpile oil, and finance major
infrastructure projects. In the international arena, the United States
bolstered economic with diplomatic support. At the UN, American
delegates consistently vetoed economic sanctions against South Africa,
despite appeals from the African National Congress (ANC) and other
anti-apartheid organizations.

The United States was not alone in supporting the apartheid
regime. Britain was a top trading partner and investor, while France,
West Germany, and Israel were important sources of military and
nuclear technology. France continued to sell weapons to Pretoria after
the imposition of a voluntary UN arms embargo in 1963. Israel sought
a closer relationship with South Africa after the 1967 and 1973 Arab-
Israeli wars, which had led to Israel's increased isolation in Africa
and the Middle East. Hoping to compensate for lost markets and
allies, Israel began to export sophisticated military equipment to the
apartheid regime, a practice that continued even after the imposition
of a mandatory UN arms embargo in 1977. Despite the international

PHOTO 5.1. Sign outside the General Motors factory in Cape Province, South Africa, January 1, 1956 (Three Lions/Getty Images).

ban, Tel Aviv and Pretoria engaged in joint military research, weapons production, and nuclear collaboration. They joined forces in military and intelligence operations, and Israeli military advisors trained SADF forces for operations in South Africa, Namibia, and Angola.

American support for apartheid was challenged not only by a domestic grassroots movement but also by forces within the government. Policies were contested internally, changed according to geopolitical circumstances, and transformed from one administration to the next. During the Kennedy administration, the Africanists, led by Assistant Secretary of State G. Mennen Williams, advocated a more forceful position against apartheid, including the imposition of an arms embargo and economic sanctions. Williams argued that existent U.S. policies undermined America's credibility with newly independent

African states, as well as the civil rights movement at home. Opposing the Africanists' position were Secretary of State Dean Rusk and the highest echelons of the State, Commerce, and Defense Departments. Rejecting any measure that might threaten the Washington-Pretoria relationship and upset NATO allies, officials in these departments championed policies that would ensure continued American access to South Africa's strategic minerals and an important missile and satellite tracking station. In Congress, anticommunist and prosegregation forces not only rejected sanctions but also advocated even closer American ties to the apartheid regime.

Under pressure from the civil rights movement at home and Africans in the OAU and UN, Assistant Secretary of State Williams proposed a compromise – a unilateral ban on weapons sales to the Pretoria regime. Williams argued that by making the first move, the United States could sidestep more radical UN measures that sought to impose mandatory economic sanctions and expel South Africa from the international body. To retain influence with African states and keep them from the communist camp, the United States had to take the lead. The compromise measure was opposed by Commerce and Defense, which fretted about its impact on relations with Britain, France, and Belgium – not to mention Portugal and South Africa. On July 31, 1963, as the South African debate brewed, Kennedy ordered his UN ambassador to join Britain and France in abstaining on a Security Council resolution imposing a voluntary arms embargo on Portugal. Williams continued to press his point, finally persuading the president and key Europeanists at State that the United States had to make a bold statement against apartheid. On August 2, the Kennedy administration announced a unilateral ban on weapons sales to Pretoria – although a "strategic exception" loophole permitted South Africa to buy weapons, spare parts, and equipment if deemed by Washington to be in the interests of common defense and international peace and security. On August 7, the American ambassador broke with Britain and France to vote in favor of a UN Security Council resolution that imposed a voluntary arms embargo on South Africa.

President Lyndon Johnson, who assumed office after Kennedy's assassination in November 1963, did not share his predecessor's African concerns. Determined not to antagonize America's European allies, he sidelined officials who supported Kennedy's attempts to cultivate moderate black regimes. His administration continued to supply

South Africa with weapons "for defense against external aggression"[3] and spare parts for military craft, as well as highly enriched uranium for Pretoria's American-built nuclear reactor.

The Nixon administration went further. Rejecting Kennedy's practice of courting Africans by publicly needling Pretoria, Nixon resurrected practices that were sympathetic to settler and colonial regimes, which he viewed as a critical bulwark against international communism. His administration relaxed compliance with the voluntary UN arms embargo, encouraged American trade with and investment in South Africa, and intensified nuclear collaboration. Washington's tilt toward Southern Africa's white-minority regimes, which continued under President Gerald Ford, antagonized African states and liberation movements. It also proved to be shortsighted, underrating African resolve and overrating the ability of the white-minority governments to hold out indefinitely. Within a matter of years, Portugal's colonies had achieved independence, and the settler regimes in the Anglophone territories were under attack.

Taking office in January 1977, President Jimmy Carter promised a transformation of U.S. foreign policy in response to global demands for justice, equality, and human rights. Embracing human rights as the cornerstone of the new American order, Carter rejected anticommunism as a justification for alliance with totalitarian regimes. With the appointment of civil rights leader Andrew Young as UN ambassador, the Carter administration intensified its public criticism of the apartheid regime and bolstered its words with action. In November 1977, following the death in detention of Black Consciousness leader Steve Biko and the banning of nearly twenty anti-apartheid organizations and publications, Young voted to render the voluntary UN arms embargo mandatory. However, reality often fell short of the president's lofty ideals. While the Carter administration halted deliveries of nuclear fuel and was more serious than its predecessors about the embargo's enforcement, it weakened the ban by exempting some dual-use equipment that had both civilian and military applications. Moreover, the Carter administration held to the longstanding practice of vetoing all Security Council resolutions that would

---

[3] "Telegram from the Department of State to the Embassy in South Africa," Washington, January 11, 1964, in *Foreign Relations of the United States, 1964–1968*, Africa, 24:575, ed. Nina Davis Howland (Washington, DC: U.S. Government Printing Office, 1999), http://history.state.gov/historicaldocuments/frus1964-68v24/d575.

impose comprehensive economic sanctions on South Africa, despite impassioned pleas from anti-apartheid leaders like Bishop Desmond Tutu, who warned, "Our last chance for peaceful change lies in the international community applying political, diplomatic and especially economic pressure."[4]

Undeterred by the relative moderateness of his predecessor's stance, President Ronald Reagan accused Carter of undermining American allies and vowed to dismantle his policies. In January 1981, Reagan's newly installed secretary of state, Alexander Haig, announced that "international terrorism will take the place of human rights in our concern because it is the ultimate abuse of human rights."[5] In consequence, the Reagan administration toned down its public rebukes of South Africa, revoked most of the tougher arms embargo enforcement standards, and stepped up previously forbidden exports. In a March 1981 interview on CBS television, the American president affirmed the desirability of a close relationship with South Africa:

> Can we abandon a country that has stood by us in every war we've ever fought, a country that strategically is essential to the free world in its production of minerals we all must have and so forth? I just feel that . . . if we're going to sit down at a table and negotiate with the Russians, surely we can keep the door open and continue to negotiate with a friendly nation like South Africa.[6]

While South African Prime Minister P. W. Botha hailed Reagan's remarks, world opinion ranged from outrage to embarrassment. Far from being the wartime ally lauded by President Reagan, the National Party, which ruled South Africa from 1948 to 1994, had vehemently opposed South Africa's entry into World War II on the side of Britain. Many prominent party members, including future Prime Minister John Vorster, were interned during the war as Nazi sympathizers.

The Washington-Pretoria rapprochement took shape in May 1981, when the Reagan administration hosted South African Foreign Minister Roelof "Pik" Botha – the first government official from sub-Saharan Africa to be received by the Reagan White House. Leaked State Department documents indicate the parameters of the new

---

4 Quoted in Father Charles Dahm, "The Case against Investment in South Africa" (New York: Interfaith Center on Corporate Responsibility, May 1979), 3C.
5 "Excerpts from Haig's Remarks at First News Conference as Secretary of State," *New York Times*, January 29, 1981, p. A10.
6 Ronald Reagan, "Excerpts from an Interview with Walter Cronkite of CBS News," March 3, 1981, http://www.reagan.utexas.edu/archives/speeches/1981/30381c.htm.

policy. Secretary Haig was urged to tell his South African counterpart that the Reagan administration was ready "to open a new chapter in relations with South Africa." The new president hoped to promote "a more positive and reciprocal relationship between the two countries based upon shared strategic concerns in southern Africa." Moreover, the United States would "work to end South Africa's polecat status in the world and seek to restore its place as a legitimate and important regional actor with whom we can cooperate pragmatically." Finally, Haig was instructed to reassure Botha that the Reagan administration "will not allow others to dictate what our relationships with South Africa will be, as evidenced by our recent veto of sanctions."[7]

In the aftermath of the Haig-Botha discussions, the Reagan administration announced a new policy of "constructive engagement" with South Africa. Abandoning Carter's human rights verbiage, Reagan's policy returned to the Nixon view that constructive change could come about only through white acquiescence. The new policy called for cooperation rather than confrontation with the white regime. "We must avoid the trap of an indiscriminate attack on all aspects of the [apartheid] system," wrote Chester Crocker, who conceptualized the policy and served as Reagan's assistant secretary of state for African affairs. This stance could mean "that the United States becomes engaged in what some observers label as only 'amelioration.'"[8] Crocker also contended that in South Africa, "it is not our task to choose between black and white.... The Reagan Administration has no intention of destabilizing South Africa in order to curry favor elsewhere."[9]

In keeping with constructive engagement, the Reagan administration distanced itself from anti-apartheid measures enacted by its predecessors. It rescinded the no-contact policy with South African military and police officials, in effect since the Kennedy administration, and brokered the delivery of nuclear fuel through European proxies. Most significant, perhaps, was Reagan's successful 1982 lobbying campaign in support of a $1.1 billion IMF loan to Pretoria – an amount that

7 Assistant Secretary Chester Crocker's "Scope Paper" for Secretary of State Alexander Haig in preparation for Haig's May 14, 1981, meeting with South African Foreign Minister Pik Botha at the State Department, reprinted in "The Secret State Department Documents," *Covert Action Information Bulletin*, no. 13 (July–August 1981), 40–41.

8 Chester Crocker, "South Africa: Strategy for Change," *Foreign Affairs* 59, no. 2 (Winter 1980–81), 327, 347.

9 Chester Crocker, *Regional Strategy for Southern Africa*, Current Policy, no. 308, August 29 (Washington, DC: U.S. Department of State, Bureau of Public Affairs, 1981), 3.

approximated the cost of South Africa's wars in Namibia and Angola between 1980 and 1982. Unlike other IMF applicants, South Africa was not required to restructure its economy in order to receive the loan – despite the fact that apartheid-linked social, economic, and military practices were responsible for much of the country's economic distress. Among South African blacks, the Reagan administration's policy was viewed as unalloyed support for the white-minority regime. The United States and capitalism were increasingly identified with apartheid, whereas Washington and Pretoria's constant reference to communists as the enemy led anti-apartheid activists to identify them as allies in struggle.

Desperate to avoid political and economic isolation, the South African government played on American Cold War fears. Posing as an ally defending Western interests, Pretoria's threats of communists on the border were, in part, a propaganda campaign directed at Western audiences to garner political support. Cold War fear-mongering also served to rally the white population inside South Africa. However, it badly misrepresented the nature of the anti-apartheid movement. The ANC, which led the civil rights and anti-apartheid struggles for more than eight decades, was the oldest liberation movement on the African continent. It was founded in 1912 – five years before the Bolshevik Revolution and nine years before the establishment of the Communist Party of South Africa. After the institution of apartheid in 1948 and the outlawing of communism in 1950, South African communists disbanded their original organization and established an underground alternative, the South African Communist Party (SACP). SACP members assumed leading positions in the Congress Alliance, of which the ANC was the dominant member. Communists also took leadership roles in the ANC itself. Following the banning of the ANC in 1960 and the commencement of armed struggle in 1961, communists played key roles in the establishment of the ANC's armed affiliate, Umkhonto we Sizwe, or "Spear of the Nation," and, together with the ANC, staffed Umkhonto's high command. The ANC worked with South African communists for a common purpose – the abolition of economic exploitation, imperialism, and white-minority rule. However, the ANC was not itself a communist organization, nor was it under communist control. Charged in 1963 with sabotage and conspiracy to overthrow the government, ANC and Umkhonto leader Nelson Mandela voiced the sentiments of many when he proclaimed from the dock, "I have cherished the ideal of a democratic and free society in which all persons live together in harmony and with equal opportunities. It is an ideal which I hope to live for and to achieve. But if needs be, it is an ideal for which I am prepared to die."[10]

From the early 1960s, the ANC sought broad-based international support for its anti-apartheid activities. A number of Western nations responded with humanitarian aid, most importantly, the Nordic countries, the Netherlands, Ireland, and Italy. The OAU Liberation Committee, the World Council of Churches, and labor and anti-apartheid organizations in Eastern and Western Europe and North America also provided academic scholarships and humanitarian support. Because Western countries refused to provide military assistance, the ANC turned to African and Eastern European countries, the Soviet Union, China, and Cuba for weapons, military equipment, and military training. From the establishment of Umkhonto we Sizwe in 1961 until the unbanning of the ANC in 1990, ANC guerrillas received military training in such countries as Morocco, Ethiopia, Algeria, Egypt, Tanzania, Zambia, and Uganda, as well as the Soviet Union, China, and Cuba. Angola became the ANC's most important African ally in 1976, when the MPLA government allowed the liberation movement to establish military camps on Angolan soil and its cadres to be trained there by Soviet, Cuban, and Eastern European instructors.

Despite the ANC's continuous appeals to the West, some members of the U.S. government, from the Eisenhower to the Reagan administrations, were convinced that the ANC was a communist-dominated organization engaged in terrorist activities. From the late 1950s, the CIA attempted to undermine the ANC by funneling money to anti-communist alternatives – including labor organizations that rejected the Congress Alliance's political trade unionism and the Pan Africanist Congress, which split from the ANC in 1959. Retired CIA and South African intelligence officials claim that the CIA provided the crucial tip that resulted in ANC leader Nelson Mandela's arrest in 1962. The Reagan administration defined terrorism so broadly that it encompassed the activities of most African liberation movements, including the ANC. In 1982, the Republican-led Senate Judiciary Committee's Subcommittee on Security and Terrorism characterized the ANC and SWAPO as "Soviet-sponsored terrorist organizations" that act "in opposition to U.S. national security interests."[11] Even

---

[10] Nelson Mandela, *No Easy Walk to Freedom* (Portsmouth, NH: Heinemann, 1973), 189.

[11] U.S. Senate, *Soviet, East German, and Cuban Involvement in Fomenting Terrorism in Southern Africa*, Report of the Chairman of the Subcommittee on Security and

the Comprehensive Anti-Apartheid Act of 1986, enacted over Presi-dent Reagan's veto, made reference to the ANC's "terrorist activities" and required a U.S. government investigation of "Communist infil-tration" into the organization.[12] As late as 2008, hundreds of South Africans, including Nelson Mandela, remained on the U.S. govern-ment's terrorist watch list for having engaged in actions against the apartheid state.

Even as Reagan administration officials and their congressional allies promoted closer links to Pretoria, grassroots activists swayed the American public toward the anti-apartheid opposition. The Com-prehensive Anti-Apartheid Act of 1986 was the culmination of decades of work by religious, labor, student, and civil rights activists who finally captured the attention of the U.S. Congress. It was passed in the wake of economic sanctions imposed by the Commonwealth, the European Community, and Japan in August and September 1986. Enacted with significant bipartisan support during a brutal crackdown and state of emergency in South Africa and just prior to U.S. congressional elec-tions, the law banned new American investments in South Africa; bank loans and computer sales to the South African government; the transfer of petroleum, nuclear, and military products; and American cooperation with the South African military and police. The sanc-tions law also prohibited the importation of South African iron, steel, coal, uranium, textiles, gold coins, and agricultural products. It ended direct flights to and from South Africa and proscribed South African aircraft from landing in the United States. In a strong rebuke to the apartheid government, the U.S. law called for an end to South Africa's state of emergency, which granted the government martial powers; it urged the release of Nelson Mandela and other political prisoners, the unbanning of the ANC and other political movements, the repeal of apartheid laws, and movement toward the establishment of a nonracial democracy. Finally, the law called on the United States to work with other industrialized democracies to end apartheid, employing further sanctions if necessary.

Although anti-apartheid activists welcomed Western sanctions, the packages imposed were far from comprehensive, and Western

Terrorism to the Committee on the Judiciary, U.S. Senate, 97th Congress, 2nd Session (Washington, DC: U.S. Government Printing Office, 1982), 28.
[12] Comprehensive Anti-Apartheid Act of 1986, Pub. Law No. 99-440, Secs. 102 (a) and 509 (a), October 2, 1986.

powers continued to buffer their South African ally. In February 1987, the United States, Britain, and West Germany vetoed a UN Security Council resolution that would have required all UN member states to impose economic sanctions against South Africa. Nonetheless, even the partial, voluntary sanctions package – combined with widespread internal unrest – took their toll. As the South African economy plummeted and capital took flight, the apartheid regime was forced to the bargaining table. In February 1990, the government unbanned the ANC, the SACP, the Pan Africanist Congress, and other opposition groups. It began to release political prisoners, including Nelson Mandela, who by that time had served twenty-seven years of a life sentence. The imminent collapse of the Soviet Union undermined the "communist threat" argument that had been key to Western support for the apartheid regime, but four more years of negotiations and bloodshed would be required before apartheid met its final demise.

Southern Rhodesia/Zimbabwe (1965–80)

As the anti-apartheid struggle intensified in South Africa, race, decolonization, and the Cold War also came into play in Southern Rhodesia, where Western powers again mistook indigenous resistance to white-minority rule for an externally backed communist insurgency. From 1890 to 1980, white settlers and their descendants dominated the political and economic structures of a territory that was successively called Southern Rhodesia, Rhodesia (from 1964), and, finally, independent Zimbabwe. Rural Africans were dispossessed of their ancestral land and forced into impoverished reserves, restricted to poorly paid jobs, and subjected to intense political repression. The situation in white-ruled Rhodesia was much like that in apartheid South Africa.

African protests against white-minority rule escalated after World War II, as trade unions and civic and youth organizations mobilized against the state. The government cracked down hard, declaring a state of emergency in 1959 and banning African political organizations in quick succession. Increasingly repressive security legislation made peaceful protest virtually impossible. From the early 1960s, the most important protest organizations were ZAPU and ZANU, which broke from ZAPU in 1963. Both organizations were outlawed and continued to operate clandestinely. Hoping to keep the nationalists out of the communist camp, the Kennedy administration gave some financial support to ZAPU and ZANU, as well as to African trade unions. However, subsequent U.S. administrations either ignored these movements or worked actively against them.

In the early 1960s, as Britain began to transfer political power to its African colonies, it pressed reluctant white Rhodesians to share power with the African majority. In 1964, London proclaimed that Rhodesia must demonstrate "unimpeded progress toward majority rule" before it could attain independence.[13] In January 1966, under pressure from African Commonwealth leaders, Britain adopted the more stringent principle of "no independence before majority rule."[14] Meanwhile, on November 11, 1965, Rhodesian Prime Minister Ian Smith, who opposed any move toward majority rule, announced a complete break with Britain. Asserting that the Unilateral Declaration of Independence (UDI) was illegal, Britain refused to recognize the Smith regime. However, having publicly rejected the use of force, in part because many Britons objected to fighting Rhodesian "kith and kin," Prime Minister Harold Wilson had discarded a powerful negotiating card.[15] Hoping to forestall more aggressive action by the UN, Britain imposed limited economic sanctions and urged the international community to follow suit.

Viewing the Rhodesian situation as a decolonization issue, the Johnson administration followed London's lead. The UN Security Council did likewise, immediately enacting selective voluntary sanctions that prohibited the sale of military equipment and petroleum products to the illegal regime. In December 1966, in the face of continued Rhodesian intransigence, the Security Council imposed selective mandatory sanctions that barred the purchase of Rhodesian asbestos, iron ore, chrome, pig iron, sugar, tobacco, copper, and animal products and prohibited the sale to Rhodesia of petroleum products; arms; ammunition; military equipment; and capital goods used to manufacture weapons, aircraft, and motor vehicles. In May 1968, two and a half

---

[13] Quoted in "Circular Telegram from the Department of State to Certain Posts," Washington, November 9, 1965, in *Foreign Relations of the United States, 1964–1968*, Africa, 24:489, ed. Nina Davis Howland (Washington, DC: U.S. Government Printing Office, 1999), http://history.state.gov/historicaldocuments/frus1964-68v24/d489.

[14] "Telegram from the Department of State to the Embassy in the United Kingdom," Washington, October 18, 1966, in *Foreign Relations of the United States, 1964–1968*, Africa, 24:544, ed. Nina Davis Howland (Washington, DC: U.S. Government Printing Office, 1999), http://history.state.gov/historicaldocuments/frus1964-68v24/d544.

[15] Quoted in Carl Watts, "Killing Kith and Kin: The Viability of British Military Intervention in Rhodesia, 1964–65," *Twentieth Century British History* 16, no. 5 (December 2005): 383.

PHOTO 5.2. Anti-Rhodesia demonstrators in London protesting British appeasement of the white-minority regime, November 25, 1971 (Frank Barratt/ Getty Images).

years after UDI, the Security Council finally imposed comprehensive mandatory sanctions, prohibiting any economic or diplomatic relationship with the rebel regime. Any breach of this embargo was a violation of international law.

While ZAPU and ZANU applauded the imposition of sanctions, claiming that economic hardship would force the Smith regime to negotiate, Rhodesian political and economic leaders engaged in a concerted effort to circumvent the international ban. They found willing partners on several continents. A number of UN member states openly flouted Rhodesian sanctions. South Africa and the Portuguese colonial regime in Mozambique served as conduits for Rhodesian imports and exports, supplying the country with petroleum, military equipment, and foreign exchange. France, Britain, and the United States looked the other way as their oil companies illegally exported petroleum to Rhodesia, and Rhodesian minerals and tobacco found their way into international markets. Moreover, these permanent members of the Security Council refused to impose sanctions on South Africa and Portugal for flagrantly violating the mandatory UN embargo.

The shift from Johnson to Nixon resulted in a transformation of U.S.-Rhodesia policy. No longer following Britain's lead, the Nixon administration embarked on a course that openly favored Southern

Africa's white-minority governments, including the illegal Rhodesian regime. The Nixon policy was strongly influenced by the emergence of a lobby similar to that which had coalesced around Katanga in the Congo. Like its predecessor, the Rhodesia lobby was an eclectic group of anticommunists, Southern segregationists, and corporations with vested interests. Encouraged by the Washington-based Rhodesian Information Office, the lobby urged Congress to open a sanctions loophole. The result was an amendment to the 1971 Military Procurement Authorization Act – the so-called Byrd Amendment – which contravened international law by allowing the importation of "strategic and critical" materials from Rhodesia so long as there was no similar ban on the importation of such materials from communist countries. The list of exempted items included seventy-two materials, among them chrome, ferrochrome, nickel, copper, tungsten, and asbestos. American companies, including Union Carbide (which owned Rhodesia's largest chrome mines), Foote Mineral, and Allegheny Ludlum, had lobbied hard for the amendment. Unwilling to challenge big business or to antagonize Southern senators before the 1972 presidential elections, Nixon signed the bill into law. In consequence, the United States joined South Africa and Portugal in openly defying UN sanctions.

The American loophole was finally closed in 1977, when the newly installed Carter administration threw its weight behind congressional liberals who had been advocating repeal since the Byrd Amendment became law. During the intervening years, the American legislation was a major boon to the Rhodesian economy and facilitated the acquisition of the foreign currency needed to buy weapons and oil. Moreover, the U.S. sanctions-busting legislation had tremendous propaganda value for the rebel regime; it was touted by the regime's supporters as an act of solidarity in the common struggle against international communism.

When it became clear that the West was unwilling to enforce sanctions or use military might to bring Rhodesia into compliance with international law, ZAPU and ZANU turned to armed struggle. The first venture, a joint operation by the ANC and ZAPU in 1967, was put down by South African and Rhodesian security forces. From 1972, ZANU collaborated with FRELIMO, operating from liberated areas inside Mozambique. After Mozambique's independence in 1975, the FRELIMO government allowed ZANU to move freely across the 700-mile border with Rhodesia. Meanwhile, ZAPU had begun to operate from bases in Zambia.

As was the case in the Portuguese territories and South Africa, the liberation movements in Rhodesia sought external support. Individual African states and the OAU Liberation Committee provided material assistance. Zambia and Mozambique closed their borders with Rhodesia and enforced UN sanctions – at great cost to themselves. Together with the other Frontline States (Tanzania, Botswana, and Angola), they attempted to unite the liberation movements and broker an equitable political settlement. Nordic countries and the World Council of Churches provided the liberation movements with humanitarian aid. When Western countries refused to provide military assistance, ZAPU and ZANU turned to the Soviet Union and China. ZAPU, which received military and political training and financial support from the Soviet Union, followed Soviet military strategy, preparing a conventional army for a cross-border invasion from Zambia. ZAPU operated in the southwestern part of the country, which was dominated by the Ndebele ethnic group. ZANU, which received military support from China, emulated Mao's strategy of mass mobilization and guerrilla warfare, infiltrating the rural population from Mozambique and relying on the peasantry for food, shelter, intelligence, and protection. ZANU operated in the northeast, home to the Shona-speaking population.

As the Rhodesian struggle intensified and Portugal withdrew from the region, Pretoria began to see the writing on the wall. No longer buffered against the "communist threat," South Africa hoped to replace the cordon sanitaire of white-ruled states with compliant black ones. In 1974, Prime Minister Vorster initiated a policy of détente with the region. Although Pretoria had been a mainstay of Rhodesia's rebel regime since UDI, Vorster worried that Smith's continued intransigence would intensify regional instability, thus enhancing prospects for revolutionary movements and jeopardizing South African security. Pretoria sought a Rhodesian solution that would install a quiescent black government, which would tamp down radical influences and allow white privilege to continue.

Vorster's Rhodesia strategy, which temporarily removed the spotlight from South Africa's own racial policies and its illegal occupation of Namibia, gained some international legitimacy when the United States signed on. Having failed to prevent the MPLA from coming to power in Angola, Secretary of State Henry Kissinger was determined to broker a "moderate" solution in Rhodesia. In 1976, he engaged in his famous brand of shuttle diplomacy in an attempt to produce a settlement that would appease Rhodesian blacks and protect white privilege. In preparation for negotiations in Geneva, ZAPU and ZANU united as the Patriotic Front, forming a formidable negotiating team. Fortified by his earlier agreements with Kissinger, Smith was determined to thwart any settlement that weakened his hold on power. The Patriotic Front, however, would accept nothing less than majority rule, and the Geneva Conference ended in failure.

Under pressure from Pretoria and Washington, Smith sought an alternative solution. Hoping to implement his own "internal settlement," he devised a plan that involved token African participation but retained real power in white hands. Circumventing the Patriotic Front, Smith allied with three internal African figures, Bishop Abel Muzorewa, Reverend Ndabaningi Sithole, and Chief Jeremiah Chirau, all of whom had rejected armed struggle. The Patriotic Front, which had no role in the negotiations, denounced the ensuing "Zimbabwe-Rhodesia" constitution and refused to participate in the April 1979 parliamentary elections. In elections marred by intimidation and violence and held under conditions of martial law, Muzorewa's United African National Council took 67 percent of the vote, and the bishop was duly installed as prime minister. Under enormous pressure from African Commonwealth members and their allies – as well as non-aligned nations and the OAU – British Prime Minister Margaret Thatcher reluctantly refrained from recognizing the new government and refused to lift economic sanctions. African influence was also evident in the position assumed by American UN ambassador and civil rights leader Andrew Young, who argued that any settlement that did not include the Patriotic Front would not end the war. Embracing the position promoted by Nigeria and the Frontline States, President Carter successfully fought off the Rhodesia lobby in Congress and declined to accord Zimbabwe-Rhodesia diplomatic recognition or to repeal American sanctions legislation.

At the urging of Commonwealth leaders, Britain pressed for another round of negotiations that would include the Patriotic Front. Hoping that the conference would result in a moderate government, the United States supported Britain's initiative. The Lancaster House Constitutional Conference was held in London during the fall of 1979. All parties were under enormous pressure to settle. Devastated by Rhodesian attacks, Mozambique informed ZANU that it could not continue to support the war. Landlocked Zambia, whose economy was ravaged by the effects of sanctions, applied similar pressure on ZAPU. Convinced that the war was lost, the Rhodesian Security

Forces and Central Intelligence Organisation were ready to concede. Hoping to force the Patriotic Front to accept proposals that fell short of unimpeded majority rule, Britain urged the United States to lift sanctions. It did so on December 16. The following day, the Patriotic Front accepted the Lancaster House Agreement. The final pact, signed on December 21, included a transitional constitution, imposed by Britain, which guaranteed whites disproportionate parliamentary representation for seven years and property, employment, and pension protection. Land redistribution would be permissible only on a "willing buyer, willing seller" basis, and the new government would be obliged to pay owners the market price.

Although both Britain and the United States had once hoped for alternatives to ZAPU and ZANU, none of the rival parties had sufficient popular support to render them viable. In the February 1980 elections, ZANU broke from the Patriotic Front to run alone. As ZANU-PF, it won fifty-seven of a hundred parliamentary seats, while the Patriotic Front (ZAPU) won twenty. Bishop Muzorewa's United African National Council won only three seats. The remaining twenty seats, reserved for whites, were won by Ian Smith's Rhodesian Front. In April 1980, ZANU-PF formed the new government of independent Zimbabwe, which also included members of the Patriotic Front and the Rhodesian Front, the two largest minority parties. The determination of Rhodesian whites to retain a monopoly on political and economic power had led to a decade-long war that killed some 20,000 to 30,000 people, the vast majority of whom were Africans. Although the war was over, its legacy would mark Zimbabwe's troubled future.

Namibia (1966–90)

Bordering both South Africa and Angola, mineral-rich Namibia was another African battleground that attracted significant foreign intervention. Formerly the German colony of South West Africa, Namibia was transferred to South Africa as a League of Nations mandate after World War I. Violating its mandatory responsibility to promote economic and social progress in the territory, South Africa divided Namibia into ethnic reserves, plundered its mineral wealth, and established an apartheid-like system of politically repressive and racially discriminatory laws. Western countries were complicit in Namibia's exploitation. While South African companies controlled Namibia's diamond mines, American firms dominated copper mining, and a consortium of British, French, Canadian, West German, and South African investors controlled the uranium industry. Western members of the UN Security Council regularly opposed sanctions intended to force South African withdrawal from the territory.

In August 1966, convinced that all peaceful avenues for change had been closed, SWAPO launched an armed struggle for Namibian independence. In October, the UN General Assembly terminated South Africa's mandate and declared that the territory was henceforth a UN responsibility. Three years later, the Security Council endorsed the General Assembly's actions and declared South Africa's continued occupation of Namibia to be illegal. In 1971, the International Court of Justice upheld the Security Council decision and ordered South Africa to leave Namibia immediately. Determined to retain Namibia as a source of mineral wealth and as a buffer against nationalist movements in Angola, Pretoria claimed that because the League of Nations had granted the mandate, only the League of Nations, defunct since 1946, could terminate it.

In 1976, SWAPO was recognized by the UN General Assembly as "the sole and authentic representative of the Namibian people" and granted observer status in the organization.[16] The liberation movement received economic and humanitarian aid from the UN, Nordic and African countries, the World Council of Churches, and Lutheran churches in Europe and the United States – as well as military and financial assistance from the Soviet Union, Eastern Europe, and North Korea. After Angola's independence in 1975, the MPLA government allowed SWAPO to establish bases in southern Angola, where its personnel received training and logistical support from Angolan, Cuban, Soviet, and East German military advisors. A smaller political movement, the South West Africa National Union (SWANU), based primarily among the Herero ethnic group, received support from China.

As world attention turned to Namibia, Prime Minister Vorster attempted to incorporate the territory into his regional détente strategy. Just as he sought to install a compliant black government in Rhodesia, Vorster hoped to establish a malleable regime in Namibia. In

---

[16] UN General Assembly Resolution 31/146, "Situation in Namibia Resulting from the Illegal Occupation of the Territory by South Africa," December 20, 1976, http://www.un.org/ga/search/view_doc.asp?symbol=A/RES/31/146&Lang=E&Area=RESOLUTION.

September 1975, government-appointed chiefs and other leaders chosen according to ethnic group met at the Turnhalle Conference to discuss the parameters of a constitution for an "independent" Namibia. Political parties, including SWAPO, were barred from participation.

It was clear to the Western powers on the Security Council that an internal settlement based on the Turnhalle talks would lack legitimacy and leave them vulnerable to pressure for stronger action against South Africa. The three powers with permanent seats – Britain, France, and the United States – had consistently obstructed punitive action. Between 1970 and 1976, the United States and Britain vetoed mandatory economic sanctions three times, while France vetoed them twice. However, these countries were under enormous pressure to force South Africa into compliance with international law. As a result, they began to prod Pretoria toward a workable settlement. In January 1976, the Security Council unanimously adopted Resolution 385, which ordered South Africa to withdraw its illegal administration and military forces and transfer power to the Namibian people through UN-supervised elections.

In 1977, as South Africa continued to obstruct the UN process, the Western members of Security Council formed a negotiating body outside the UN framework. Composed of Britain, France, the United States, West Germany, and Canada, the Western Contact Group sought a compromise that would protect its members' economic interests in Namibia and undermine the drive for UN sanctions against South Africa. Toward this end, the Western Contact Group pressed SWAPO to make concessions favorable to Pretoria. The result was UN Security Council Resolution 435, adopted in September 1978, which gave Pretoria more control and the UN less control over the transition process. In contrast to Resolution 385, the new resolution permitted the South African military and police to remain in Namibia during the transition period. Elections would be supervised by the UN but with the assistance of the South African administrator general. Both SWAPO and South Africa agreed to the new plan. The devil would be in the details.

South African Defense Minister P. W. Botha, who replaced Vorster as prime minister in September 1978, was determined to retain a compliant Namibia as a buffer against Angola's radical government to the north. Ignoring the UN resolution, he resumed plans for a South African–controlled internal settlement and hastily scheduled elections for December 1978. When the Security Council passed a resolution that condemned South African defiance and declared the elections null and void, the Western Contact Group members abstained. Their continued refusal to impose sanctions on South Africa for noncompliance with UN mandates gave Pretoria the upper hand in subsequent negotiations.

By early 1980, Pretoria could no longer hide the fact that its client regime was viable only with massive South African military support. Privately, South African military officials indicated that the war in Namibia was unwinnable, and authorities in Pretoria admitted that SWAPO would win any free UN-supervised elections. Then, in November, Ronald Reagan was elected president of the United States. Anticipating solidarity from the soon-to-be-inaugurated Reagan administration, South Africa stalled. In January 1981, during another round of implementation negotiations, South Africa revoked its support for Resolution 435 and walked out of the talks. In March, the Western Contact Group members abstained on ten General Assembly resolutions that condemned South Africa and called on the Security Council to impose sanctions. In April, the United States, Britain, and France vetoed four Security Council resolutions that would have imposed economic sanctions, an oil embargo, and a stronger arms ban on Pretoria.

The South African position elicited a sympathetic response from the new American administration. In January, Secretary of State–designate Alexander Haig had told the Senate Foreign Relations Committee that the United States wished "to bring about a solution which is not going to put in jeopardy the interest of those who share our values and [interests], above all, in a broad, strategic sense."[17] He privately assured his South African counterpart that Pretoria would not be "steamrolled on Namibia."[18] Within months, Assistant Secretary Crocker was promoting a revised Namibian independence plan. Although the UN plan had stipulated that the Namibian constitution be drafted after the UN-supervised elections – when South Africa was no longer in control – Crocker proposed the adoption of constitutional

[17] Quoted in *Nomination of Alexander M. Haig, Jr.*, Hearings before the Committee on Foreign Relations, U.S. Senate, 97th Congress, 1st Session, on the Nomination of Alexander M. Haig, Jr. to be Secretary of State, January 9–10, 12–15, 1981, part 2 (Washington, DC: U.S. Government Printing Office, 1981), 9.

[18] Quoted in "Prepared Statement of Randall Robinson, Executive Director, TransAfrica," *Controls on Exports to South Africa*, Hearings before the Subcommittees on International Economic Policy and Trade and on Africa, Committee on Foreign Affairs, U.S. House of Representatives, 97th Congress, 2nd Session, February 9 and December 2, 1982 (Washington, DC: U.S. Government Printing Office, 1983), 97.

principles before the elections. These principles would enshrine white-minority rights, protect (white-owned) private property, and otherwise limit the authority and independence of the future Namibian government. In May, Crocker advised Haig to tell the South African foreign minister that "we are willing to work with them toward an internationally acceptable settlement which will safeguard their interests and reflect our mutual desire to foreclose Soviet gains in southern Africa." Haig should assure his South African counterpart that "we share your view that Namibia should not be turned over to the Soviets and their allies. A Russian flag in Windhoek is as unacceptable to us as it is to you."[19] In August, South Africa launched its largest invasion into Angola since 1975, using more than 5,000 troops to attack SWAPO bases, create a buffer zone north of the Namibian border, and occupy southern Angola. Thousands of Namibians and hundreds of Angolans were killed in the operation, and two Angolan towns were destroyed by South African bombs. In the UN Security Council, Britain, France, and West Germany joined those who condemned South Africa aggression; the United States alone vetoed the resolution.

In 1982, undeterred by the fact that the UN Security Council had already approved a Namibian independence plan, the Reagan administration introduced a new issue that would delay Namibian independence for another eight years. Arguing that the presence of Cuban troops in Angola constituted a legitimate security concern for South Africa, the Reagan administration insisted that independence in Namibia be contingent on prior Cuban troop withdrawal from Angola. SWAPO, Angola, and the Frontline States denounced "linkage" for arbitrarily tying Namibia's fate to the prior resolution of a regional conflict – which Pretoria now had even greater interest in perpetuating. Although the other Western Contact Group members refused to endorse the linkage plan, they did little to bring the United States back into line. With a green light from Washington, Pretoria commenced regular assaults against southern Angola, where it established permanent military bases staffed with more than 1,000 South African soldiers. Simultaneously, it intensified its support for UNITA as a proxy force, causing Cuba and the Soviet Union to increase their assistance to the MPLA government. The growing threat ensured that

---

[19] Chester Crocker's "Scope Paper" for Secretary of State Alexander Haig in preparation for Haig's May 14, 1981, meeting with South African Foreign Minister Pik Botha at the State Department, reprinted in "The Secret State Department Documents," *Covert Action Information Bulletin*, no. 13 (July–August 1981), 41.

Cuban troops would remain in Angola and that Namibia would not gain its independence. Angola's sovereign right to determine its own defense policy and Namibia's fundamental right to independence were thus sacrificed to the American linkage policy.

The United States further sabotaged Namibian independence by resuming open support for UNITA after a decade-long official hiatus.[20] In the summer of 1985, at the urging of President Reagan, Congress repealed the Clark Amendment, which had banned the use of U.S. government funds for military and paramilitary activities in Angola. In 1986, following a vigorous lobbying campaign by anti-Castro Cuban Americans and other anticommunist groups, Congress restored U.S. military aid to UNITA, supplying the rebel force with some of the most sophisticated American weapons on the market, including several hundred heat-seeking Stinger antiaircraft missiles. The value of American military aid to UNITA rose from $15 million in 1986 to $30 million in 1987. Renewed U.S. support for the antigovernment insurgency guaranteed the continued presence of Cuban combat forces in Angola.

In the fall of 1987, South Africa launched its largest military venture in Angola to date, eventually involving some 6,000 SADF soldiers. Cuba responded with an influx of 15,000 more soldiers, while the Soviet Union provided sophisticated weapons and equipment that soon destroyed South African air superiority. The tide began to turn toward Angola in March 1988, when South African forces, rendered vulnerable by the lack of air cover and thwarted by MPLA and Cuban soldiers, were forced to concede a stalemate at the town of Cuito Cuanavale. No longer able to control the buffer zone that separated Angola and Namibia and unwilling to accept the high white casualty rates that would result from an intensified land assault, South Africa finally accepted the inevitability of Namibian independence.

By summer, South Africa had seriously begun to negotiate its withdrawal from Namibia and southern Angola, signing a ceasefire with Angola and Cuba in July. In December, the three countries signed the U.S.-brokered Tripartite Agreement, which required South Africa and Cuba to withdraw their troops from Angola and South Africa to

---

[20] Although direct American support for military and paramilitary activities in Angola had been outlawed, the United States continued to supply UNITA indirectly through third countries during the period that the Clark Amendment was in effect.

implement UN Security Council Resolution 435 – the Namibian independence plan that had languished for a decade. Although SWAPO was a signatory to the UN resolution, it had not been party to the 1988 negotiations and, thus, was not a signatory to the December accords. Once again, outsiders had determined the future of the Namibian people. The sidelining of SWAPO in the final hour led to confusion and tragedy, the most serious of which was the April 1989 slaughter of nearly 300 SWAPO soldiers as they tried to reach UN forces so that they could be confined to base inside Namibia. The killings were perpetrated by the SADF in an operation authorized by the understaffed UN, whose own forces had been drastically reduced by the permanent members of the Security Council, who did not want to foot the bill.

Despite these setbacks, Namibian elections were held in November 1989 and judged free and fair by the UN and other international observers. SWAPO won 57 percent of the vote and a majority of seats in the Constituent Assembly that was tasked with writing a new constitution. Namibia became independent in March 1990, with SWAPO leader Sam Nujoma as its first president. Although the Reagan administration proclaimed the December 1988 Namibian settlement to be a victory for constructive engagement, it was in fact another case of justice delayed. Across the African continent, the United States was viewed as the South African ally that had stalled Namibian independence for more than a decade.

Destabilization in Southern Africa (1975–90)

As Southern Africans struggled to build new nations in the aftermath of colonialism and white-minority rule, they faced a new wave of foreign intervention. This time the aggressor was an intracontinental rather than extracontinental power. From 1975 to 1990, South Africa's apartheid regime waged wars of destabilization against neighboring states, destroying infrastructure and supporting insurgent movements that threatened their governments. It held hostage countries whose economies were heavily dependent on South Africa, forcing them to expel South African refugees and political activists.

Pretoria's goals were twofold. The apartheid regime targeted countries that sought to undermine white-minority rule and those that menaced South Africa's economic domination of the region.

Threatened by the emergence of nonracial societies built on socialist economic models and by regional collaboration that challenged
South Africa's political and economic hegemony, Pretoria sponsored
rebel movements and military incursions that killed hundreds of thousands of people in Angola and Mozambique. It launched cross-border
raids into Lesotho, Swaziland, Botswana, Zimbabwe, and Zambia,
and it thwarted Namibian independence for several decades. Framing its actions in Cold War national security rhetoric – the protection
of its borders against communist infiltration – Pretoria won the tacit
complicity, if not the outright support, of important Western powers.

Once Portugal had departed from the region and Zimbabwe had
attained its independence, South Africa was no longer buffered by
white-ruled states to the north. Convinced that South Africa was sur-
rounded by hostile neighbors that were determined to install a Marxist
government in Pretoria, Prime Minister P. W. Botha abandoned his
predecessor's policy of regional détente. His new policy assumed that
enemies were infiltrating South Africa through neighboring states in
a communist onslaught coordinated by the Soviet Union. Internal
unrest and regional hostility were believed to be the result of external
subversion rather than the nature of the apartheid system.

Botha's response to the "total onslaught" was a two-pronged "total
strategy" that involved both co-optation and destabilization. In accor-
dance with the first prong, Botha attempted to seduce South Africa's
neighbors into a regional economic and security alliance, dubbed
the "Constellation of Southern African States" (CONSAS), in which
South Africa would be the dominant partner. CONSAS members
would be forced to accept military and economic agreements that
increased their dependence on South Africa and rendered them vulnerable to South African pressure. They would be expected to police
South African refugees and activists on their soil, cease aid to South
African and Namibian liberation movements, avoid socialist economic
models, and sever ties to socialist countries. Pretoria's ability to coerce
its neighbors was bolstered by regional economic structures that were
rooted in the colonial era. The region's transportation networks converged on South Africa, the economic hub. In 1981, half of the trade
leaving landlocked Southern African states passed through South
African ports. South African businesses dominated in the production and distribution of goods throughout the region, with significant investments in mining, manufacturing, agriculture, and services.
South Africa was the main trading partner of five Southern African

states (Botswana, Lesotho, Swaziland, Zimbabwe, and Malawi), and proceeds from their citizens' labor in the South African mines was an important source of income for three (Botswana, Lesotho, and Swaziland).

Despite the odds in Pretoria's favor, the CONSAS plan was still-born. In response to the South African initiative, nine Southern African states (Angola, Botswana, Lesotho, Malawi, Mozambique, Swaziland, Tanzania, Zambia, and Zimbabwe) formed the Southern African Development Coordination Conference (SADCC) in April 1980. Their objective was to create alternative networks of trade, transportation, communications, energy, and agricultural and industrial development that would break South Africa's economic stranglehold on the region. Supported primarily by Nordic countries, small contributions from Western Europe, and a lesser amount from the United States, SADCC threatened South Africa both politically and economically. Its members would become the focus of the second prong of Pretoria's total strategy.

Unable to co-opt its neighbors, Pretoria increasingly chose military aggression and destabilization as its preferred option. South Africa targeted the Frontline States to deter their assistance to the South African and Namibian liberation movements and to prevent their development of alternative political, economic, and social models that might inspire anti-apartheid activists and threaten South African regional hegemony. Pretoria also armed and trained local forces, particularly in Angola and Mozambique, using them to attack civilians and destroy infrastructure. To some extent, these tactics were successful. Fearing military reprisals, countries bordering South Africa refused to allow ANC bases or training facilities on their soil – denying the South African liberation movement the kind of rear bases that Mozambique and Zambia had provided to Zimbabwean guerrillas or that Angola had provided to SWAPO. As a result, the ANC was forced to establish its training camps in more distant countries (Tanzania and Angola) and to locate its political headquarters in Zambia. Although they would not sanction military bases, the border states initially provided ANC partisans with safe haven and allowed guerrillas, weapons, and supplies to move through their territories en route to South Africa.

Pretoria retaliated, engaging in targeted assassinations and regular attacks on ANC residences and refugee camps in Botswana, Lesotho, Swaziland, Mozambique, Angola, Zimbabwe, and Zambia. The apartheid regime also supported rebel forces in Angola,

Mozambique, Lesotho, Zimbabwe, and Zambia that attempted to overthrow or destabilize those countries' governments. Coerced into signing nonaggression pacts with Pretoria in the 1980s, several Southern African countries evicted ANC cadres and withdrew permission for transit into South Africa. Mozambique and Angola were by far the greatest victims of South African destabilization, either through direct aggression or surrogate forces. Between 1980 and 1988, wars in Angola and Mozambique took as many as 2 million lives, forced another 7.5 million people from their homes, destroyed the countries' infrastructures, and devastated their economies. Land mines laid by Pretoria's proxies gave Angola and Mozambique the unenviable distinction of possessing some of the world's highest amputee rates.

Shortly after Mozambique's independence, an insurgent organization, Mozambique National Resistance (RENAMO), launched a devastating war against the FRELIMO government. Although the rebels were portrayed by Rhodesia, South Africa, and right-wing supporters in the United States as an anticommunist liberation movement, the organization was in fact the brainchild of the Rhodesian Central Intelligence Organisation and the Portuguese secret police. It was created not to emancipate Mozambicans but to harass their government, in the hope of severing its support for ZANU, and to conduct raids on ZANU camps in Mozambique. When white-ruled Rhodesia became the independent nation of Zimbabwe in 1980, RENAMO's headquarters were transferred to South Africa, which viewed Mozambique's socialist policies and support for South African liberation as a threat to its political, economic, and military hegemony in the region. Henceforth, South Africa trained, equipped, and funded RENAMO forces.

Without a political platform or ideology, RENAMO's sole objective was to undermine popular support for FRELIMO. The insurgents targeted the country's infrastructure, including roads, bridges, electricity pylons, and transmission lines from the country's massive hydroelectric dam. In addition, RENAMO rebels attacked the Beira oil pipeline that supplied both Zimbabwe and Mozambique, as well as the Beira oil refinery and storage facility. They bombed rail lines leading to three Mozambican ports, forcing six landlocked SADCC countries to use South African alternatives. RENAMO forces destroyed rural schools, stores, and medical clinics. They kidnapped and killed teachers, health-care workers, and development assistants. They undermined Mozambique's food supply by laying land mines in the fields and rural pathways and attacking trucks that hauled food to market. They terrorized the rural population, attacking peasants with machetes, amputating their noses, lips, ears, breasts, and limbs. They press-ganged child soldiers and forced women and girls into sexual slavery. RENAMO's depredations resulted in widespread malnutrition and starvation and weakened popular support for the FRELIMO government, which could not protect the population.

Framing its mission as a crusade against communism, RENAMO attempted to garner U.S. government support. The RENAMO lobby in the United States won the allegiance of some members the defense and intelligence communities, Congress, the religious right, and other organizations, but it failed to convince the Reagan administration that RENAMO was anything other than a bandit organization. The lack of Cuban troops on the ground and the Soviet Union's relative disinterest reduced the Cold War profile of the conflict. British Prime Minister Margaret Thatcher's support for the FRELIMO government, in gratitude for its facilitation of the Lancaster House settlement, also helped convince the Reagan administration that Mozambique was to be wooed rather than subverted.

By the early 1980s, Mozambique had turned toward the Western powers, including Britain and the United States. Its economy was devastated by insurgency, drought, and inexperience, and the Soviet Union was unresponsive to its appeals. After it signed a nonaggression pact with Pretoria in 1984, FRELIMO was rewarded with desperately needed aid from Western nations. The Nkomati Accord required FRELIMO to expel all ANC military personnel and to prevent ANC guerrillas and weapons from moving through Mozambican territory, and it drastically curtailed the number of ANC political activists permitted inside the country. In return, South Africa pledged to end support for RENAMO – a promise it failed to keep. Despite overwhelming evidence of Pretoria's duplicity, the Reagan administration refused to punish South Africa and did nothing to undercut RENAMO, which continued to enjoy quiet support in the U.S. intelligence community.

Simultaneous with its surrogate war against Mozambique, South Africa waged war against Angola, using both proxies and conventional armed forces. Calling the conflict a "border war," Pretoria engaged in unremitting assaults on southern Angola between 1975 and 1988 while providing massive support for UNITA's insurgency. Initially, South Africa's purpose was to prevent the installation of an MPLA government in Angola. When that failed, its primary concern became the preservation of South African control over Namibia. To destroy SWAPO bases and supply lines and to pressure the MPLA government to cut off support, Pretoria subjected Angola to regular bombing campaigns, incursions across the Namibian border, and large-scale invasions involving thousands of South African troops who set up a permanent military occupation in southern Angola. Its own interests coinciding with those of Pretoria, UNITA, like RENAMO, targeted economic infrastructure – roads, railway lines, oil refineries, and electricity pylons – as well as rural schools, clinics, and farms. As a result of UNITA sabotage, the Benguela railroad, which linked the copper fields of Zambia and Zaire to the Angolan port city of Lobito – was closed for more than a decade. Not only did the Reagan administration refuse to impose sanctions on South Africa for its devastation of Angola, it actively supported Pretoria's campaign. Where the RENAMO lobby failed, the UNITA lobby was successful. Between 1986 and 1991, the United States provided UNITA with more than $250 million in military assistance, and support for UNITA became a central feature of Reagan's Southern Africa policy.

The dismantling of apartheid in the early 1990s and the inability of Pretoria to continue financing its regional wars led to new opportunities for peace. In Mozambique, the initiative was seized by the Italian Catholic Community of Sant'Egidio, which, in collaboration with the archbishop of Beira and a representative of the Italian government, brokered a settlement between RENAMO and FRELIMO. Following the signing of the Rome General Peace Agreement in October 1992, a UN peacekeeping force supervised a two-year transitional period and international observers monitored multiparty elections in October 1994. FRELIMO won the presidency and more than the half parliamentary seats. RENAMO, which won a substantial minority, accepted the results that maintained FRELIMO's dominance.

In Angola, the outcome was far less successful. Following the withdrawal of South African and Cuban troops according to the terms of the December 1988 Tripartite Agreement, Portugal mediated a settlement between the MPLA and UNITA. The Bicesse Accords, signed in May 1991, led to a UN-monitored ceasefire and internationally supervised multiparty elections in September 1992. In elections judged by international observers to be free and fair, the MPLA won a solid parliamentary victory and a plurality of the presidential ballots. In contrast to his Mozambican counterpart, UNITA leader Jonas Savimbi repudiated the election results. Declaring the elections fraudulent, he refused to participate in the presidential runoff and plunged the country back into war. His American and South African pipelines having

PHOTO 5.3. President Reagan with UNITA leader Jonas Savimbi in the Oval Office, January 30, 1986 (Bettmann/Corbis).

dried up with the disintegration of the Soviet Union and apartheid, Savimbi sought new sources of support. Following the imposition of a UN arms, fuel, and financial embargo against UNITA in 1993, the rebel organization turned to illicit diamond trading. From 1992 until 1998, when the UN embargo was expanded to include the sale of conflict diamonds, UNITA dominated the Angolan diamond market, selling an estimated $4 billion worth of gems. The Angolan government, in turn, financed the war with its oil revenues, leaving little for the country's enormous reconstruction and development needs. The Angolan war continued for a decade beyond the thwarted 1992 elections, ending only with Savimbi's death in combat in February 2002. As the twenty-first century entered its second decade, both Mozambique and Angola were technically at peace. However, neither had recovered from the devastating destabilization wars.

Southern Africa's White-Minority Regimes: A Unique Case

In contrast to other cases considered in this book, international involvement in Southern Africa was more prolonged and varied than a Cold War framework would suggest. International intervention for regime change in the white-ruled countries involved coalitions of African and non-African states and of nongovernmental organizations that crossed Cold War boundaries. Southern Africa solidarity networks focused on issues of decolonization and antiracism, as well as those involving the Cold War. In some ways, the Southern Africa solidarity movement resembled the eclectic anti-Nazi alliance of World War II while echoing the ideals of the postwar UN, the African and Asian anticolonial struggles, and the American civil rights movement.

Foreign coalitions working for regime change varied from one Southern African case to the next. The Commonwealth played a critical part in Rhodesia's transition to majority rule, while the UN took a leading role in Namibia and South Africa. Although grassroots organizations mobilized around the Zimbabwean and Namibian struggles, only the South African anti-apartheid struggle generated an enormous transnational movement composed of student, labor, religious, civil rights, and antiracism organizations.

The struggle against white-minority rule in Rhodesia was a concern not only for African states but also for the Commonwealth, which comprised former British possessions in Africa and other continents. African leaders such as Julius Nyerere of Tanzania and Kenneth Kaunda of Zambia were prominent voices in Commonwealth deliberations in support of Zimbabwean majority rule. Their connections to British and Nordic socialists, rather than Eastern Bloc or Chinese communists, undermined the charge that support for Zimbabwean liberation was part of a communist plot. Commonwealth members from Africa, the Caribbean, and countries like India and Malaysia, ensured that decolonization rather than the Cold War dominated debates about Zimbabwe's future.

Namibia's special status as a ward of the UN resulted in deep, ongoing attention by that organization and by UN member states that might otherwise have paid scant attention to a small African territory. Despite South African and American efforts to frame Namibian independence in Cold War terms, that perspective was rejected by the vast majority of UN members. Moreover, the strong ties of the Namibian liberation movement to Nordic countries and to Lutheran churches worldwide invalidated claims that the call for regime change was communist inspired.

By far the widest and most varied international involvement occurred in the case of South Africa. The UN Special Committee against Apartheid played a central role in the international anti-apartheid movement, working not only with governments around the world but also with activist organizations in scores of countries. The World Council of Churches' Programme to Combat Racism, the British Anti-Apartheid Movement, and the American Free South Africa Movement are but a few of the many nongovernmental organizations that joined the international struggle against apartheid. Together with resistance inside South Africa and the work of the ANC in exile, the international anti-apartheid movement helped to rally world opinion and reduce Western countries' political, economic, and military support for the apartheid regime.

The inadequacy of the Cold War framework did not stop the white-minority regimes from attempting to employ it. The ruling powers in Rhodesia, Namibia, and South Africa all sought to present their opposition to equal rights in Cold War terms. In so doing, they gained support from some constituencies in the United States and other Western countries. However, their efforts ultimately failed, as a wide range of international actors – including governments, intergovernmental organizations, and civil society – rejected the Cold War framework and endorsed that of the liberation movements. These external actors embraced the notion that the struggle in Southern Africa was a battle for basic human rights that deserved support regardless of Cold War alignments.

Suggested Reading

Several important books focus on U.S. policy toward Southern Africa. Thomas J. Noer's *Cold War and Black Liberation: The United States and White Rule in Africa, 1948–1968* (Columbia: University of Missouri Press, 1985) explores the evolution of American policy toward the region from the Truman through the Johnson administrations, when the early commitment to oppose colonialism was overshadowed by Cold War concerns and, finally, declining interest in Africa. Thomas Borstelmann's *Apartheid's Reluctant Uncle: The United States and Southern Africa in the Early Cold War* (New York: Oxford University Press, 1993) focuses on the Truman administration and examines the role of racism, as well as Cold War concerns, in U.S.-South Africa policy. Alex Thomson brings these works up to date in *U.S. Foreign Policy towards Apartheid South Africa, 1948–1994: Conflict of Interests* (New York: Palgrave Macmillan, 2008), which assesses the conflicts inherent in U.S.-South Africa policy throughout the apartheid era. Kenneth Mokoena has compiled an invaluable collection of declassified documents in *South Africa and the United States: The Declassified History* (New York: New Press, 1993), which provides insight into U.S.-Southern Africa policies from the Kennedy through the George H. W. Bush administrations. Two works by Assistant Secretary of State for African Affairs Chester Crocker provide a glimpse into the thinking and internal workings of the Reagan administration's Africa policy network. "South Africa: Strategy for Change," *Foreign Affairs* 59, no. 2 (Winter 1980–81): 323–51, outlines the constructive engagement policy that became the cornerstone of the administration's South Africa policy. *High Noon in Southern Africa: Making Peace in a Rough Neighborhood* (New York: W. W. Norton, 1993), a memoir written in response to his critics, is a defense of constructive engagement and provides an insider's account of policy battles within the administration. International relations scholar J. E. Davies provides a counterpoint to Crocker in *Constructive Engagement? Chester Crocker & American Policy in South Africa, Namibia & Angola, 1981–1988* (Athens: Ohio University Press, 2007), in which he outlines the aims of Crocker's strategy, examines its implementation, and argues that it failed in its objectives.

A number of important studies examine the political and economic interests and roles of other outsiders in the region. William Minter's *King Solomon's Mines Revisited: Western Interests and the Burdened History of Southern Africa* (New York: Basic Books, 1986) is a highly readable overview of the role of Western governments and businesses in creating and sustaining white-minority rule in Southern Africa. Sasha Polakow-Suransky provides an in-depth exposé of the military and nuclear ties that bound South Africa and Israel in *The Unspoken Alliance: Israel's Secret Relationship with Apartheid South Africa* (New York: Pantheon, 2010). Sue Onslow's edited collection, *Cold War in Southern Africa: White Power, Black Liberation* (New York: Routledge, 2009), includes case studies by leading scholars of the region who have used archival sources from the United States, the former Soviet Union, Cuba, Britain, Zambia, and South Africa. One of the contributors, Vladimir Shubin, has published his own book, *The Hot "Cold War": The USSR in Southern Africa* (London: Pluto Press, 2008), an insider's view of the Soviet role in Southern Africa, bolstered by documents recently made available in the Russian archives. The Nordic countries were among the few Western states to support Southern African liberation struggles. For their involvement, see the Nordic Africa Institute's six-volume series, *National Liberation in Southern Africa: The Role of the Nordic Countries*, http://www.liberationafrica.se/publications. The role of neighboring African states in struggles against white-minority rule in Rhodesia and Namibia are assessed in Carol B. Thompson's *Challenge to Imperialism: The Frontline States in the Liberation of Zimbabwe* (Boulder, CO: Westview Press, 1986) and Gilbert M. Khadiagala's *Allies in Adversity: The Frontline States in Southern African Security, 1975–1993* (Athens: Ohio University Press, 1994).

The dynamics of the negotiated settlements in Angola, Mozambique, Rhodesia, Namibia, and South Africa, including the roles of foreign powers, are examined in two recommended books: Thomas Ohlson and Stephen John Stedman, with Robert Davies, *The New Is Not Yet Born: Conflict Resolution in Southern Africa* (Washington, DC: Brookings Institution, 1994) and Thomas Ohlson, *Power Politics and Peace Policies: Intra-State Conflict Resolution in Southern Africa* (Uppsala, Sweden: Department of Peace and Conflict Research, Uppsala University, 1998). South African journalist Allister Sparks offers an in-depth account of years of negotiations between the ANC and the government of South Africa in *Tomorrow Is Another Country: The Inside Story of South Africa's Road to Change* (New York: Hill and Wang, 1995).

A number of works provide important insights into South African political, economic, and social dynamics and the long struggle for majority rule. In *The Mind of South Africa* (New York: Ballantine Books, 1990), South African journalist Allister Sparks provides a highly accessible comprehensive history of South Africa from white settlement through the uprisings of the 1980s. Thomas G. Karis, Gwendolen M. Carter, Gail M. Gerhart, and others have edited an invaluable compendium of primary documents covering a range of organizations and 100 years of opposition to white-minority rule: *From Protest to Challenge: A Documentary History of African Politics in South Africa, 1882–1990*, 6 vols. (Stanford, CA: Hoover Institution Press, 1972–). Tom Lodge's *Black Politics in South Africa since 1945* (New York: Longman, 1983) offers a comprehensive, well-documented analysis of internal and external struggles against political and racial oppression from 1945 to the aftermath of the 1976 Soweto uprising. In contrast, Gordon Winter's *Inside BOSS: South Africa's Secret Police* (Harmondsworth, UK: Penguin Books, 1981), by a veteran of South Africa's Bureau of State Security, offers an insider's view of the internal workings of the police state.

Several books examine the role of the African National Congress in the struggle against apartheid. Nelson Mandela's *Long Walk to Freedom: The Autobiography of Nelson Mandela* (Boston: Little, Brown, 1994), much of which was written covertly while the author was in prison, is a seminal firsthand account by the ANC leader and first president of postapartheid South Africa. Raymond Suttner, a former member of the ANC underground and political prisoner, offers a unique view into the workings of the outlawed ANC inside South Africa in *The ANC Underground in South Africa, 1950–1976* (Boulder, CO: Lynne Rienner, 2009). Two journalists provide a window into the ANC's armed struggle. Stephen M. Davis's *Apartheid's Rebels: Inside South Africa's Hidden War* (New Haven, CT: Yale University Press, 1987) is a highly readable account based on extensive written documents and hundreds of interviews. Howard Barrell's *MK: The ANC's Armed Struggle* (New York: Penguin Books, 1990) brings the story to the beginnings of the negotiations that ended apartheid. A more critical view of the ANC's armed struggle and the party's relationship to the South African Communist Party is offered by Stephen Ellis, a former editor of *Africa Confidential,* and Tsepo Sechaba, a pseudonym for an ANC insider, in *Comrades against Apartheid: The ANC and the South African Communist Party in Exile* (Bloomington: Indiana University Press, 1992). The Ellis-Sechaba book is heavily criticized in Soviet activist-scholar Vladimir Shubin's *ANC: A View from Moscow* (Bellville, South Africa: Mayibuye Books, 1999), which is based on ANC and South African Communist Party documents and the archives of the Communist Party of the Soviet Union and the Soviet Afro-Asian Solidarity Committee. Leading American authority Thomas G. Karis traces the evolution of the ANC and its program and rejects the notion that the ANC was communist dominated in "South African Liberation: The Communist Factor," *Foreign Affairs* 65, no. 2 (Winter, 1986–87): 267–87.

The role of international solidarity movements in the struggle against apartheid is investigated in numerous works. The most comprehensive assessment to date is *The Road to Democracy in South Africa,* vol. 3, *International Solidarity,* ed. South African Democracy Education Trust (Pretoria: UNISA Press, 2008), http://www.sadet.co.za/road_democracy_vol3.html and http://www.noeasyvictories.org/research/sadet_usa.pdf. *The Road to Democracy in South Africa,* vol. 5, *African Solidarity,* ed. South African Democracy Education Trust (Pretoria: UNISA Press), http://www.sadet .co.za/road_democracy.html is forthcoming. Håkan Thörn's *Anti-Apartheid and the Emergence of a Global Civil Society* (New York: Palgrave Macmillan, 2009) focuses on the transnational character of the anti-apartheid movement, with special emphasis on the Swedish and British organizations. Roger Fieldhouse's *Anti-Apartheid: A History of the Movement in Britain: A Study in Pressure Group Politics* (London: Merlin Press, 2005) examines the roles of the British Anti-Apartheid Movement and the International Defence and Aid Fund. William Minter, Gail Hovey, and Charles Cobb Jr.'s *No Easy Victories: African Liberation and American Activists over a Half Century, 1950–2000* (Trenton, NJ: Africa World Press, 2008) is an invaluable edited collection that includes reflections, interviews, and photographs involving key participants in the American solidarity movement, focusing not only on South Africa but also on liberation struggles throughout the region. Francis Njubi Nesbitt's *Race for Sanctions: African Americans against Apartheid, 1946–1994* (Bloomington: Indiana University Press, 2004) zeros in on the critical role of African Americans in moving the anti-apartheid struggle from the periphery to the mainstream of American politics. Elizabeth Schmidt's *Decoding Corporate Camouflage: U.S. Business Support for Apartheid* (Washington, DC: Institute for Policy Studies, 1980), http://africanactivist.msu.edu/document_metadata.php?objectid=32-130-24F is an example of activist scholarship that was intended for use by the grassroots divestment movement that mobilized against American corporate involvement in South Africa. An exposé of the way in which a highly touted fair employment code was used to disguise U.S. business support for apartheid, the book was banned in South Africa.

Several books provide penetrating insights into the struggle for majority rule in Rhodesia/Zimbabwe. David Martin and Phyllis Johnson's *The Struggle for Zimbabwe: The Chimurenga War* (New York: Monthly Review Press, 1981) is a well-documented account of the unfolding of the liberation struggle by journalists with unusual access to secret documents and key players in the ZANU camp. The contributions of ZAPU, in contrast, tend to be understated. For a deeper look at the roles of both liberation movements, as well as that of the rural populace more generally, readers should refer to Ngwabi Bhebe and Terence Ranger's two-volume edited collection, *Soldiers in Zimbabwe's Liberation War* and *Society in Zimbabwe's Liberation War* (Portsmouth, NH: Heinemann, 1995–96). American journalist Julie Frederikse explores the Rhodesian regime's propaganda war in *None but Ourselves: Masses vs. Media in the Making of Zimbabwe* (New York: Penguin Books, 1984), which includes a wealth of photographs, songs, posters, newspaper accounts, and interviews that provide a unique grassroots perspective of the war. Participants' views are further evident in three firsthand accounts. Maurice Nyagumbo's *With the People: An Autobiography from the Zimbabwe Struggle* (London: Allison & Busby, 1980) was written by a ZANU stalwart who spent nearly two decades in prison, jail, or detention. Joshua Nkomo's *Nkomo, The Story of My Life* (London: Methuen, 1984), authored by ZAPU's founding leader, focuses on his role in the liberation struggle and his experiences with the ZANU-dominated government that took office in 1980. In *Serving Secretly: An Intelligence Chief on Record: Rhodesia into Zimbabwe, 1964–1981* (London: John Murray, 1987), Ken Flower, head of Rhodesia's Central Intelligence Organisation, offers insight into Rhodesian government actions during the liberation war and its role in the creation of RENAMO, the insurgent organization in Mozambique.

Three books focus on U.S.-Rhodesian relations in the post–World War II period; each notes the importance of the American civil rights movement in the shaping of American policies. Gerald Horne's *From the Barrel of a Gun: The United States and the War against Zimbabwe, 1965–1980* (Chapel Hill: University of North Carolina Press, 2001), which is based on archival research in Zimbabwe and the United States, explores the transformations in American policy, especially during the intensification of the armed struggle in the 1970s. Anthony Lake's *The "Tar Baby" Option: American Policy toward Southern Rhodesia* (New York: Columbia University Press, 1976), which focuses on the policies of the Nixon and Ford administrations, is especially useful in its analysis of the Byrd Amendment's passage and implementation. Andrew DeRoche's *Black, White, and Chrome: The United States and Zimbabwe, 1953–1998* (Trenton, NJ: Africa World Press, 2001), which examines U.S.-Rhodesian relations from the Eisenhower to the Clinton administrations, offers the most complete diplomatic history to date. Two works focus on the role of UN sanctions in bringing about majority rule. William Minter and Elizabeth Schmidt's article, "When Sanctions Worked: The Case of Rhodesia Reexamined," *African Affairs* 87, no. 347, (April 1988): 207–37, http://www.africafocus.org/editor/aa1988.php, was among the first to challenge the accepted wisdom that sanctions had been ineffective, if not counterproductive. Based on contemporary journalists' accounts and extensive interviews in postindependence Zimbabwe, the article was followed by more in-depth studies such as David M. Rowe's *Manipulating the Market: Understanding Economic Sanctions, Institutional Change, and the Political Unity of White Rhodesia* (Ann Arbor: University of Michigan Press, 2001), which provides a comprehensive analysis of the ways in which economic sanctions influenced the transition to majority rule.

For Namibia, three books about South African occupation and the liberation struggle are especially recommended. David Soggot's *Namibia: The Violent Heritage* (New York: St. Martin's Press, 1986) was written by a defense lawyer who had close contact with many of the participants. Peter H. Katjavivi's *A History of Resistance in Namibia* (London: James Currey, 1988) was written by a scholar who was also a leading SWAPO official and participant in the events. Denis Herbstein and John Evenson's *The Devils Are among Us: The War for Namibia* (Atlantic Highlands, NJ: Zed Books, 1989) is particularly useful for its focus on South African methods for countering popular resistance and Western political and economic involvement in Namibia. Also recommended is John Ya-Otto's *Battlefront Namibia: An Autobiography* (Westport, CT: Lawrence Hill, 1981), a firsthand account by a SWAPO leader of the organization's first fifteen years and his own initiation into the struggle.

Focusing on the role of outsiders, Allan D. Cooper's edited collection, *Allies in Apartheid: Western Capitalism in Occupied Namibia* (New York: St. Martin's Press, 1988), explores Western economic interests in Namibia and the grassroots campaigns against them. Peter H. Katjavivi, Per Frostin, and Kaire Mbuende's *Church and Liberation in Namibia* (Winchester, MA: Pluto Press, 1989) examines the role of the church in Namibia, investigating in particular its support for the liberation struggle. Written by two SWAPO members (Katjavivi and Mbuende) and a Swedish theologian (Frostin), the book includes a range of important church documents on the issue. In *Namibia and the Nordic Countries* (Uppsala, Sweden: Scandinavian Institute of African Studies, 1981), Hans-Otto Sano and his coauthors explore Nordic countries' political and humanitarian support for the liberation struggle.

Three recommended works explore Namibia's transition to independence. G. R. Berridge's "Diplomacy and the Angola/Namibia Accords," *International Affairs* **65**, no. 3 (Summer 1989): 463–79, analyzes the circumstances on the ground that led to the 1988 accords between Angola, Cuba, and South Africa. Charles W. Freeman, Jr., the American deputy assistant secretary of state for African affairs during the negotiations, provides a U.S. government view of the events leading up to the 1988 agreement in "The Angola/Namibia Accords," *Foreign Affairs* 68, no. 3 (Summer 1989): 126–41. In *The Transition to Independence in Namibia* (Boulder, CO: Lynn Rienner, 1994), Lionel Cliffe and a team of scholars of the Namibian independence struggle describe their experiences as observers of the 1989 elections for the Constituent Assembly that drafted Namibia's new constitution; their book includes important historical contextualization.

The militarization of South African society and its role in regional destabilization are the subjects of several important works. Kenneth W. Grundy's *The Militarization of South African Politics* (Bloomington: Indiana University Press, 1986) and Jacklyn Cock and Laurie Nathan's edited collection, *Society at War: The Militarisation of South Africa* (New York: St. Martin's Press, 1989), examine the dominance of the military in South African politics and society and the country's total mobilization for domestic and foreign wars. A comprehensive analysis of South Africa's push for regional domination through the military and economic destabilization of neighboring states can be found in Joseph Hanlon's *Beggar Your Neighbours: Apartheid Power in Southern Africa* (Bloomington: Indiana University Press, 1986); Phyllis Johnson and David Martin's edited collection, *Frontline Southern Africa: Destructive Engagement* (New York: Four Walls Eight Windows, 1988); and James Barber and John Barratt's *South Africa's Foreign Policy: The Search for Status and Security, 1945–1988* (New York: Cambridge University Press, 1990). Robert S. Jaster and his colleagues provide similar analyses in *Changing Fortunes: War, Diplomacy, and Economics in Southern Africa* (New York: Ford Foundation and Foreign Policy Association, 1992), which also includes appendices of key documents. Zeroing in on the former Portuguese colonies, William Minter's *Apartheid's Contras: An Inquiry into the Roots of War in Angola and Mozambique* (Atlantic Highlands, NJ: Zed Books, 1994) investigates the wars of destabilization and use of proxy forces in Angola and Mozambique.

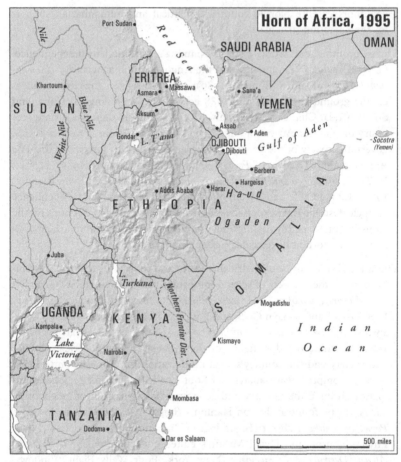

MAP 6.1. Horn of Africa, 1995. (Map by Philip Schwartzberg, Meridian Mapping, Minneapolis.)

CHAPTER 6

Conflict in the Horn, 1952–1993

Simultaneous with the struggle for Southern Africa was the Cold War battle for the Horn. Bordering on the critical Red Sea and Indian Ocean sea-lanes and in close proximity to Middle Eastern oil, Ethiopia and Somalia were both regional rivals and objects of competition between the United States and the Soviet Union. While the dynamics of decolonization established the framework for Cold War battles in North Africa, the Congo, the Portuguese colonies, and the white-ruled regimes of Southern Africa, superpower involvement in the Horn of Africa was primarily linked to postcolonial regional competition. Like African actors elsewhere on the continent, contenders for power in the Horn sought support from Cold War antagonists in order to promote their own national and regional endeavors. Although the effects of American and Soviet intervention were at times decisive, Washington and Moscow responded to African internal dynamics; they did not cause them.

African-superpower alliances in the Horn were complex and fluid. In the early 1970s, the United States helped sustain Emperor Haile Selassie's feudal order in Ethiopia while the nominally socialist military regime of Mohamed Siad Barre in Somalia was supported by the Soviet Union. However, by 1978, after a military coup in Ethiopia had brought a self-proclaimed Marxist regime to power and Somalia had attempted to annex Somali-inhabited territory in Ethiopia, Moscow and Washington had switched sides. Each had done so with reluctance, having initially hoped to maintain relations with both countries. Meanwhile, the collapse of Haile Selassie's regime had resulted in a surge of separatist movements among peoples subjugated by the Ethiopian empire. Most significantly, the nationalist movement in the former Italian colony of Eritrea, which had been annexed by Ethiopia in 1962, escalated its war for independence. Although the Soviet Union had long promoted the Eritrean cause, it withdrew its support after shifting its allegiance from Somalia to Ethiopia. Cuba, in contrast, supported Ethiopia in many capacities but refused to support its war against Eritrea. Although the conflicts in the Horn had deep local roots, they were exacerbated by the Cold War interventions of the superpowers and their allies. Without the vast quantities of weapons provided by the United States and the Soviet Union, local conflicts would not have escalated into regional ones that took an enormous toll in human life. The militarization and destabilization of the Horn during the Cold War are at the root of the conflicts that continue to devastate the region in the twenty-first century.

Ethiopia and the United States

A large multi-ethnic empire in the Horn of Africa, Ethiopia was the only African territory to successfully resist Western conquest during the late-nineteenth-century Scramble for Africa.[1] Ethiopia also participated in the scramble. Expanding its domain through the subjugation of smaller political entities, Ethiopia rapidly became the largest regional power, dominating the interior while confining European interlopers to the coast. Armed with the latest European weapons, purchased with proceeds from the East African slave trade, Emperor Menelik II defeated Italian would-be conquerors in 1896. However, Ethiopia's access to the Red Sea was blocked by the Italian colony of Eritrea, which had been established in the wake of an Ethiopian-Italian treaty in 1889 and included some lands that had been part of earlier Ethiopian kingdoms. For the following century, Ethiopia would attempt to gain control of this strategic territory.

In an expansionist campaign that presaged World War II, Italian forces occupied Ethiopia in 1936 and merged the Somali-inhabited Ogaden and Haud regions with Italian Somaliland. The Allies expelled

---

[1] Liberia, though nominally independent, was ruled for 133 years by an Americo-Liberian elite comprising freed American slaves and their descendents, who were Western in their ideas and practices.

the Italians in 1941 and reinstated the exiled Ethiopian emperor, Haile Selassie. However, Britain, as the dominant power in the region, continued to administer the disputed Ogaden and Haud territories as well as the Italian colony of Eritrea. With much of Africa controlled by Britain and France, the United States viewed Ethiopia as a strategic entrée to the continent. After the war, Washington initiated a mutually beneficial alliance with Ethiopia that lasted nearly four decades. It pressed Britain to return the disputed Ogaden and Haud regions to Ethiopia and supported Ethiopian claims to Eritrea. When the UN slated the Italian colonies of Libya and Italian Somaliland for independence, the United States urged the UN to place Eritrea under Ethiopian control. Although many Eritreans had agitated for independence, the UN acquiesced to American wishes, and Eritrea was formally federated with Ethiopia in 1952. Haile Selassie was not satisfied with this arrangement, however, and continuously eroded the parameters of Eritrean autonomy. In 1962, he annexed the territory outright, making it a province of Ethiopia. Although Selassie's maneuver violated the UN agreement, the United States condoned it, and the UN took no punitive action.

America's protégé in the Horn was no democrat, but he was a dependable Cold War ally. Like his predecessors, Haile Selassie presided over a feudal system in which an aristocracy wielded enormous power over the land and the peasant class that worked it. Christian Amharas of the northern and central highlands ruled over multiethnic Muslim and Christian populations in other parts of the empire. Convinced that the best bulwark against communism was regional stability under the Selassie regime, the United States became the emperor's primary outside backer. Central to U.S. interests in the region were the Kagnew communications station in Asmara and naval facilities in Massawa, both located in Eritrea. During the Cold War, the communications station would play a critical role in American intelligence gathering in Africa and the Middle East. In exchange for access to these two facilities, the United States provided Ethiopia with more than $280 million in military aid between 1953 and 1977 and trained thousands of military personnel, building a 47,000-man army that was used to quell internal dissent, oppose the Eritrean independence struggle, and ward off Somali expansionism.

Although the United States turned a blind eye to most Ethiopian human rights abuses, it could not ignore its ally's role in the horrific famine of 1972–73. Even after the famine began, Ethiopian farmers were forced to produce food for export rather than domestic consumption. Embarrassed by his government's inability to handle the crisis, Selassie attempted to hide it and turned away international assistance that might have averted a catastrophe. As a result, some 100,000 to 200,000 people died. In the famine's aftermath, the emperor refused to implement reforms, even in the face of internal unrest and international condemnation. The United States did not press the point. However, the famine would have long-term repercussions for the Selassie regime.

The famine debacle; the worldwide economic crisis precipitated by dramatic oil price increases in 1973–74; and mounting inflation, unemployment, and a balance-of-payments deficit led to the popular protests of 1974 that culminated in the overthrow of the Selassie regime. Between June and September 1974, a group of junior military officers known as the Derg (committee) gradually usurped power. Hundreds of officials from the former government were arrested; fifty-seven were later executed. Although some members of the Derg responded to Ethiopia's internal crisis by promoting an African form of socialism, others, including an American-trained major, Mengistu Haile Mariam, eventually embraced Marxism-Leninism. A bloody power struggle within the Derg in February 1977 would leave Mengistu as the sole man in charge. Meanwhile, in December 1974, the Derg introduced the notion of Ethiopian socialism. During the year that followed, the regime abolished the monarchy and nationalized much of the economy, including banks, industries, commercial enterprises, and land. A major land-reform program broke large feudal estates into peasant cooperatives. A highly effective mass literacy campaign spread education into the countryside. However, beneath the Marxist rhetoric lay the old imperial structures, whereby the military clique concentrated power in its own hands through a highly centralized decision-making process. While former aristocrats criticized the Derg from the right, other opponents of the monarchy – particularly trade unionists and students – condemned military rule from the left and called for the institution of a democratic people's government. The result was a hard-hitting campaign against government opponents from 1977 to 1978 that left tens of thousands of Ethiopians imprisoned, exiled, or dead. The primary targets of the regime's so-called Red Terror were members of the Marxist Ethiopian People's Revolutionary Party, which claimed that the military regime had hijacked the revolution.

Determined to maintain its longstanding relationship with Ethiopia and to undermine Soviet-backed Somalia, the Ford administration, under the influence of Secretary of State Henry Kissinger, supported the military regime that toppled Selassie in 1974 – despite its socialist rhetoric and flagrant human rights abuses. From 1974 to 1977, U.S. military aid to Ethiopia actually increased; through loans, grants, and sales, Washington provided the new regime with weapons, tanks, and fighter aircraft worth $180 million. Nonetheless, the Derg considered American assistance to be insecure, especially after Jimmy Carter's election to the presidency in November 1976. Concerned by Carter's vow to link foreign assistance to human rights practices, the Derg began to look elsewhere for military aid. In December, it signed a secret weapons agreement with the Soviet Union. It thus was Ethiopia, rather than the Soviet Union, that initiated the shift in allegiances.

In February 1977, shortly after Mengistu's ascent to power, the newly inaugurated Carter administration announced that it would reduce military aid to Ethiopia as a result of its gross human rights abuses. In April, a month after Soviet weapons began to arrive, Ethiopia announced the closure of the Kagnew communications station and four other American facilities, as well as the expulsion of 300 American personnel, including all military advisors. The Kagnew shutdown was purely symbolic, as the United States had already made plans to abandon it. By 1977, the facility had been rendered obsolete by satellite technology and new American naval facilities on the Indian Ocean island of Diego Garcia. Nonetheless, the Carter administration responded to the snub by canceling all remaining arms shipments and a military sales credit program worth $100 million. By the end of the year, Washington had announced that it would sell arms to Ethiopia's regional rivals, Somalia and Sudan.

Somalia and the Soviet Union

Somalia, like Ethiopia, was a tinderbox of tensions that exploded during the Cold War. An awkward union of British and Italian colonies that had been joined at independence in 1960, Somalia was also prized for its strategic location. With the Gulf of Aden to the north and the Indian Ocean to the east, Somalia controlled access to the Red Sea and Middle Eastern oil. Although most of the country's inhabitants were ethnic Somalis who shared a language, culture, and religion, they were sharply divided by clan rivalry. Ethnic minorities, such as the Somali Bantu, whose ancestors had been brought to Somalia as slaves, were harshly discriminated against. Moreover, as a result of colonial boundary treaties in which Somalis had no part, millions of ethnic Somalis lived beyond Somalia's borders – in Ethiopia, Kenya, and Djibouti. The campaign to unite all ethnic Somalis in one country would lead to regular border disputes as well as devastating regional wars.

Fearing Somali designs on friendly governments in Ethiopia and Kenya, Western governments responded reluctantly to Somali appeals for military aid. In early 1961, the Kennedy administration turned down a request for $9 million to upgrade the 2,000-man Somali army. In November 1963, the United States, Italy, and West Germany offered a paltry $10 million to bolster Somalia's internal security capacity but refused to assist in the development of its offensive forces. Moreover, the offer stood only if Somalia agreed not to seek aid elsewhere – an attempt by Western powers to thwart Soviet influence in the Horn. Somalia then turned to the Soviet Union, which countered with a $32 million package – later increased to $55 million – to train and equip a Somali army of 10,000 men. When Somalia accepted the Soviet bid, the Western monopoly on arms sales in the Horn was broken.

Somalia, like Ethiopia, was beset by internal problems during the Cold War. Its brief experience with civilian rule ended badly. Its early postindependence governments were marked by corruption, clan rivalry, and disputes over the country's expansionist goals. Somalia's second president, Abdirashid Ali Shermarke, was assassinated in October 1969. Less than a week later, Major General Mohamed Siad Barre, commander in chief of the Somali army, seized power in a military coup. In 1970, following the expulsion of a number of American diplomats, military attachés, and the Peace Corps, the United States terminated all economic aid. The Soviet Union, in contrast, intensified its military and economic assistance programs and augmented the number of Soviet advisors to nearly 1,000. By the end of the year, Siad Barre had announced that Somalia would follow the tenets of scientific socialism.

During the first few years of his rule, Siad Barre implemented a major public works program and Somalia made real strides in mass literacy, primary education, public health, and economic development, particularly in the rural areas. However, he also suspended the constitution, banned political parties, and assassinated rivals. Three clans dominated his government, which was rife with clan patronage. In 1974–75, a drought swept through Somalia, threatening a famine on the scale of Ethiopia's 1972–73 disaster. However, Siad Barre, unlike Haile Selassie, welcomed foreign assistance and avoided a catastrophe of the same magnitude. The Soviet Union was Somalia's most generous provider, supplying food, medicine, medical staff, and development aid, as well as airplanes, trucks, and personnel to transport 90,000 famine victims to safety.

The Soviet Union was also Somalia's main source of military assistance, including highly sophisticated weapons, tanks, fighter planes, and bombers. Between 1971 and 1974, the value of Soviet military aid increased tenfold and the number of Soviet military advisors reached 1,400. In July 1974, Somalia and the Soviet Union signed a friendship and cooperation treaty, the first between Moscow and a sub-Saharan African state. Over the following three years, Moscow supplied Mogadishu with weapons and military equipment valued at some $300 million. By 1976, Somalia boasted a 22,000-man army and was the fourth most heavily armed nation in sub-Saharan Africa, surpassed only by Nigeria, Zaire, and Ethiopia. While Cuban technicians trained Somali troops in the use of Soviet armaments, the Soviet Union and East Germany helped bolster Somalia's National Security Service, which was notorious for arresting and torturing opponents of the Siad Barre regime. Moscow also developed the port of Berbera into a sophisticated naval and air base with long-range communications capabilities and gained access to port and air facilities in Mogadishu. The facilities on the Gulf of Aden (Berbera) and Indian Ocean (Mogadishu) provided the Soviet Union with an important counterweight to American power in the region.

Even as it strengthened its relationship with Somalia, Moscow worried about the growing influence of conservative Arab regimes, particularly Saudi Arabia and Kuwait. In February 1974, Somalia had joined the Arab League, sponsored by Saudi Arabia, which was intent on diminishing Soviet influence in the Middle East. In April 1977, Saudi Arabia began to make good on its promise of $350 million for the purchase of military supplies – in exchange for Somalia's agreement to sever its military ties to the Soviet Union. By that time, the Kremlin was convinced that the Derg had stronger Marxist credentials than its Somali counterpart, and it had began to supply Ethiopia as well as its Somali rival. After Somalia attempted to advance territorial claims by invading the Ogaden region of Ethiopia in July 1977, the Soviet Union threw its full support to Ethiopia.

The Somali-Ethiopian War, 1977–78

By 1978, Somalia and Ethiopia had effectively switched sides in the Cold War. It was the Somali-Ethiopian War of 1977–78 that solidified the new alliances. During the late-nineteenth-century Scramble for Africa, the historical Somali homeland had been divided among Britain, Italy, France, and Ethiopia. Establishing its own Somali colony on the Gulf of Aden, Britain had administered the Somali-inhabited Northern Frontier District as part of British East Africa (later, Kenya) and ceded the Somali-inhabited Ogaden and Haud regions to Ethiopia. Italy carved out a Somali colony along the Indian Ocean coast, while French Somaliland was established at the mouth of the Red Sea. Following the expulsion of Italy from Ethiopia during World War II, Britain again administered the Ogaden and Haud regions, which it hoped to unite with British and Italian Somaliland under British governance. American pressure induced Britain to relinquish the territories to Ethiopia after the war, despite strong Somali protests. In 1960, British and Italian Somaliland were joined together as independent Somalia while the other Somali territories remained under foreign control. Somalia's campaign to reunite the Somali people led to numerous border conflicts with pro-Western governments in Ethiopia and Kenya during the 1960s and full-scale wars in 1964 and 1977–78.

Within Africa, Somalia was widely condemned for refusing to respect the territorial integrity of neighboring states. The fact that Somalia was considered the aggressor was closely linked to the heavy influence of imperial Ethiopia in the African decolonization process. In May 1963, thirty-two independent African nations met in Addis Ababa to establish a body to promote African unity and emancipation. The charter of the resultant Organization of African Unity was drafted by a committee under the influence of Ethiopian Emperor Haile Selassie. Deaf to the likes of Kwame Nkrumah and Sékou Touré, who warned of the dangers of balkanization and called for the creation of larger territorial entities, the OAU endorsed the principle of independence within old colonial boundaries, however unjust or wrongheaded they might be. Determined to prevent destructive border wars and ethnically based secessionist movements that would plague the continent with endless conflict – and threaten the power base of established leaders – the OAU determined in 1964 that colonial boundaries must be respected. Haile Selassie, whose Christian, Amhara-dominated regime suppressed numerous ethnic minorities, many of whom were Muslim, and who maintained a tenuous hold on Somali-inhabited territories as well as the former Italian colony of Eritrea, was particularly anxious to write this principle in stone.

Few African states had sympathy for Somalia, whose expansionist aims raised concerns about the sanctity of their own borders. Thus, Somalia was forced to look elsewhere for allies and suppliers. For most of the 1970s, the Soviet Union was its main source of support. However, the quest for a Greater Somalia ultimately destroyed that relationship as well. In 1975, the Somali government established the Western Somali Liberation Front (WSLF) to promote secession in the Ogaden. Although the WSLF was able to recruit a substantial number of fighters from the Ogaden region, Somali army regulars also bolstered their ranks. In the spring of 1977, the Soviet Union, which had grown increasingly sympathetic to the Ethiopian revolution and hoped to promote socialist unity throughout the Horn, urged Somalia to relinquish its claims to Ethiopian territory and joined Cuba in an unsuccessful attempt to broker peace between the two countries. With the Ethiopian regime preoccupied by internal conflicts, domestic protests, and an escalating war in Eritrea, Somalia perceived an opening. In July, the Soviet-built Somali army invaded the Ogaden. The Kremlin was livid.

As far as Moscow was concerned, Ethiopia was the prize. It was far more populous than Somalia and, since the acquisition of Eritrea, more strategically located along the Red Sea oil transit lanes. Moreover, its Marxist revolution seemed to be more promising. In response to Somalia's unilateral action, the Soviet Union immediately transferred 1,200 military advisors from Somalia to Ethiopia. By October, it had halted all weapons and fuel deliveries to Somalia and pledged its full support to Ethiopia. In November, Somalia annulled its friendship treaty with the Soviet Union, expelled all Soviet and Cuban military and technical personnel, prohibited Soviet use of the Berbera and Mogadishu military facilities, and severed diplomatic relations with Cuba. Convinced that the Ethiopian government would collapse without foreign assistance, Cuba agreed to send troops and Moscow launched a massive military supply effort, airlifting $1 billion

PHOTO 6.1. Somali residents of Mogadishu protest Soviet support for Ethiopia in the Somali-Ethiopian War, April 5, 1978 (Keystone-France/Gamma-Keystone via Getty Images).

worth of military supplies and 1,000 Soviet military personnel between September 1977 and March 1978, as well as providing transport for nearly 12,000 Cuban soldiers and 6,000 Cuban advisors and technicians. As the Soviet-backed Ethiopian army countered the Soviet-built Somali army, 400 East German advisors arrived to train Ethiopian intelligence and internal security forces.

Ethiopia won a clear victory in the court of international opinion. OAU members generally viewed Ethiopia as the victim of Somali aggression. The United States, Britain, France, West Germany, and Italy took a similar stance – despite Siad Barre's attempt to play up the notion of a communist threat. Fearing the consequences of an Arab-backed Somali victory, Israel escalated its aid to the Mengistu regime. Although Saudi Arabia and Iran provided Mogadishu with some aid, without massive assistance from the West Somalia could not counter its loss of Soviet support. Ultimately, Mogadishu was unable to sustain its war in the Ogaden, and in March 1978, it agreed to withdraw. The war ended with a resounding victory for the Ethiopian, Soviet, and Cuban forces – only two years after the Soviet-Cuban-MPLA triumph in Angola. The military operation in Ethiopia was

Moscow's most significant engagement outside Eastern Europe since the Korean War.

Ethiopia and the Soviet Union

Ironically, Moscow's initial response to the Ethiopian revolution had been somewhat hesitant. The Kremlin had been concerned about the Derg's continued links to the West, particularly its reliance on the United States for military aid. The regime's growing relationship with China and some of the perceived Maoist influences in Ethiopia's brand of socialism had also irked the Kremlin. Most importantly, Moscow had not wanted to jeopardize its relationship with Somalia by aiding the new socialist government in Addis Ababa. By mid-1976, however, the Soviet Union was unhappy with the progress of Somalia's socialist program, the prominent role of Islam in Somali society, Mogadishu's close relations with conservative Arab regimes, its failure to develop a true vanguard party, and the nature of its economic policies. The belief that Ethiopia, rather than Somalia, was the true representative of Marxism-Leninism in the Horn had gained strong support in the Kremlin. In the best of all possible worlds, the Soviet Union would find a way to support Ethiopia without abandoning Somalia. The ideal solution would be a Marxist-Leninist confederation in the Horn that would unite Somalia, Ethiopia, Djibouti, and the People's Democratic Republic of Yemen (South Yemen).

The election of Jimmy Carter to the American presidency in November 1976, and Washington's growing disenchantment with the Mengistu regime, provided the Soviet Union an opening. A secret Ethiopian-Soviet arms deal was signed in December 1976. In March 1977, Soviet weapons, tanks, and MiG fighter planes began to arrive, followed by some 200 Cuban technicians who would train the Ethiopian military to use them. During the intra-Derg struggles of February 1977, Moscow supported the Mengistu faction, and during the Red Terror campaign of 1977–78, the Kremlin applauded Mengistu's eradication of "counterrevolutionary" elements. When Somali actions forced the Soviet Union to pick sides, it chose Ethiopia. By 1979, Ethiopia was firmly in the Soviet camp – and the beneficiary of the largest Soviet foreign assistance program since Moscow's massive transfer of aid, technology, and know-how to China in the 1950s. More than 7,000 technicians and other personnel arrived

from Cuba, the Soviet Union, and Eastern Bloc countries to help
Ethiopia build a revolutionary socialist society. However, Mengistu's
campaign of terror had decimated the ranks of the educated elite and
killed or forced into exile most civilian Marxists. Although few of these
had direct connections to the Soviet Union – many had studied in the
United States, Western Europe, China, or Yugoslavia – Moscow was
convinced that a successful revolution required a civilian base and
that the Ethiopian regime was destroying it. The Kremlin criticized
Mengistu's wanton killing of rivals and urged him, unsuccessfully, to
reconcile with those who remained.

Despite Soviet concerns, military assistance to Ethiopia continued.
After the Ogaden victory, Ethiopia harnessed Soviet aid in a futile
attempt to crush the growing Eritrean liberation movement and the
Tigrayan and Oromo insurgencies. By 1984, Moscow had provided
Addis Ababa with more than $4 billion in military assistance, as well
as some 2,600 Soviet and Eastern Bloc military advisors who trained
and commanded the Ethiopian troops. The international spotlight
again turned on Ethiopia in 1984–85, when another famine, caused by
drought, poorly executed land reform, retaliation against Mengistu's
opponents, and war, took hundreds of thousands of lives. For the
Soviet Union, the turning point came in March 1985, when Mikhail
Gorbachev rose to power as the Soviet Communist Party leader. From
mid-1987, the Soviet Union was preoccupied with its losing battle
and imminent withdrawal from Afghanistan and its internal economic
and political crisis. Moreover, the Kremlin was disillusioned with the
nonsocialist attitudes and practices of its Third World allies and no
longer felt compelled to fund them. As a result, Mengistu's regime,
whose human rights abuses particularly disgusted the Soviet leader,
suffered massive funding cuts. When internal forces brought about
Mengistu's overthrow in May 1991, the United States and Canada,
not the rapidly disintegrating Soviet Union, facilitated the Ethiopian
leader's exile in Zimbabwe.

Somalia and the United States

When Moscow refused to support Somalia's attack on Ethiopia in
1977, Somalia turned to the United States. The newly installed Carter
administration was deeply divided over the crisis in the Horn. National
Security Advisor Zbigniew Brzezinski viewed the Ogaden conflict

primarily in Cold War terms. He was concerned about increased Soviet involvement in Ethiopia, with its close proximity to the Suez Canal and oil-rich Saudi Arabia and the Persian Gulf. He worried that American inaction, following what he considered to be a Soviet-Cuban victory in Angola, would make the United States appear weak to its allies. Given these considerations, Brzezinski favored a strong show of support for Somalia and actions that would render the costs of war untenable for the Soviet Union. Secretary of State Cyrus Vance, in contrast, maintained that the Ogaden conflict was fundamentally local in character. He argued that the United States should not assist Somalia, which was undeniably the aggressor nation. Support for a country whose actions had clearly violated the OAU Charter would jeopardize America's standing with other African countries. Vance's position, supported by the Defense Department and the Joint Chiefs of Staff, ultimately carried the day, and the United States withdrew an earlier offer of defensive weapons.

Following Somalia's departure from the Ogaden in 1978, the Carter administration reevaluated its hands-off policy. The overthrow of the pro-Western Shah of Iran in January 1979, the taking of American hostages in November, followed by the Soviet invasion of Afghanistan in December, propelled the Carter administration into action. It increased aid to the Siad Barre regime and encouraged pro-Western Muslim countries and China to do likewise. Seeking replacements for lost facilities in Ethiopia, Washington obtained rights to naval, port, and air facilities in Berbera and Mogadishu that had been recently vacated by the Soviet Union. In return, the United States provided Somalia with $500 million worth of military and economic assistance between 1981 and 1986, making Mogadishu one of the largest recipients of U.S. military aid in sub-Saharan Africa. Despite its human rights pronouncements, the Carter administration ultimately allowed Cold War concerns to govern its policy in Somalia. The Reagan administration followed suit, although moderates prevailed over those who advocated increasing Somali military aid to match Soviet assistance to Ethiopia.

U.S. aid notwithstanding, the Siad Barre regime was in crisis by the time the George H. W. Bush administration took office. Somalia's external isolation was compounded by internal troubles. The Ogaden war had run the economy into the ground, dissipating the development achievements of 1969–75. Siad Barre's practice of political oppression also came back to haunt him. The Somali president had squelched all political opposition – imprisoning or killing government critics or drafting them into the Somali army to fight insurgencies that were threatening his regime. Central to his divide-and-rule strategy was the encouragement of clan rivalry, which he hoped would disrupt his opponents and allow him to retain his hold on power. His plan back-fired. The repression of dissent and attempts to raise funds through intensified taxation served to mobilize the clans and stimulate rural unrest. By the late 1980s, clan-based militias and Islamic militants who had been repressed by the Siad Barre dictatorship were united in their hatred of his regime. Because American support had been key to Siad Barre's survival, his opponents were generally hostile to the United States and distrustful of its motives.

As the Soviet Union collapsed and the Cold War drew to a close, the American alliance with Somalia diminished in importance, and American policy was revised. In 1989, the Bush administration expressed newfound concern for Siad Barre's human rights abuses, and Congress suspended military and economic aid. With weakening American support, the Siad Barre regime was an easy target. In January 1991, the clan-based militia of General Mohamed Farah Aideed, one of Somalia's most powerful warlords, overthrew the Siad Barre regime. With the central government gone, rivalries promoted by Siad Barre surfaced with a vengeance. As Somalia descended into clan-based warfare, the economy collapsed and Mogadishu and the rest of southern Somalia disintegrated into fiefdoms ruled by warlords and their militias. By 1993, tens of thousands of civilians had been killed and hundreds of thousands had starved to death as warlords diverted food supplies to buy weapons and to increase their power. Somalia had been transformed from a Cold War battleground into free-for-all among local warlords.

The Eritrean Independence War, 1961–93

While Ethiopia and Somalia competed for regional dominance, Eritrea waged a war for independence. During the Cold War, both the United States and the Soviet Union made choices that favored Ethiopia. Only after the Cold War ended was Eritrea able to exercise its right to self-determination.

Although Ethiopia had taken advantage of the turbulence in the late nineteenth century to expand its empire in the interior, Italy had acquired the prized coastal areas along the Red Sea and Indian Ocean, leaving the Ethiopian empire landlocked. Thus began Eritrea's most recent history of foreign domination. Between 1890 and 1941, Eritrea was an Italian colony. Following Italy's defeat by Britain and its allies in the 1940–41 East Africa Campaign, Eritrea became a British protectorate. When World War II ended, the UN was charged with disposing of Italy's African colonies. It determined that Libya and Somaliland would be granted independence, while Eritrea would be joined in a federation with Ethiopia, despite significant popular sentiment in Eritrea for independence. Although the Soviet Union, a number of Arab states, and other UN members also favored Eritrean independence, U.S. Secretary of State John Foster Dulles argued that American strategic interests took precedence over Eritrean popular opinion. In consequence, no referendum was held. Instead, as the dominant power in the UN, the United States was able to impose its desires. In 1952, the UN General Assembly federated Eritrea with Ethiopia, America's regional ally. Ethiopia, meanwhile, was determined to absorb Eritrea outright, claiming that the territory was part of its historical empire.

Just as nationalist movements emerged to oppose colonial rule in other parts of Africa, they also appeared in Eritrea. In 1958, the Eritrean Liberation Movement was established by Eritrean students, workers, and intellectuals to mobilize strikes, demonstrations, and other mass actions inside Eritrea. The ranks of the movement were soon decimated by government repression. In 1961, the newly formed Eritrean Liberation Front (ELF) opted for armed struggle. Rather than consider independence, Ethiopia dug in deeper. Having systematically eroded Eritrean autonomy over the previous decade, Haile Selassie, assured of American military backing, dissolved the federation and in November 1962 annexed Eritrea as an Ethiopian province. The acquisition of Eritrea was the culmination of a decades-long effort spearheaded by Selassie's American international affairs advisor, John H. Spencer. The United States and other Western powers turned a blind eye, and the UN ignored Ethiopia's illegal action.

During the 1960s, the largely Muslim ELF was the beneficiary of funding, training, and arms from radical Arab League states, particularly Syria and South Yemen, which supplied the movement with Soviet weapons. After a 1969 military coup brought Colonel Jaafar Nimeiri to power in Sudan, that country served as a major conduit of Soviet weaponry, countering Ethiopian support for southern Sudanese secessionists, who were primarily Christian and animist. When a 1971 agreement between Sudan and Ethiopia temporarily blocked that source, Iraq and Syria took up the slack. China assisted the ELF with weapons and military training until 1972, when Ethiopian recognition of Beijing as the legitimate Chinese government led to China's abandonment of the Eritrean struggle. On the Ethiopian side, Israel and Ethiopia, united by their mutual distrust of their Arab neighbors, made common cause. By the mid-1960s, Israel was training thousands of Ethiopian soldiers in counterinsurgency techniques. In the 1970s, Israeli-trained Ethiopian forces cracked down on Eritrean guerrillas and civilians – operating first on behalf of Haile Selassie and then the Derg.

Concerned by the growing influence of Arab and other pan-Islamic states in the Eritrean nationalist struggle, the secular Eritrean People's Liberation Front (EPLF) emerged from ELF splinter groups in the early 1970s. The new organization focused its efforts on Tigrinya-speaking Christians in Eritrea's southern highlands, although it had both Muslim and Christian members. Avowedly Marxist, the EPLF advocated social transformation as well as political independence. Like the PAIGC in Portuguese Guinea and FRELIMO in Mozambique, the EPLF established schools, cooperatives, hospitals, and women's and youth organizations in the liberated areas. Until 1975, the EPLF received material support from the Soviet Union, East Germany, and South Yemen, as well as military training from Cuba. The Eritrean diaspora also provided significant resources.

After the establishment of a Marxist government in Ethiopia, the Soviet Union promoted the notion of Eritrean autonomy within a socialist Ethiopia and ended its support for the EPLF. Although the Marxist theory and practice of the Eritrean movement was better developed than that of the Ethiopian Derg, a unified Ethiopia with the Red Sea coastline intact was better suited to Soviet interests. However, when Moscow threw its support to Ethiopia and its war against Eritrea, Cuba balked. Sensitive to the views of African and Arab states and the Non-Aligned Movement in general, Cuba refused to support Ethiopia's war effort.

Even after the cessation of Soviet aid, the ELF and EPLF met with success. With Ethiopia distracted by the Ogaden war, the Eritrean liberation movements had gained control of nearly all of the rural areas and most of the towns by mid-1978. Ethiopian forces retained only the capital, Asmara, the port cities of Massawa and Assab, and a few other urban centers. However, the rebels' fortunes were reversed after the resolution of the Ogaden war. Strengthened by a large infusion of Soviet military aid during the Somali-Ethiopian War, Ethiopia again turned its attention to Eritrea. Addis Ababa's offensives, backed by the Soviet Union, East Germany, and South Yemen, began in May 1978, causing a military stalemate that lasted until 1984. Meanwhile, internecine fighting between the ELF and the EPLF also took an enormous toll. By 1981, the fragmented ELF had collapsed, and the EPLF carried on the struggle alone. Although the EPLF officially abandoned Marxism for democratic pluralism in 1987, it received little material support from the West. Soviet weapons, tanks, and trucks, discarded by defeated Ethiopia forces, served as its main source of military hardware.

By 1989, Ethiopia was again desperate for military assistance. Apart from the Eritrean independence war, Ethiopia was beset by a number of internal insurgencies. In the south, the Oromo Liberation Front fought for the right to self-determination, with some factions favoring political representation in a reformed Ethiopia and others advocating secession. In the northern highlands adjacent to Eritrea, Tigrinya-speakers established the Marxist Tigray People's Liberation Front (TPLF), which agitated for political change within Ethiopia. The Soviet Union's political and economic decline and the rise of the East German prodemocracy movement had resulted in major cuts in military aid. When Ethiopia appealed for further assistance, Israel stepped into the gap. Concerned about Arab support for the EPLF and the TPLF, Tel Aviv provided the Mengistu regime with arms, equipment, and advisors. However, Israeli intervention could not compensate for the loss of Soviet and East German support. As the decade closed, the situation on the ground had shifted to the rebels' advantage. In a joint operation conducted in February and March 1989, the EPLF and the TPLF defeated Ethiopian forces in western Tigray, resulting in the Derg's withdrawal from most of the province. Ethiopia's land bridge to Eritrea was severed. In February 1990, the EPLF captured the port of Massawa, thereby cutting the sea link that had supplied Ethiopian troops in Asmara and central Eritrea. In late January 1991, the Ethiopian Popular Revolutionary Democratic Front (EPRDF), a TPLF-dominated umbrella organization composed of multiple guerrilla armies, began to move toward Addis Ababa, mobilizing Amhara and Oromo peasants along the way.

Chastened by recent events in Somalia and concerned that a collapse of the Ethiopian government would be devastating for regional stability, the Bush administration brokered talks between the Mengistu regime and the EPLF in October 1990 and February 1991. Another round of talks was scheduled for May 27. By that time, the Ethiopian government was in the final stages of disintegration. On May 21, as the EPRDF advanced toward the capital, President Mengistu fled into exile. He found refuge in Zimbabwe, where, with the help of the U.S. government, his asylum had been prearranged. Without its leader, the Ethiopian army collapsed. The EPLF occupied Eritrea's capital on May 24, while the EPRDF took Addis Ababa on May 28. At the May 27 talks, Ethiopia and Eritrea agreed to a ceasefire, and the EPLF agreed to delay an independence referendum for two more years. Thus, it was in April 1993 that the UN, which had imposed federation on Eritrea in 1952 and condoned annexation a decade later, sponsored the long-postponed referendum. The vote in favor of independence was overwhelming, and in May 1993, Eritrea became an independent nation.

Regime change in Somalia and Ethiopia and independence in Eritrea did not bring peace to the troubled Horn. The stresses and divisions wrought by colonialism, Cold War, and regional rivalries continued into the twenty-first century. Somalia, which had descended into anarchy following the collapse of the Siad Barre regime, witnessed the rise of warlord militias and Islamic insurgencies that precluded the establishment of a central government. The governments of Ethiopia and Eritrea, led respectively by former TPLF leader Meles Zenawi and former EPLF leader Isaias Afewerki, discarded their democratic constitutions and continued the repressive practices of their predecessors. Their quests for personal and regional power culminated in a bloody fratricidal war from 1998 to 2000 that took the lives of some 70,000 people and devastated their countries' fragile economies. Current conflicts in the Horn are part of a process that began more than a century ago. Although local actors took the lead in destabilizing the region, their work was accomplished only with outside assistance.

Suggested Reading

For Ethiopia, two historical surveys are especially recommended. An exceptionally good overview is Bahru Zewde's *A History of Modern Ethiopia, 1855–1991*, 2nd ed. (Athens: Ohio University Press, 2001), which incorporates primary research, secondary literature, and firsthand experience by an Ethiopian scholar. Also recommended is Paul B. Henze's *Layers of Time: A History of Ethiopia* (New York: Palgrave, 2000), which covers ancient times to the 1990s and is informed both by extensive scholarship and personal experience.

Other recommended books focus on specific historical periods. Christopher S. Clapham's *Haile-Selassie's Government* (New York: Praeger, 1969) is among the very best books on the subject. His *Transformation and Continuity in Revolutionary Ethiopia* (New York: Cambridge University Press, 1988) provides an insightful analysis of the revolutionary state and its program and is considered a seminal work. Other solid introductions to revolutionary Ethiopia include John W. Harbeson's *The Ethiopian Transformation: The Quest for the Post-Imperial State* (Boulder, CO: Westview, 1988), which examines the imperial regime and those who opposed it, the revolutionary process, and the postimperial state; and Edmond J. Keller's *Revolutionary Ethiopia: From Empire to People's Republic* (Bloomington: Indiana University Press, 1988), which provides a comprehensive analysis of the Selassie regime, the causes of the revolution, and its aftermath. Finally, Dawit Wolde Giorgis's *Red Tears: War, Famine and Revolution in Ethiopia* (Trenton, NJ: Red Sea Press, 1989) covers the end of imperial rule, the revolution and postimperial state, ethnic conflict and secessionist movements, and famine. Written by a military officer in Selassie's government who continued to serve as a high official in the revolutionary government, *Red Tears* provides a unique view from an insider who became a critic of the government.

For Somalia, two historical surveys are especially recommended. I. M. Lewis's *A Modern History of the Somali: Nation and State in the Horn of Africa*, 4th ed. (Athens: Ohio University Press, 2002) is considered by many to be the seminal study of Somali politics and society from ancient times through the early 1990s. David D. Laitin and Said S. Samatar's *Somalia: Nation in Search of a State* (Boulder, CO: Westview Press, 1987), a state-centered study, surveys the precolonial and colonial periods but focuses especially on events after independence. For a concise, readable analysis of Somalia under Siad Barre, see Ahmed I. Samatar's *Socialist Somalia: Rhetoric and Reality* (Atlantic Highlands, NJ: Zed Press, 1988).

For Eritrea, several important books focus on the independence struggle. Ruth Iyob's *The Eritrean Struggle for Independence: Domination, Resistance, Nationalism, 1941–1993* (New York: Cambridge University Press, 1993) traces the evolution of Eritrean nationalism over a half century, situating it within the regional and international political context. Written by a political scientist whose family was involved in the political and armed struggles, the book includes both insider and scholarly perspectives. Bereket Habte Selassie's *Conflict and Intervention in the Horn of Africa* (New York: Monthly Review Press, 1980), another insider and scholarly account, focuses on regional conflict, foreign intervention, and the Eritrean independence struggle. An attorney general of Ethiopia under Haile Selassie, the author participated in the underground opposition to the regime; the Derg's Commission of Enquiry into the wrongdoings of the Selassie government; and, finally, the Eritrean independence struggle as a member of the EPLF. Selassie's two-volume critical memoir is also highly recommended: Bereket Habte Selassie, *The Crown and the Pen: The Memoirs of a Lawyer Turned Rebel* (Trenton, NJ: Red Sea Press, 2007) and Bereket Habte Selassie, *Wounded Nation: How a Once Promising Eritrea Was Betrayed and Its Future Compromised* (Trenton, NJ: Red Sea Press, 2010). Hagai Erlikh's *The Struggle over Eritrea, 1962–1978: War and Revolution in the Horn of Africa* (Stanford, CA: Hoover Institution Press, 1983), based on interviews and journalistic accounts in several languages, focuses on the development of Eritrean nationalism and conflicts within the nationalist movement. Finally, Dan Connell's *Against All Odds: A Chronicle of the Eritrean Revolution*, 2nd ed. (Trenton, NJ: Red Sea Press, 1997) provides the unique perspective of an American journalist who traveled with Eritrean guerrilla armies in the 1970s and made many subsequent trips to the country.

A number of books provide insight into American involvement in the Horn during the Cold War. Jeffrey A. Lefebvre's *Arms for the Horn: U.S. Security Policy in Ethiopia and Somalia, 1953–1991* (Pittsburgh, PA: University of Pittsburgh Press, 1991) uses declassified government documents and interviews to examine U.S. relations with Ethiopia and Somalia, focusing especially on the massive influx of weaponry and its societal impact. David A. Korn's *Ethiopia, the United States and the Soviet Union* (Carbondale: Southern Illinois University Press, 1986) examines the relations of revolutionary Ethiopia with the superpowers from 1974 to 1985. The American chargé d'affaires in Ethiopia from 1982 to 1985, Korn provides a detailed account of U.S.-Ethiopian diplomacy from the perspective of a high-level American government official. Marina Ottaway's *Soviet and American Influence in the Horn of Africa* (New York: Praeger, 1982), an authoritative account based on firsthand observations and scholarly analysis, focuses on superpower influence in Somalia and Ethiopia. From a vantage point on the ground, Ottaway argues that local people and governments were not simply manipulated by outsiders but had a great deal of influence over the course of events. For debate within the Carter administration concerning the proper response to Somali aggression against Ethiopia, see the memoirs of National Security Advisor Zbigniew Brzezinski and of Secretary of State Cyrus Vance: Zbigniew Brzezinski, *Power and Principle: Memoirs of the National Security Advisor, 1977–1981* (New York: Farrar, Straus & Giroux, 1983), and Cyrus R. Vance, *Hard Choices: Critical Years in America's Foreign Policy* (New York: Simon and Schuster, 1983).

Besides Korn and Ottaway (mentioned above), an important work on Soviet involvement in the Horn is Robert G. Patman's *The Soviet Union in the Horn of Africa: The Diplomacy of Intervention and Disengagement* (New York: Cambridge University Press, 1990), which provides unique insight into Soviet policy, including conflict within the state bureaucracy over Soviet prospects in the Horn.

Cuba's involvement in Ethiopia is explored in Piero Gleijeses's "Moscow's Proxy? Cuba and Africa, 1975–1988," *Journal of Cold War Studies* 8, no. 4 (Fall 2006): 98–146, which challenges the widely held view that Cuba's policy toward Ethiopia and Eritrea was subservient to that of the Soviet Union.

For a new assessment of Israel's relationship with Ethiopia, see Zach Levey, *Israel in Africa, 1956–1976* (Dordrecht, the Netherlands: Republic of Letters, 2012).

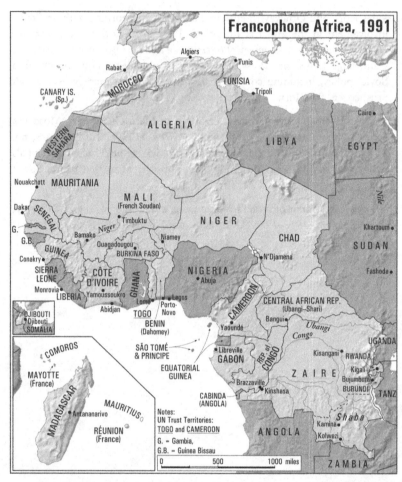

MAP 7.1. Francophone Africa, 1991. (Map by Philip Schwartzberg, Meridian Mapping, Minneapolis.)

CHAPTER 7

France's Private African Domain, 1947–1991

This chapter, unlike Chapters 2–6, does not focus on a regional case study. Rather, it examines Francophone sub-Saharan Africa during the period 1947–91, exploring the dynamics of a decolonization process that was intended to bind African territories to France politically and economically. Although Cold War concerns influenced this process, the greatest perceived threat was not the Soviet Union but French communists and their allies, along with the United States, which embodied a perceived Anglophone menace to French interests. From 1944 to 1958, France implemented a series of colonial reforms that were intended to thwart the growth of radical nationalism and to forestall any movement toward independence. While the majority parties in most territories ultimately embraced the French reform programs, those in Madagascar, Cameroon, and Guinea resisted French prescriptions and suffered strong reprisals as a result. Their experiences are described here. Although France was eventually forced to concede independence to the majority of its territories, most of them established neocolonial states in which French interests continued to dominate politically, economically, and even militarily.

During the periods of decolonization and the Cold War, France, like the superpowers, intervened in African countries to protect its interests, shoring up allies and subverting enemies. During the period 1960–91, France was second only to Cuba in the number of troops deployed on African soil, and Paris conducted more than three dozen military interventions in sixteen African countries. The cases of Cameroon, Niger, Gabon, the Central African Republic, Chad, and

Zaire are considered in this chapter. Even after African nations gained their independence, Paris assumed that interference in the affairs of its former territories was its natural right. Its Western allies generally concurred, considering only Eastern Bloc and Cuban involvement to be "foreign aggression" and preferring French to Soviet influence. Despite their commonality of interests, France and its Anglophone allies experienced considerable tension as they jockeyed for position in postcolonial Africa. As a result, they sometimes supported opposing factions in African power struggles.

The waning years of the Cold War coincided with an economic crisis in Africa and the continent's declining economic importance to France. As unrest brewed and indigenous prodemocracy movements threatened French allies in the early 1990s, Paris distanced itself from dictators it had long sustained. However, the collapse of authoritarian regimes rarely led to democratic governance, despite popular demands. Instead, rival factions, rebel organizations, and warlords fought over the spoils, leading to new crises in postcolonial Africa.

Radical Nationalism, Decolonization, and the Cold War

Although French involvement in African affairs was linked, first and foremost, to its imperial enterprise, Cold War concerns profoundly altered the playing field. The PCF was France's largest political party after World War II, its popularity heightened by its leadership in the anti-Nazi resistance. As such, it was a powerful member of the post-liberation coalition government that took office in 1944. French communists were closely identified with emerging protest movements in subordinate territories, where they helped to develop the organizing capabilities and leadership skills of trade unions and political organizations. In the French parliament, the PCF consistently supported African demands for rights and treatment equal to those of other French citizens – and it was the only metropolitan party to do so.[1] Anticommunist forces in France found an ally in the United States. As the major benefactor in France's postwar reconstruction, Washington

---

[1] The PCF believed that African emancipation would occur when the communist party came to power in France and overhauled the economy and the state to benefit the French working class and all colonized peoples. As a result, the PCF supported movements for colonial reform but not those agitating for national independence.

made it clear that in return for critical economic aid, communists must be eliminated from French political, economic, and military spheres. In May 1947, after PCF parliamentarians protested French repression in Indochina and Madagascar and criticized domestic economic policies, the socialist prime minister ousted all communist ministers from the government. The coalition government disintegrated, and the crackdown on communists and their allies began.

Reform and Resistance

Until its defeat by Germany in 1940, France was one of the world's great powers, its empire surpassed only by that of Britain. Because the people and resources of the empire had helped France to survive the war, Paris was convinced that maintenance of the empire would permit France to reassume its position as a great power in the postwar era. However, French plans for renewed greatness were threatened on several fronts. The republic's economy was in shambles and its political system broken. France's hold on its empire was endangered both by indigenous nationalist movements, which gained strength in the war's aftermath, and by the emergence of the United States and the Soviet Union as the new world powers.

American pressure on European imperial powers began during World War II. In exchange for wartime assistance, the United States sought access to European colonies in Africa and Asia for the purchase of raw materials, the exploitation of markets, and the establishment of military bases. To guarantee permanent access, the United States demanded a full-scale transformation of the old imperial order. The resulting Atlantic Charter, signed by the United States and Britain in August 1941, underscored the right of all nations to free trade and to "access, on equal terms, . . . to the raw materials of the world which are needed for their economic prosperity." Following a critique of the actions of the Axis powers, the charter further declared "the right of all peoples to choose the form of government under which they will live" and the "wish to see sovereign rights and self-government restored to those who have been forcibly deprived of them."[2] These principles

---

[2] "The Atlantic Charter," August 14, 1941, http://www.nato.int/cps/en/natolive/official_texts_16912.htm?selectedLocale=en.

were subsequently endorsed by the Soviet Union, China, and dozens of other allied nations, including France after its liberation in 1944.

Because France considered its empire to be an integral part of its sovereign domain, it saw no contradiction in calling for the restoration of "sovereign rights and self-government" and its status as an imperial power. After the war, France sought the return of Indochina, which had been liberated from Japanese occupation by the indigenous Viet Minh nationalist coalition, which then fought the reimposition of French rule. Similarly, it sought to regain possession of Madagascar, which had been ruled by Vichy collaborators until seized by the British in 1942. To the dismay of many anticolonial liberation movements, the United States conceded the notion of increased self-government within reformed European empires, as long as the reforms included free trade.

France was faced with multiple demands to implement reforms. The United States pressed for changes both to gain economic advantage and to thwart communist influence. Colonized peoples, who had sustained the war effort at great human and material cost, demanded a greater voice in the management of their own affairs. Having long justified empire as part of a great "civilizing mission," France was determined to convince the world of the worthiness of its stewardship. At the Brazzaville Conference in 1944, Free French leader General Charles de Gaulle proposed a program of imperial reform that was to be implemented after the war. In 1946, forced labor was abolished, colonial subjects became citizens of a French Union that embraced both metropolitan France and the old empire, and a new constitution granted overseas citizens token representation in French political bodies and a voice in their own affairs.

According to the terms of the 1946 constitution, the French Union was composed of the "indivisible" French Republic – which included metropolitan France, overseas departments, and overseas territories – as well as associated territories and states. Algeria included four overseas departments, while Guadeloupe, Martinique, French Guiana, and Réunion each constituted a single overseas department. The overseas territories included the former colonies of French West and Equatorial Africa, Madagascar, and French Somaliland. Joining Morocco, Tunisia, and Indochina as associated territories were the portions of the former German colonies of Cameroon and Togo that were administered by France as League of Nations mandates after World War I and UN trust territories after World War II. Because overseas territories were considered an integral part of the French Republic, any agitation for independence was tantamount to secession – and, thus, a treasonous offense. Although associated territories were technically separate from the republic, in practice, they were treated like the overseas territories. Any attempt on their part to assert independence and withdraw from the French Union was deemed an equally serious affront.

The Indian Ocean island of Madagascar was the first African territory to challenge its status under the new constitution. Having been freed from Vichy authority in 1942, Malagasy nationalists demanded independence after the war, rather than reversion to colonial status, and appealed to the United States for assistance. Steeped in the Western tradition of democratic rights and liberties, they based their claims on American President Franklin D. Roosevelt's "Four Freedoms,"[3] the Atlantic Charter, and the UN Charter, which championed the right of all peoples to "equal rights and self-determination."[4] Convinced that nationalist agitation would lead to chaos and an opening to communist penetration, the Truman administration rebuffed nationalist demands and supported the return to France of its liberated colonies in Southeast Asia, North Africa, and the Indian Ocean.[5]

---

[3] In his 1941 State of the Union Address, President Roosevelt described what would become known as the Four Freedoms: "In the future days, which we seek to make secure, we look forward to a world founded upon four essential human freedoms. The first is freedom of speech and expression – everywhere in the world. The second is freedom of every person to worship God in his own way.... The third is freedom from want.... The fourth is freedom from fear.... Freedom means the supremacy of human rights everywhere. Our support goes to those who struggle to gain those rights or keep them." President Franklin D. Roosevelt, "State of the Union Address to Congress," January 6, 1941, http://www.wwnorton.com/college/history/ralph/workbook/ralprs36b.htm.

[4] Chapter 1, Article 1, "Charter of the United Nations," San Francisco, June 26, 1945, http://www.un.org/en/documents/charter/chapter1.shtml.

[5] Nationalists from French Indochina, who also asked for American help in ending French colonial rule, were similarly dismissed. The Vietnamese nationalist, Ho Chi Minh, first petitioned for American assistance at the 1919 Paris Peace Conference, which established the framework for a new world order after World War I. He based his claims on the principles of democracy and self-determination elaborated on in President Woodrow Wilson's "Fourteen Points." At the end of World War II, Ho and his associates in the Viet Minh liberation movement freed Vietnam from a Japanese-imposed ruler and appealed to the United States to support their claims for independence. Instead, President Truman endorsed the return of Vietnam to French rule. The Viet Minh waged an eight-year battle for independence before forcing France to begin its withdrawal in 1954. When the United States assumed the French mantle in 1955, the war was transformed from a decolonization to a Cold War conflict. Vietnamese nationalists fought American military intervention for two more decades.

The Democratic Movement for Malagasy Restoration (MDRM) was established in early 1946 to promote independence through legal means. Decrying French refusal to consider the independence option, MDRM deputies in the 1946 Constituent Assembly refused to vote on the final constitutional draft. Meanwhile, in Madagascar, MDRM youth teamed up with disenchanted rural dwellers angered by the burdens of the war effort and the poverty that followed in its wake. In late March 1947, a revolt broke out in the eastern coastal areas, eventually consuming one-third of the island. The insurgents attacked government buildings, military garrisons, French settlers, and Malagasies whom they deemed collaborators. Claiming that the revolt was part of a communist plot to undermine France, the French government arrested the MDRM deputies, stripped them of their parliamentary immunity, and banned their party.

In Madagascar, French troops, eventually numbering 30,000, waged a brutal counteroffensive. Employing scorched-earth tactics, they bombed villages, burned fields, and killed livestock. Untold numbers of civilians were tortured, mutilated, and slaughtered. By the time the insurrection ended in November 1948, some 90,000 Malagasies – approximately 2 percent of the population – had died as a result of violence, hunger, and disease. Seventy-seven MDRM leaders were put on trial, although few had been involved in the rebellion and many had condemned it. Two MDRM parliamentarians and four other leaders were sentenced to death, although their sentences were later commuted to life in prison. Among the general population, 5,765 Malagasies were convicted of crimes related to the rebellion, and some two dozen were executed. Early in the decolonization period, Madagascar stood out as a stark example. France would not tolerate any challenge to the legitimacy of the French Republic or the French Union. It would brook no claims to independence.

Activists in other territories were also critical of the new constitution – approved in an October 1946 referendum in which few Africans had been allowed to vote. Shortly after the referendum, African delegates from a number of Francophone sub-Saharan African territories met in Bamako, French Soudan, to discuss the inadequacies of the constitution and to establish an organization to address them. The result was the African Democratic Rally (RDA), an interterritorial alliance of political parties that eventually had affiliates in most of the twelve territories of French West and Equatorial Africa, as well as the two UN trusts of Togo and Cameroon. Although its detractors portrayed the RDA as radical, the organization was committed to working within the confines of the French Union. Within that framework, it strove to win greater political autonomy for the overseas territories and UN trusts, as well as equality of political, economic, and social rights for overseas and metropolitan peoples. The RDA advocated increased local autonomy rather than independence. However, it rejected the notion that African territories constituted an integral part of an "indivisible" French Republic or that a French Union that had been imposed on its members could be legitimate.

In the French parliament, RDA deputies established an alliance with the PCF, the only French party that consistently supported its emancipatory program. However, communists were ousted from the French government only months after the RDA's formation, and the RDA found itself aligned with a much-maligned opposition party rather than a member of the ruling coalition. With its parliamentary ties to the PCF and its links to the communist-affiliated General Confederation of Labor (CGT), the RDA rapidly fell victim to mounting anticommunist fervor. Between 1947 and 1951, the official policy toward the RDA in all the African territories was repression. The brutal crackdown began in Côte d'Ivoire, home of the RDA interterritorial president and parliamentary deputy, Félix Houphouët-Boigny. During 1949–50, when the terror reached its peak, more than fifty RDA activists in Côte d'Ivoire were killed, including Senator Biaka Boda. Several hundred more were injured, and thousands were imprisoned.

Because the pretext for government repression was the RDA's communist affiliations, some party leaders argued that the RDA-PCF alliance should be abandoned. In October 1950, RDA parliamentarians, under Houphouët-Boigny's leadership, severed all ties to the PCF and began to forge an alliance with the ruling coalition. The parliamentarians' action sowed serious division within the ranks. In some territorial branches, there were strong feelings of confusion and betrayal. Determined to reassert control over the movement, Houphouët-Boigny convened a congress of the RDA coordinating committee on July 8–12, 1955, during which the committee resolved to exclude from the party all dissident branches still operating with communist sympathies. The Nigerien Democratic Union, Senegalese Democratic Union, and Union of the Peoples of Cameroon (UPC) were expelled for refusing to toe the anticommunist line.

After Madagascar, Cameroon was the second recalcitrant territory to bear the brunt of sustained French repression. The UPC, like a number of RDA branches, had emerged from Marxist study groups, communist-affiliated trade unions, and various political organizations that proliferated in Africa after World War II. However, unlike other RDA branches, the UPC never strove for equal status within the French Union. Instead, it demanded independence for the reunited territories of French and British Cameroon, which had constituted the German colony of Kamerun until the end of World War I, when they were divided into separate League of Nations mandates. The UPC's appeals were largely based on Cameroon's special status as a UN trust territory, a status it had achieved after World War II. The party charged that the absorption of Cameroon into the French Union and its administration like any other colony was a violation of the UN Charter, which stipulated as an objective of the trusteeship system the advancement of entrusted peoples toward "self-government or independence."[6] The UPC's appeals, unlike those of other RDA branches, threatened the sanctity of the French Union. As a radical movement with close ties to the PCF and to British African nationalists, the UPC also played into Paris's dual fears of communist and Anglophone encroachment. Finally, the party brought unwanted attention to French practices in its subject territories. In the UN General Assembly, UPC claims generated widespread support among African, Asian, and Eastern European states, which promoted resolutions criticizing French misrule in Cameroon.

Refusing to acknowledge Cameroon's distinctiveness as a UN trust, France considered UPC agitation for self-government and independence to be subversive. By 1955, UPC members and sympathizers numbered some 100,000 in an electorate of 747,000. The party had structures in most parts of the territory and was represented among all sectors of the population. Although the UPC had more influence and followers than any other party, it had no representatives in Cameroon's local assembly or the French parliament. Repression and fraud had prevented any electoral victories. Tensions escalated during the week of May 22–30, when anticolonial protests and government repression resulted in the deaths of 21 UPC activists and the injury of 114. The violence was followed by the mass arrest of UPC sympathizers, convictions without due process, the torture and killing of prisoners, and a scorched-earth policy in UPC rural strongholds. On July 13,

---

[6] Charter of the United Nations, Chapter 12, Article 76, http://www.un.org/en/documents/charter/chapter12.shtml.

immediately after the RDA excluded the UPC from its ranks, the French government outlawed the party. With no legal means to achieve their goals, hundreds of UPC members fled to British Cameroon and thousands more joined the underground resistance. In December 1956, the UPC began a campaign of sabotage, attacking telephone lines, railways, roads, and bridges, in an attempt to disrupt elections from which the UPC was barred. As sabotage evolved into targeted assassinations, the UPC became the only nationalist movement in Francophone sub-Saharan Africa to adopt tactics of armed struggle. Thousands of UPC supporters went into exile, where they rallied support from Ghana, Guinea, Algeria, the United Arab Republic, and other members of the Afro-Asian Peoples' Solidarity Organization.

Meanwhile, in other Francophone African territories, military veterans, trade unionists, and members of nascent political parties responded to incremental colonial reforms by demanding equal rights for all French citizens. The rights and privileges of citizens in the metropole became their new yardstick, and the persistent agitation of these groups resulted in significant material gains for some. In an effort to demonstrate the success of reformed imperialism – and to justify the continuation of empire – France began to invest heavily in African economic development. By the mid-1950s, these expenditures were taking their toll on the national budget, and some critics argued that the costs of empire far outweighed the benefits. To meet these challenges, Paris was determined to transfer local political control – and responsibility for paying the new expenses – to elected African governments. In 1956, a new legal framework (*loi-cadre*) granted limited self-government to individual overseas territories, which were expected to shoulder a greater share of the burden of economic development – and to bear the brunt of political discontent.

Until the mid-1950s, France considered the maintenance of empire to be critical to its economic well-being and diplomatic status. However, defeat by nationalist forces in Indochina and the commencement of armed struggle in Algeria in 1954, and the escalation of anti-colonial unrest elsewhere, forced France to reconsider its options. In 1958, Prime Minister Charles de Gaulle spearheaded the enactment of yet another constitution to address the crisis. French territories were offered two choices: accept the constitution, which prescribed junior partnership in a French Community, or reject the constitution in favor of immediate independence. In an empire-wide referendum on September 28, 1958, only Guinea chose independence.

In fact, the French prime minister had never meant to pose a real choice. As the treatment of Madagascar and Cameroon had made brutally clear, secession was not an option – whether from the French Union or the French Community. Openly threatening those territories that were considering independence, de Gaulle declared:

> It is well understood, and I understand it, one can desire secession. [Secession] imposes duties. It carries dangers. Independence has its burdens. The referendum will ascertain if the idea of secession carries the day. *But one cannot conceive of an independent territory and a France that continues to aid it. The* [independent] *government will bear the consequences, economic and otherwise, that are entailed in the manifestation of such a will.*[7]

Thus, de Gaulle made it clear that any declaration of independence would be cause for retribution. Denouncing any constitution that failed to guarantee Africans their "legitimate and natural right to independence," Guinean nationalist leader, Sékou Touré, responded, "We prefer poverty in liberty to riches in slavery."[8] On referendum day, 94 percent of Guinean voters cast their ballots for independence.

For Guinea, the consequences of that choice were devastating, as France retaliated politically and economically, and the new country's attempts to establish relations as a coequal partner were rebuffed. Even before the anticipated no vote, French teachers and other civil servants were withdrawn and capital was transferred to other territories. Commercial transactions and credits were suspended, and cargo ships bound for Conakry were rerouted to Dakar or Abidjan. Immediately after the referendum, the French government severed most of its economic ties to Guinea, suspending all bank credits, development assistance, and cooperative endeavors. French technical and administrative personnel were ordered to leave the territory and to take or destroy all materials and archives. Technical services and equipment were sabotaged. Telephone wires were cut. Cranes at the port of Conakry disappeared. Military camps were stripped of their equipment and hospitals of their medicines. Ships filled with food and medicine were diverted from their course. Merchandise was rerouted

---

[7] Quoted in Georges Chaffard, *Les Carnets Secrets de la Décolonisation* (Paris: Calmann-Lévy, 1967), 2:189 (passage translated by Elizabeth Schmidt).

[8] Quoted in Chaffard, *Carnets Secrets de la Décolonisation*, 2:197 (passage translated by Elizabeth Schmidt).

to other destinations. Large sums of money were transferred out of the country. The Bank of France canceled Guinea's old currency, rendering its reserves worthless, while the French intelligence agency – the External Documentation and Counterespionage Service (SDECE) – created panic by peppering the country with counterfeit bills. All of these measures were designed to provoke economic panic, political discontent, and civil unrest.

France also embarked on a campaign to isolate Guinea internationally. When Guinea became independent on October 2, 1958, Paris refused to recognize the new nation and instructed its allies to do likewise. As a result, Britain, West Germany, and the United States delayed recognition and stalled on offers of economic, technical, and military assistance. Ghana and Liberia were the first countries to recognize the sovereign state, followed by the Soviet Union, China, Bulgaria, and Czechoslovakia. Ironically, France's isolation of Guinea pushed it toward the Soviet Union, the Eastern Bloc, and China, with which it concluded agreements for loans, lines of credit, trade, and military cooperation.

Neocolonialism in Francophone Sub-Saharan Africa

In the decade following World War II, three sub-Saharan African territories threatened the French project of maintaining its empire as the reformed French Union or French Community. In targeting Madagascar and Cameroon, Paris strove to preserve the French Union. In making an example of Guinea, which had refused junior partnership in the French Community, Paris hoped to demonstrate that nation's inability to assume the responsibilities of independence and to dissuade other territories from following its path. French victories were short lived. By the end of 1960, virtually all French sub-Saharan African territories had become sovereign independent nations. The UN trust territories of Cameroon and Togo claimed their independence in January and April 1960, respectively. In June, Senegal, French Soudan, and Madagascar declared independence. They were followed in August by Dahomey, Niger, Upper Volta, Côte d'Ivoire, Chad, Ubangi-Shari, Middle Congo, and Gabon. Finally, in November, Mauritania became a sovereign state. Thus, by the end of 1960, the eight territories of French West Africa, the four of French Equatorial Africa, the two UN trusts, and Madagascar had declared their independence from France. Having devised the means to maintain dominance through economic and military agreements, France was ready to relinquish political control – and to unburden itself of the onus of colonial rule. None of the territories that achieved independence in 1960 was subjected to the dire consequences imposed on Guinea two years previously.

The French African territories were independent but weak. Most of the new nations were small and impoverished, and France remained a significant force in their political and economic affairs – in a relationship that typified neocolonialism. Africa remained France's most important source of raw materials and, after Europe, its second most important market for exports. French state-owned enterprises invested heavily in African oil and minerals. In a number of former colonies, France continued to control the radio, telecommunications, and military communications networks. In many countries, French citizens retained important positions in government and influenced economic, foreign policy, and military decisions. Thousands of government-sponsored teachers, technicians, and medical and military personnel, as well as tens of thousands of private entrepreneurs, lived and worked in the former colonies. Decades after the colonies became independent, France exploited their natural resources, profited from investments in their economies, and propped up or overthrew their governments. No other former imperial power intervened to the same extent in the internal affairs of its onetime possessions.

Once African territories became independent, French-African affairs were directed from the Africa Cell, a secretive body that was separate from the Foreign Ministry and worked under the personal direction of the French president. From 1960 to 1974, the Africa Cell was headed by Jacques Foccart, who not only shaped France's Africa policy but also directed the activities of the French intelligence agency, SDECE, throughout Francophone Africa. As such, Foccart had enormous power in making or breaking African governments. Successive French presidents and heads of the Africa Cell cultivated close personal ties with the leaders of Francophone African states and established pacts that stressed loyalty and reciprocity. Until the early 1990s, the personalization of politics bound France to its African clients, even after the extent of their corrupt, repressive, and authoritarian practices had been exposed. Personal ties were strengthened by annual Franco-African summits that included French presidents and their Francophone African counterparts.

France's ties to its former colonies were formalized by a number of cooperation agreements signed in the early 1960s and subsequently updated. The agreements covered economic, monetary, and foreign affairs; defense and security; strategic minerals; and other domains. Whereas the French Community agreement of 1958 gave France sole authority in these areas, the new cooperation agreements were billed as giving African nations a voice. In reality, they perpetuated French dominance. Although most former French territories signed such agreements, four of them – Côte d'Ivoire, Senegal, Cameroon, and Gabon – constituted the pillars of the postcolonial system. Their political and economic policies were crafted to protect French interests, and their rulers, boasting close personal ties to France, reigned supreme for periods ranging from two to four decades. If the regimes or their policies were threatened, Paris used its political, economic, and military clout to restore the balance.

The postindependence economic cooperation agreements preserved the mercantilist relationship between Paris and its former colonies. For France, they guaranteed markets for exports and privileged access to Africa's raw materials, the most important of which were critical to French aeronautical, nuclear energy, and armaments industries. The former colonies agreed to limit their imports from other countries. As a result, France remained the dominant supplier of goods and services, even though French prices generally exceeded the world average by substantial amounts. Even after the 1963 Yaoundé Convention opened Francophone African markets to all members of the European Economic Community, France continued to maintain a large trade surplus with Africa, in part because French foreign aid and loans to African governments were tied to French goods and services. Large French trading companies still controlled the import-export market, and French industries continued to dominate African manufacturing sectors.

Economic cooperation agreements were complemented by monetary accords. Most former French colonies joined the African Financial Community (CFA) or franc zone, a monetary union whose participants shared a common currency, the value of which was linked to the French franc. Membership in the franc zone bestowed a number of benefits on its African participants. The CFA franc was convertible – unlike the currencies of many individual African countries. The currency's convertibility meant that the French Treasury would exchange any quantity of CFA francs for hard currency. Moreover, the CFA franc was guaranteed by the Bank of France. Countries with balance-of-payments difficulties were able to draw on the foreign exchange reserves of members with a surplus. However, membership in the franc zone also had drawbacks. African participants surrendered their economic autonomy. Monetary and financial regulations – and, by extension, economic policies – were determined in Paris. The issue and circulation of currency was under French control. France was permitted to devalue the CFA currency without consulting African governments, and French administrators could veto the decisions of African central banks. Lack of restrictions on capital transfers meant that French firms repatriated significant portions of their profits rather than reinvesting them in African economies.

These shortcomings were not merely theoretical. In the late 1980s, when many African countries were in economic crisis, the French Treasury was forced to bail out a number of clients threatened with bankruptcy, repaying their IMF and World Bank debts. The bailouts constituted a huge expense for French taxpayers and resulted in a dramatic revision to French policy. In 1993, Paris took the unprecedented step of suspending the free convertibility of the CFA franc and announced that, henceforth, prospective aid recipients must implement IMF and World Bank structural adjustment and good governance programs before receiving French aid. Moreover, France would no longer bail out corrupt countries with failing economies. In January 1994, France made another unforeseen move, unilaterally devaluing the CFA franc by 50 percent. Shock waves spread across the franc zone. Import costs doubled, and foreign exchange earnings plummeted. Household income and living standards declined precipitously. These critical actions were taken without input from African governments.

Like the postindependence economic and monetary accords, military cooperation agreements provided the framework for permanent French involvement in the former colonies. Parties to the agreements were required to buy French weapons and equipment and to hire French military and technical advisors. They could also appeal for French military intervention to quash internal or external threats to their regimes. In exchange, France was guaranteed access to strategic raw materials in the signatory countries. Most important among these were oil, natural gas, and uranium, the critical element in nuclear-power production. France was granted a priority right to buy such strategic materials and to limit or prevent their export to other

PHOTO 7.1. French and African soldiers marching together in Middle Congo shortly before independence, August 1, 1960 (Terrence Spencer/Time Life Pictures/Getty Images).

countries if such actions were determined to be in "the interests of common defense."[9] Related military training and technical assistance agreements guaranteed French training to African armed forces, while the French intelligence agency trained African intelligence operatives as well as local police forces. From the early 1960s through 1992, France trained some 40,000 African military officers. In some instances, French officers remained after independence to organize, train, and advise the new national armies. In others, African soldiers were sent for training in France. These agreements gave France enormous influence over the size and capabilities of African armies. As the major weapons supplier in its former colonies, France also had significant influence over the regional balance of power.

The military accords granted France enormous clout by permitting the former imperial power to retain military bases and keep large numbers of troops on African soil. In 1960, when most French African colonies attained their independence, more than 60,000 French troops were lodged in some ninety garrisons in

[9] Quoted in Pierre Lellouche and Dominique Moisi, "French Policy in Africa: A Lonely Battle against Destabilization," *International Security* 3, no. 4 (Spring 1979), 116n15.

sub-Saharan Africa and Madagascar. The number of troops in North Africa was far greater – with 500,000 French troops in Algeria alone. In the context of widespread decolonization, France determined that it was politically risky to station such large numbers of troops in Africa. As a result, when the Algerian war ended in 1962, France began to diminish its military presence on the continent. Between 1962 and 1964, some 300,000 French troops departed, leaving more than 23,000 French troops in nearly forty garrisons. France closed most of its military bases, retaining only those in Senegal, Côte d'Ivoire, Chad, and Madagascar. In the mid-1970s, after its ejection from the bases in Chad and Madagascar, France established new ones in Gabon, the Central African Republic, Djibouti, and on the Indian Ocean island of Réunion.

Despite these moves, France retained a considerable military presence in Africa. By the late 1970s, some 15,000 French troops were still garrisoned in more than twenty African states and territories, and France continued to maintain transit, refueling, and support facilities across the continent. Nor did the removal of hundreds of thousands of troops herald the end of French military intervention. Contingents in Africa were supplemented by rapid deployment forces composed of mobile airborne troops, which were stationed in France and ready to intervene whenever and wherever necessary. As late as 1993, a rapid deployment force of 44,500 men was ready to leave France on short notice to protect French interests in Africa.

French Military Intervention in African Affairs

During the first three decades of African independence, France was involved in some three dozen military interventions in sixteen African countries, including Benin, Cameroon, the Central African Republic, Chad, the Comoros, Congo-Brazzaville, Côte d'Ivoire, Djibouti, Gabon, Madagascar, Mauritania, Niger, Rwanda, Senegal, Togo, and Zaire. In most cases, France acted to protect allied regimes from internal threats to their power rather than from external aggression. In some instances, French intervention was sparked by concern about communist subversion or intrusion into France's privileged domain by Anglophone or Arab interests.

French government concerns about communist subversion were nearly matched by its antipathy toward American political and economic expansion into France's "traditional" spheres of influence. Hostility toward the United States had been preceded by centuries of competition with Britain. Paris's aversion to Anglophone influence in Africa, the so-called Fashoda complex, is frequently attributed to a 1898 incident at Fashoda, Sudan, where a British military challenge thwarted French dreams of building an empire from the Atlantic to the Indian Ocean. Even after the dissolution of its empire in the 1950s and 1960s, France considered its former colonies to be a *pré carré* (private domain) or *chasse gardée* (private hunting ground) – off limits to other powers, much as the United States applied the Monroe Doctrine to Latin America. To safeguard its supremacy, France expanded its sphere of influence to include Francophone countries that had been colonized by Belgium (Congo/Zaire, Rwanda, and Burundi) and sought to undermine the influence of Anglophone countries such as Nigeria and Uganda, which it considered to be British and American surrogates. Thus, during the Nigerian Civil War of 1967–70, France was the main source of arms for the Biafran secessionist movement. In the 1990s, France supported a Hutu extremist regime in Rwanda in its bid to destroy the Uganda-backed Rwandan Patriotic Front (RPF), a rebel movement composed primarily of Rwandan Tutsi refugees and their descendants, who had been exiled in Anglophone Uganda. It was these Hutu extremists who perpetrated the 1994 Rwandan genocide that claimed nearly one million lives. Paris also supported Zaire's brutal dictator, Mobutu Sese Seko (formerly, Joseph-Désiré Mobutu), until he was driven from power in 1997 by a Zairian rebel movement supported by Uganda and RPF-led Rwanda.

Six cases of French military intervention are briefly considered here, including those in Cameroon, Niger, Gabon, the Central African Republic, Chad, and Zaire. In each case, French predominance was believed to be threatened by communist, Anglophone, or pan-Arab interests. Two countries, Cameroon and Gabon, were among France's four political and economic pillars on the continent. All six countries possessed important deposits of strategic minerals, particularly uranium, which France desired for both weapons and energy production.[10] Protection of France's privileged access to uranium was

---

[10] Convinced that American-dominated NATO would not protect it from a Soviet attack, France had begun to develop its own nuclear defenses in the 1950s. With limited domestic energy resources and heavily dependent on foreign oil, it was also concerned about energy security. Following the 1973 Arab oil embargo, imposed

a factor in French intervention in Niger, Gabon, the Central African Republic, Chad, and Zaire. Gabon and Chad also possessed important oil reserves. Diamonds were found in the Central African Republic and Zaire, while the latter also claimed rich deposits of copper, cobalt, and a plethora of other strategic minerals.

Although all six cases displayed a number of commonalities, they also exhibited differences. In Cameroon, France engaged in a long-term counterinsurgency operation, which diverged from the more common pattern of thwarting or supporting military coups. Following its expulsion from the RDA and banning by the French government in 1955, the UPC had transformed itself into a guerrilla movement. With longstanding ties to the PCF and to nationalists in British Cameroon, the UPC sparked French concerns about both communist and Anglophone infringement. Immediately after Cameroon's independence, President Ahmadou Ahidjo, who was closely tied to metropolitan interests, requested French assistance in quashing the UPC insurrection. France sent 300 military officers to orchestrate the Cameroonian government's response and five French battalions to enact it. In the ensuing months, some 3,000 rebels were killed, and thousands of civilians died as a result of the war. Ahidjo subsequently banned all opposition parties and, with SDECE support, established an extensive domestic security apparatus. The insurgency was quelled in the mid-1960s, and Ahidjo clung to power until 1982.

French intervention in Niger included thwarting a coup d'état, supporting a coup d'état, and waging a counterinsurgency operation. In 1963, French troops helped crush an attempted coup against Hamani Diori's government, which had granted France priority access to uranium deposits and other strategic minerals. In 1964–65, France assisted Diori in putting down a rebellion led by Sawaba, an outlawed organization that had emerged from the Nigerien Democratic Union, Niger's renegade RDA branch. Sawaba, like the UPC, played into French fears of communist and Anglophone infiltration. The organization's guerrillas were trained and equipped by the Soviet Union, Eastern Bloc countries, Cuba, China, and North Vietnam. They also received support from radical African states, including Algeria and Ghana. Equally worrisome, Sawaba's popular base was linked

on Western countries that had supported Israel during the Arab-Israeli War, France launched a major program to revamp its energy industry and to produce the bulk of its electricity from nuclear power.

PHOTO 7.2. Cameroonian President Ahmadou Ahidjo, French President General Charles de Gaulle, and French Africa advisor Jacques Foccart leaving the Élysée Palace, Paris, June 21, 1967 (AFP/Getty Images).

ethnically, culturally, and economically to Nigeria, France's Anglophone nemesis in the region. French intelligence officers, who continued to dominate Niger's security apparatus, kept close tabs on Sawaba's activities, while French security officers supervised the beating and torture of captured Sawaba guerrillas. French soldiers were stationed in several Nigerien cities, and Paris retained military bases in Niger until the end of 1964, when the conclusion of the Algerian war rendered their presence less crucial. French support for Diori waned with his loyalty. In 1974, the Nigerien president attempted to negotiate more favorable terms for uranium sales, at a time when Nigerien uranium constituted two-thirds of that used by French nuclear reactors and French firms held significant shares in Niger's uranium exploration and production. Shortly after negotiations began, Diori was overthrown by a military coup. The French military did not intervene to support him.

In Gabon, where France had extensive investments in uranium, oil, natural gas, manganese, iron, and timber, Paris supported a client regime by suppressing domestic dissent and restoring the president to power following a military coup. In 1960, SDECE intervened in Gabon's presidential elections to ensure the victory of Léon M'ba, who was willing to cater to French interests. In 1960 and 1962, France helped M'ba put down internal unrest aimed at his increasingly repressive government. In February 1964, 600 French paratroopers reinstated M'ba after he was toppled by a coup d'état, which French President Charles de Gaulle believed was orchestrated by the CIA to give the United States access to Gabon's oil, uranium, and other strategic resources. In Gabon, there were widespread protests against the dictator's reinstatement.

After M'ba's death in 1967, his successor, Omar Bongo, was handpicked by SDECE's Africa chief, Jacques Foccart. During Bongo's forty-two year reign, French paratroopers and pilots were permanently stationed near the Gabonese capital, and French officers trained the country's military and intelligence networks. Notoriously repressive and corrupt, Bongo siphoned off Gabon's oil wealth to become one of Africa's richest rulers. The year after its client was installed in Gabon, France intervened in the Nigerian Civil War, hoping to undermine the power of the Anglophone giant. SDECE agents convinced Bongo to recognize the Biafran secessionists and to permit France to use Gabon as a resupply area. Over the course of the war, France covertly supplied the Biafrans with 350 tons of weapons, transferred through both Gabon and Côte d'Ivoire.

In the Central African Republic, France supported regime change to safeguard its interests – failing to intervene in some cases and aggressively intervening in others. In 1960, France actively supported David Dacko as the nation's first president. Military and economic cooperation agreements permitted France to station troops in the country and to control uranium exploration and production. Dacko quickly instituted a one-party state that was rife with corruption. Hoping to gain popular support by demonstrating his independence, Dacko eliminated French monopolies on diamonds and lumber and accepted Chinese aid. On New Year's Eve in 1965, Dacko was overthrown in a military coup led by army chief of staff Colonel Jean-Bédel Bokassa. French troops in the capital did not intervene.

Claiming that he was saving the country from international communism, Bokassa began a decade and a half of brutal dictatorial rule. He changed the name of his country to the Central African Empire and was crowned emperor in a ceremony reputed to have cost $30 million. Concerned that Bokassa's repressive policies and erratic behavior threatened French interests, SDECE planned another coup. In September 1979, in what Jacques Foccart called "France's last colonial expedition," French paratroopers and intelligence agents deposed the emperor and restored Dacko to power.[11] As before, Dacko permitted a strong French military and bureaucratic presence in the country. However, in September 1981, when Dacko was overthrown by army chief of staff General André Kolingba, who had important French military connections, France again chose not to intervene. Another in a long line of corrupt dictators, Kolingba maintained close relations with France through the end of the Cold War.

French intervention in Chad, which occurred in 1968–75, 1977–80, and 1983–84, was perhaps the most drawn-out of France's military actions in postcolonial Africa. Bordering on six states, Chad was rich in uranium and oil and an important source of cotton for the French textile industry. Concerned about Soviet, Libyan, and American intrusion, Paris acted to ensure the survival of a regime friendly to French interests. During the colonial period, France had focused its development efforts in Chad's predominantly Christian and Sara south, neglecting the heavily Muslim northern region. As a result, Sara and other southerners dominated the state at independence. In 1962, President Ngartha François Tombalbaye, a southerner, outlawed all political parties except his own and appointed primarily southerners to the government and civil service. Discrimination against the Muslim north led to the establishment of the multi-ethnic Front for the National Liberation of Chad (FROLINAT) in 1966 and the commencement of armed struggle. Between 1968 and 1971, the French military helped Tombalbaye's regime recapture most of the rebel-held regions. In the meantime, Captain Muammar al-Qaddafi came to power in neighboring Libya following a 1969 coup d'état. When Nasser

---

[11] Quoted in "Central African Republic," http://www.royalafricansociety.org/country-profiles/141-central-african-republic.html.

died in September 1970, Qaddafi assumed the leadership of the pan-Arab movement, which supported Arab emancipation and unity in Africa and the Middle East. Hoping to draw Chad into the Libyan sphere, Qaddafi openly supported the Chadian rebels, contributing to tensions between FROLINAT's primarily Arab leadership and Tubu fighters on the ground.

By 1975, when Tombalbaye was killed in a coup d'état, Chad's north-south division had been replaced by a more complex pattern of ethnic and intra-ethnic conflict. At one time or another, France and Libya supported most of the factions with military and economic aid. Although the factionalism was domestic in origin, foreign involvement made it particularly lethal. General Félix Malloum, chair of the newly established military junta, incorporated more northern and eastern Muslims in his government, but southern Sara continued to dominate. Among the northern rebels, rivalry between Arabs and Tubus was further complicated by divisions among Tubu groups. Goukouni Oueddei's Tubu faction, residing near the Libyan border, identified strongly with the peoples of southern Libya. Hissène Habré's Tubu faction, located further south, was oriented toward Sudan in the east. Under Valéry Giscard d'Estaing's center-right government (1974–81), France provided covert assistance to Habré, while Libya supported Goukouni Oueddei. The United States, which considered Libya to be a Soviet proxy as well as a sponsor of international terrorism, supported whichever side was opposed by the Libyans.

By the spring of 1978, half of Chad was under rebel control. Malloum appealed for the return of French troops and made an alliance with Habré, who joined the government as prime minister. France supplied 2,000 troops and Jaguar fighter-bombers to stem Goukouni's advance. By March 1979, more than 10,000 Chadians had died in the violence. A peace accord was signed in August, followed by the establishment of a Transitional Government of National Unity (GUNT), which was recognized by the OAU as Chad's legitimate government. Goukouni assumed the position of president, and Habré was named minister of national defense. By late March 1980, it was clear that GUNT had failed. French troops and OAU peacekeepers stood by as Habré's forces took control of part of the capital. Libya responded to GUNT's appeal for assistance, providing money, training facilities, and troops.

Under François Mitterrand's socialist government (1981–95), France again changed course. Committed to backing the OAU solution, the new French government threw its support to Goukouni, offering economic aid and support for an OAU peacekeeping force in exchange for Libyan withdrawal from Chad. Goukouni agreed, and Libyan soldiers departed. The Reagan administration, however, believed that Qaddafi was an agent of international communism. Worried that Chad, Sudan, Egypt, and Nigeria would fall like dominos, President Reagan authorized the CIA to funnel large amounts of cash, arms, and vehicles to Habré's rebels, undermining the OAU peacekeeping operation. In June 1982, largely as a result of American covert funding and military support, Habré returned to power. In another about-face, France recognized the Habré government as a fait accompli and the one most likely to protect French interests.

Goukouni again turned to Libya for assistance. In June 1983, Goukouni's forces, armed with sophisticated military equipment and backed by 2,000 Libyan regulars, attacked Habré's forces in Chad. France, the United States, and their regional proxy – Zaire – came to Habré's rescue. While the United States provided military advisors and aid, and Zaire sent aircraft and paratroopers, France supplied some 3,000 troops, as well as weapons, equipment, and logistical support. The Chad campaign of August 1983 to September 1984 was France's largest military intervention in Africa since Algeria. Habré ruled Chad from 1982 to 1990, when he was ousted by his former chief military advisor, Idriss Déby. Habré's brutal eight-year reign was marked by the systematic use of torture and thousands of political murders.

Paris also had a strong presence in Zaire, which followed France as the world's second most populous Francophone country. French businesses had important interests in the copper and cobalt mines of Shaba (formerly Katanga) Province. They helped build the massive hydro-electric dams near the capital city and assisted in the construction of ports, airports, and telecommunications infrastructure. In the 1970s and 1980s, France bailed out the nearly bankrupt Mobutu regime and provided it with sophisticated military equipment – including Mirage F1 fighter jets, Alouette III helicopters, armored cars, and weaponry – as well French instructors to teach Zairian soldiers how to use them.

France also intervened in Zaire militarily. In 1977 and again in 1978, Zairian rebels based in Angola attacked the mineral-rich Shaba Province. Claiming that it was repelling a Soviet-backed invasion from MPLA territory, France helped Mobutu ward off the first wave of attacks in April 1977 by transporting Moroccan troops and military vehicles to the embattled region. In May 1978, Paris sent 1,000 French paratroopers to break the siege of Kolwezi, an important Shaba mining center. In a strategic region challenged by Anglophone interests, Zaire was France's final hope. As a result, the French courtship of Mobutu endured for two decades. Having "lost" Rwanda in 1994 to the English-speaking RPF, Paris was determined to retain Zaire for "la francophonie." In 1997, as Mobutu's regime crumbled under a rebel onslaught backed by Uganda and RPF-led Rwanda, France ran a covert military operation against the rebels that included three combat aircraft and some eighty European mercenaries. While the United States distanced itself from Mobutu, who had little value in the post–Cold War world, France supported its protégé to the bitter end.

New Developments in the 1990s

From the 1960s to the 1990s, France was closely linked to a number of unsavory but anticommunist dictators who protected French interests in Africa. With the end of the Cold War, France could afford to cut many of these ties, and the emergence of popular prodemocracy movements across Francophone Africa made severing them a necessity. Beginning in February 1990, trade unionists, civil servants, religious leaders, students, and other democratic forces pressured unelected governments to hold national conferences in a number of Francophone African states, including Benin, Gabon, Congo-Brazzaville, Mali, Togo, Niger, Zaire, Chad, the Central African Republic, Cameroon, Madagascar, Burkina Faso, and Mauritania. Civil society organizations demanded that the conferences honestly assess past government practices, evaluate ongoing political and economic crises, and write new constitutions that enshrined multiparty democracy and the accountability of leaders.

Pressured by national conferences held in Benin and Gabon and widespread agitation elsewhere, President Mitterrand unveiled a new Africa policy in June 1990. At the Franco-African summit held in La Baule, France, Mitterrand declared that there could be no development without democracy and announced that, henceforth, French aid would be tied to human rights practices. However, in an ambiguous escape clause, Mitterrand also affirmed that France would continue to help its allies ward off external threats and would refrain from interfering in internal conflicts. Throughout Francophone Africa, wary dictators embarked on superficial reforms to bring about "multi-party democracy" that would protect their relationships with France, then resumed rigging elections and cracking down on dissent without fear of the consequences.

The changing political climate of the 1990s was accompanied by economic transformations at home and abroad. Reformers in the French bureaucracy argued that Africa's economic importance to France had diminished and that military and economic aid should be similarly curtailed. By the late 1990s, less than 5 percent of French foreign trade was with Africa, and African countries absorbed less than 20 percent of France's direct foreign investment – although French businesses still dominated mining, agribusiness, building and public works, telecommunications, insurance, banking, and electricity supply. Moreover, when France joined the European Economic and Monetary Union in 1993, it was required to reduce its government deficit, which resulted in diminished military and economic aid to African countries; the suspension of the free convertibility of the CFA franc; and a year later, its dramatic devaluation.

French military presence in Africa was also overhauled in the 1990s. In 1994, nearly 9,000 French troops were in stationed in seven African countries, while approximately 800 French military advisors operated in twenty more. By 2008, Paris had reduced the number of troops on the ground to approximately 6,000 and had eliminated all but three bases – retaining only those in Djibouti, Senegal, and Gabon. Instead of the permanent presence that had characterized the 1960s to 1990s, French troops in the new millennium would be moved in and out of African countries on short-term assignments.

Suggested Reading

For an overview of decolonization in French sub-Saharan Africa, three books are especially recommended. Ruth Schachter Morgenthau's classic, *Political Parties in French-Speaking West Africa* (Oxford, UK: Clarendon Press, 1964), is an in-depth political history that focuses on local, territorial, and international levels and provides unique insights into African parties and activists. Edward Mortimer's *France and the Africans, 1944–1960: A Political History* (New York: Walker and Co., 1969), a more traditional political history with an expansive view from above, offers a detailed account of colonial reforms and their implementation. Tony Chafer's *The End of*

Empire in French West Africa: France's Successful Decolonization? (New York: Berg, 2002) examines the wider political context of decolonization, the growth of popular pressures for reform and independence, and the French response.

Several authors examine political movements in territories that resisted French reform programs and the consequences they suffered. For Madagascar, see Raymond K. Kent, *The Many Faces of an Anti-Colonial Revolt: Madagascar's Long Journey into 1947* (Albany, CA: Foundation for Malagasy Studies, 2007); Martin Shipway, "Madagascar on the Eve of Insurrection, 1944–47: The Impasse of a Liberal Colonial Policy," *Journal of Imperial and Commonwealth History* 24, no. 1 (January 1996): 72–100; and Douglas Little, "Cold War and Colonialism in Africa: The United States, France, and the Madagascar Revolt of 1947," *Pacific Historical Review* 59, no. 4 (November 1990): 527–52. For Cameroon, see Richard A. Joseph, *Radical Nationalism in Cameroun: Social Origins of the U.P.C. Rebellion* (New York: Oxford University Press, 1977); Meredith Terretta, "Cameroonian Nationalists Go Global: From Forest *Maquis* to a Pan-African Accra," *Journal of African History* 51, no. 2 (2010): 189–212; and Meredith Terretta, *Nation of Outlaws, State of Violence: Nationalism, Grassfields Tradition, and State-Building in Cameroon* (Athens: Ohio University Press, forthcoming 2013). For Guinea, see Elizabeth Schmidt, *Cold War and Decolonization in Guinea, 1946–1958* (Athens: Ohio University Press, 2007).

For background on Franco-American competition in Africa during the periods of decolonization and the Cold War, see Asteris C. Huliaras, "The 'Anglosaxon Conspiracy': French Perceptions of the Great Lakes Crisis," *Journal of Modern African Studies* 36, no. 4 (December 1998): 593–609. See also Philip E. Muehlenbeck's *Betting on the Africans: John F. Kennedy's Courting of African Nationalist Leaders* (New York: Oxford University Press, 2012), which includes an insightful chapter titled "The Kennedy-de Gaulle Rivalry in Africa."

For further reading on neocolonialism in former French Africa, a number of works are recommended. Victor T. Le Vine's *Politics in Francophone Africa* (Boulder, CO: Lynne Rienner, 2004) examines continued French domination of the political, economic, and military spheres of fourteen former territories in sub-Saharan Africa. Bruno Charbonneau's *France and the New Imperialism: Security Policy in Sub-Saharan Africa* (Burlington, VT: Ashgate, 2008) explores continuities in Franco-African relations from conquest through the postcolonial period, focusing especially on military, business, and personal connections. Alexander Keese's "First Lessons in Neo-Colonialism: The Personalisation of Relations Between African Politicians and French Officials in Sub-Saharan Africa, 1956–66," *Journal of Imperial and Commonwealth History* 35, no. 4 (December 2007): 593–613, assesses the French policy of cultivating personal relationships with postindependence African leaders as a way of maintaining influence. Several older articles, which focus on continued French involvement in African political, economic, military, and cultural spheres, provide useful summaries. See especially Richard Joseph, "The Gaullist Legacy: Patterns of French Neo-Colonialism," *Review of African Political Economy*, no. 6 (May–August 1976): 4–13; Guy Martin, "The Historical, Economic, and Political Bases of France's African Policy," *Journal of Modern African Studies* 23, no. 2 (June 1985): 189–208; and Martin Staniland, "Francophone Africa: The Enduring French Connection," *Annals of the American Academy of Political and Social Science* 489 (January 1987): 51–62.

A number of articles focus specifically on Franco-African military cooperation agreements, the presence in Africa of French troops and bases, and French military intervention in independent African states. Four are especially recommended: Pierre Lellouche and Dominique Moisi, "French Policy in Africa: A Lonely Battle against Destabilization," *International Security* 3, no. 4 (Spring 1979): 108–33; Robin Luckham, "French Militarism in Africa," *Review of African Political Economy*, no. 24 (May–August 1982): 55–84; James O. Goldsborough, "Dateline Paris: Africa's Policeman," *Foreign Policy*, no. 33 (Winter 1978–79): 174–90; and Shaun Gregory, "The French Military in Africa: Past and Present," *African Affairs* 99, no. 396 (July 2000): 435–48. Douglas Porch's *The French Secret Services: From the Dreyfus Affair to the Gulf War* (New York: Farrar, Straus & Giroux, 1995) includes information on the role of the French secret services in destabilizing, toppling, or maintaining African governments. Alexander Keese's "Building a New Image of Africa: 'Dissident States' and the Emergence of French Neo-Colonialism in the Aftermath of Decolonization," *Cahiers d'Études Africaines* 48, no. 3 (2008): 513–30, in contrast, focuses on cases in which France chose not to intervene.

A number of works focus on French political, economic, and military intervention in specific countries. For Cameroon, see Joseph and Terretta (mentioned above). For Niger, see three important studies by Klaas van Walraven: "Decolonization by Referendum: The Anomaly of Niger and the Fall of Sawaba, 1958–1959," *Journal of African History* 50, no. 2 (July 2009): 269–92; "From Tamanrasset: The Struggle of Sawaba and the Algerian Connection, 1957–1966," *Journal of North African Studies* 10, nos. 3–4 (September–December 2005): 507–27; and *The Yearning for Relief: A History of the Sawaba Movement in Niger* (Leiden: Brill, 2013). For Gabon, see Michael C. Reed, "Gabon: A Neo-Colonial Enclave of Enduring French Interest," *Journal of Modern African Studies* 25, no. 2 (June 1987): 283–320. For the Central African Republic, see Brian Titley, *Dark Age: The Political Odyssey of Emperor Bokassa* (Montreal: McGill-Queen's University Press,

1997). For French involvement in Chad's civil wars, see J. Millard Burr and Robert O. Collins, *Africa's Thirty Years' War: Libya, Chad, and the Sudan, 1963–1993* (Boulder, CO: Westview Press, 1999), and René Lemarchand, "The Crisis in Chad," in *African Crisis Areas and U.S. Foreign Policy*, ed. Gerald J. Bender, James S. Coleman, and Richard L. Sklar (Berkeley: University of California Press, 1985): 239–56. For French intervention in Zaire during the Shaba invasions, see Piero Gleijeses, "Truth or Credibility: Castro, Carter, and the Invasions of Shaba," *International History Review* 18, no. 1 (February 1996): 70–103.

Franco-African relations at the end of the Cold War are explored in Guy Martin's "Continuity and Change in Franco-African Relations," *Journal of Modern African Studies* 33, no. 1 (March 1995): 1–20, which examines the impact of the end of the Cold War, European integration, and globalization on Franco-African relations. Pearl T. Robinson's "The National Conference Phenomenon in Francophone Africa," *Comparative Studies in Society and History* 36, no. 3 (July 1994): 575–610, explores the impact of popular prodemocracy movements and French pressure in the implementation of political reforms in French-speaking Africa.

CHAPTER 8

From the Cold War to the War on Terror, 1991–2010

When the Soviet Union disintegrated in 1991 and the Cold War ended, African client states were economically devastated, fraught with political divisions, and awash in weapons. No longer propped up by outside powers, dictators were driven from power and fragile states collapsed. In many instances, nascent prodemocracy movements were trampled as warlords, criminal gangs, and paramilitary groups devoid of political ideology or program moved into the power vacuums. The pervasive violence of the first post–Cold War decade was rooted in the political and economic crises of the Cold War era. As states and economies fragmented, opportunists mobilized the alienated, impoverished, and unemployed to claim their share of power and resources on the basis of their race, ethnicity, clan, or religion. Those who did not share these identities were excluded as unworthy and their claims as illegitimate. Marginalized out-groups were easy scapegoats for the countries' enormous political and economic problems. Thus, the politics of exclusion laid the groundwork for intergroup violence, ethnic cleansing, and genocide. Foreshadowed by the Cold War era wars of destabilization in Angola and Mozambique, in which antigovernment forces controlled indigenous populations through terror, the wars of the 1990s were characterized by widespread violence and atrocities against civilians.

Foreign intervention after the Cold War also assumed new characteristics. The state and its foreign backers no longer monopolized the means of coercion. The new wars were both privatized and globalized. Contests for control over power and resources were waged by private factions – warlords, criminal gangs, rebel groups, renegade soldiers, and old-fashioned foreign mercenaries and their new transformations as private military companies. Foreign intervention during this period involved neighboring states as well as non-African powers. Intervention was sometimes bilateral, just as it was when former colonial powers or Cold War superpowers policed their privileged domains. In other instances, it was multinational, characterized by the involvement of UN, African Union, regionally based peacekeeping forces, or international humanitarian organizations.[1] Some of these bodies intervened to monitor and enforce peace accords or to facilitate humanitarian relief operations. In other cases, foreign powers and peacekeeping forces took advantage of state disintegration to promote their own strategic goals and to abscond with natural resources. They, too, preyed on local populations in actions that bore a striking resemblance to those of the warlords, rebel armies, and criminal gangs they came to oppose. Funding sources were also diversified in the post–Cold War period. The new wars were generally financed not by foreign patron states but by looting natural resources, pillaging local populations, commandeering international humanitarian aid, gunrunning, money laundering, and drug smuggling. Because many groups profited from the continuation of war, peace accords often failed.

In contrast to the Cold War period, during the late twentieth and early twenty-first centuries foreign states were criticized as much for their failure to intervene as for their intervention. Following the refusal of the international community to act to prevent genocide in Rwanda in 1994 and ethnic cleansing in Darfur in 2003–4, the UN took an unprecedented action. In 2005, the General Assembly adopted a resolution that held states responsible for protecting their citizens "from genocide, war crimes, ethnic cleansing and crimes against humanity" and granted the international community the right to intervene militarily if states failed to meet their "responsibility to protect."[2] The resolution contravened the principle of state sovereignty embedded in international law since the seventeenth century and enshrined in the UN Charter. In theory, respect for state sovereignty could no longer be used as an excuse to allow mass killings to proceed unhindered. In reality, the situation was far more complicated.

---

[1] The African Union replaced the OAU in 2002.
[2] UN General Assembly, "2005 World Summit Outcome," paragraphs 138–9, adopted September 15, 2005, http://www.who.int/hiv/universalaccess2010/worldsummit.pdf.

Governments remained reluctant to set precedents that might be used against them in the future, and powerful nations rarely committed the resources or personnel necessary to implement the resolution. Notable exceptions occurred in 2011, when UN and French forces conducted military strikes against government strongholds in Côte d'Ivoire and NATO launched UN-approved air strikes against government tanks and artillery in Libya to protect the lives of civilians under attack by state security forces. While foreign intervention was justified on the grounds of protecting civilian lives, the application of external military power also supported local insurgencies that paved the way for regime change.

This chapter begins with an overview of the economic crisis that engulfed sub-Saharan Africa in the 1970s and 1980s, severely weakening a number of American Cold War clients. Examining the cases of Liberia, Somalia, Sudan, and Zaire, it explores the relationship between political and economic practices during the Cold War and the traumas of the first post–Cold War decade (1991–2001). Despite the large degree of American responsibility for the devastation these countries faced, concern for Africa was low on the U.S. agenda, and foreign aid and development assistance declined precipitously during the 1990s. Following the terrorist attacks on the United States in September 2001, however, terrorism replaced communism as the rallying cry for American overseas involvement. During the first decade of the global war on terror (2001–10), the United States revamped its Cold War African strategy, increasing support for repressive regimes in strategic states in exchange for cooperation on counterterrorism.

Economic Decline, State Collapse, and Competition for the Spoils

As the Cold War drew to a close in the late 1980s and early 1990s, African states were in crisis, both politically and economically. Despite a massive influx of U.S. military and economic aid during the Cold War years, American clients such as Liberia, Somalia, Sudan, and Zaire were bankrupt. Although corruption, war, and economic mismanagement were responsible for much of the devastation, the position of these countries in the global political economy was also a crucial factor. In the decades after independence, most African countries continued the colonial practice of exporting low-priced primary commodities and importing expensive manufactured goods from the West. Lacking developed oil resources of their own, they were forced to import petroleum products critical to their economic development. As a result, the worldwide economic crisis of the 1970s and 1980s had a catastrophic impact on much of the African continent.

Two economic traumas sparked the crisis. The first stemmed from dramatic increases in oil prices in 1973–74 and 1979–80, which forced African countries to deplete their foreign exchange reserves and intensify their debt burdens to pay for petroleum products. The second trauma – a sharp global decline in commodity prices – coincided with the second oil price increase. As worldwide prices for copper, cocoa, cotton, and coffee plummeted, African economies were devastated. Between 1980 and 1989, sub-Saharan African countries suffered from low export prices, high import prices, and mounting trade deficits, which resulted in a 28 percent decline in their terms of trade. Unable to produce the ever-greater amounts of cash crops and minerals needed to buy the oil, manufactured goods, and capital equipment required for development, African countries borrowed heavily from foreign commercial banks and governments. In many cases, the amount required for annual debt servicing was equivalent to the bulk of a country's gross domestic product or export earnings. As interest rates rose in the mid-1980s, many African countries were unable to pay the yearly principal and interest owed on their debts. Faced with insoluble debt crises, their governments turned to international financial institutions for assistance. Although these institutions were willing to help African governments repay their debts, their loans came with strings attached.

Driven by free market ideologies aimed at strengthening global capitalism, Western-dominated international financial institutions such as the IMF and the World Bank imposed stringent conditions on their loans. The IMF, which concerns itself with trade and currency imbalances, focuses on both short-term stabilization measures and long-term structural adjustment. To stimulate exports and decrease imports, the IMF typically requires currency devaluations. To promote free market ideals, it mandates reductions in government spending. The World Bank also focuses on the long term, stipulating changes to economic structures that are intended to remove the government from economic affairs. The IMF and World Bank structural adjustment programs invariably emphasize free trade (an end to government subsidies, price controls, tariffs, and marketing boards) and free enterprise (privatization of government-owned economic entities and reduction in the number of government employees). Recipients of IMF and World Bank largesse are frequently compelled to implement measures that stimulate foreign investment, including currency devaluation, reduced taxation of foreign firms, and liberal profit repatriation arrangements.

By the late 1980s, economic decline and external prescriptions for addressing the crisis had led to severe political instability in many African countries. The IMF and World Bank stabilization and structural adjustment programs, imposed from above by unrepresentative regimes, sparked significant social unrest. People took to the streets in protest as compliant African governments ended food, seed, and fertilizer subsidies; cut spending on health and education; and laid off public employees. If these free market measures caused the greatest harm to the most vulnerable members of society, currency devaluations spread the pain more broadly, reducing profits on exports and increasing the cost of imports critical to development. Externally imposed reforms also disrupted longstanding patronage networks as retrenched soldiers and civil servants lost access to state resources. Although some elites benefited from privatization measures by snatching up state-owned enterprises, others were forced to seek new sources of income and power. Like the rulers of these weakened states, some ousted elites partnered with foreign entities, engaging in illicit economic activities such as money laundering and drug, weapons, and minerals trafficking. Some became warlords whose power was rooted in their control over commercial networks and the populations that produced the wealth.

Foreign policies and practices in Africa during the Cold War had much to do with this troubling scenario, and the United States bore a major share of the responsibility. During the four decades of U.S.-Soviet competition, anticolonial nationalists, prodemocracy activists, and issues of good governance and development were ignored or opposed if they interfered with U.S. strategic interests. No regime was deemed too corrupt or repressive for American support so long as it allied with the United States in the Cold War. However, with the disintegration of the Soviet Union and the end of the Cold War, the United States cut loose many of its longtime clients. Without American military and economic aid, repressive governments were vulnerable to the pressures of popular movements agitating against poverty, oppression, and corruption. As dictators were driven from power in the 1990s, either by popular democratic forces or by armed insurrection, a number of countries lapsed into violent conflict. Unstable nation-states were flooded with weapons left over from the Cold War. In many instances, warlords stepped into the void, manipulating ethnicity, clan, or religion to establish new bases of power, while neighboring countries intervened to support proxy forces that would allow them to gain control over lucrative resources. The cases of Liberia, Somalia, Sudan, and Zaire, discussed here, are emblematic of many others.

Liberia

A virtual colony since its founding by freed American slaves in the early nineteenth century, Liberia was a vital U.S. Cold War ally. For 133 years, Americo-Liberian settlers and their descendants, who constituted a mere 5 percent of the population, monopolized power and imposed a near feudal system on the indigenous population. In exchange for their services as regional policemen, a succession of Americo-Liberian dictators received substantial U.S. military and economic support. President William Tubman, who ruled Liberia from 1944 to 1971, built a powerful network of secret police and regarded the public treasury as his private bank. During his reign, the United States built or enhanced a number of important facilities in Liberia: a Voice of America relay station, which broadcast American propaganda throughout Africa, the Middle East, and Southeast Asia; the Omega navigation station, which facilitated shipping along the West African coast; a critical CIA listening post; and Roberts Field, where American military planes landed and refueled on twenty-four hours' notice.

During the presidency of William Tolbert (1971–80), deteriorating economic conditions culminated in the rice riots of 1979. After Tolbert announced a major price increase in the dietary staple, unarmed protesters took to the streets. Police opened fire, killing at least forty and injuring hundreds more. As unrest mounted, dissidents in the Liberian army, led by Master Sergeant Samuel Doe, a member of the indigenous Krahn ethnic group, overthrew the Tolbert regime. Described as a strike against repressive Americo-Liberian rule, the coup d'état was initially applauded in Liberia and elsewhere. However, in short order, Doe suspended the constitution, declared martial law, banned political activities, and imprisoned or executed his rivals.

During his decade in power, Doe continued his predecessors' corrupt practices, as he and his associates stole some $300 million from public coffers.

Throughout this period, Liberia remained one of America's most important African allies. During the Reagan administration, Liberia served as a staging ground for a CIA task force operating against Qaddafi's Libya, which the United States had designated a "state sponsor of terrorism."[3] The United States upgraded Roberts Field, which, along with the Kamina and Kinshasa air bases in Zaire, served as a key transit point for covert aid to the Angolan rebel movement, UNITA. In return, the Doe regime received enormous financial support. In 1982, Liberia was the largest per capita recipient of U.S. aid in sub-Saharan Africa. It received nearly $500 million in military and economic aid from 1980 to 1985 – amounting to one-third of its operating budget.

In 1985, General Thomas Quiwonkpa, whom Doe had removed from his position as commanding general of the Liberian armed forces, attempted another coup d'état. Whereas most of the president's associates were members of his Krahn ethnic group, Quiwonkpa was of Gio origin. Doe responded to the failed coup with a brutal crackdown on the Gio and related Mano populations. When the reprisals were over, as many as 3,000 people were dead. With Washington standing behind Doe and all moderate opposition quashed, warlords seized on popular anger. The most notorious of these was Charles Taylor, an American-educated member of the Americo-Liberian elite. In December 1989, Taylor and his Libyan-trained rebels in the National Patriotic Front of Liberia (NPFL) launched an attack from Côte d'Ivoire. Exploiting the rage of the brutalized Gio and Mano civilians, Taylor distributed weapons to alienated young men – including hundreds of boys whose parents had been killed in government raids. These recruits formed the first Small Boy Units – child soldiers, emboldened by drugs, who were urged to seek revenge against the Krahn and Mandingo populations. While Krahn soldiers had been responsible for many of the anti-Gio and Mano atrocities, Mandingos – who were primarily traders and small-scale entrepreneurs and possessed 60 percent of Liberia's wealth – were targeted for having prospered under the Doe regime. Taylor also stoked religious hatred, encouraging Christian

---

[3] The criteria for and consequences of the designation "state sponsor of terrorism" can be found on the State Department website, http://www.state.gov/j/ct/list/c14151.htm.

Liberians to attack Mandingos because they were Muslim. His crusade eventually attracted high-profile support from leaders of the American religious right. In the meantime, Doe's American-trained army responded to the rebel invasion with a brutal counterinsurgency campaign against Gio and Mano civilians. American Navy ships staffed with more than 2,000 Marines evacuated American citizens and other foreigners but refused to intervene to stop the slaughter, characterizing it an internal Liberian affair.

While the U.S. armed forces stood by, neighboring countries entered the fray, driven by diverse motives. As members of the Economic Community of West African States (ECOWAS), Nigeria, Ghana, Guinea, Sierra Leone, and Gambia were united in their desire for regional stability. Specific national interests were also at stake. Nigeria, under pressure to protect Liberian Muslims, demonstrated its regional dominance by leading the ECOWAS action. Ghana intensified its involvement to counter Nigerian domination. Guinea was also worried about the fate of Liberian Muslims, many of whom had Guinean business and family ties. Sierra Leone and Gambia were troubled by Taylor's recruitment and training of their own dissident nationals, whom he had incorporated into his rebel forces. In August 1990, ECOWAS sent troops to Monrovia to effect a ceasefire. Operating under the name Economic Community Monitoring Group (ECOMOG), the 4,000-man force – which rose to 16,000 three years later – was led by Nigeria and Ghana, with important contributions from Guinea and, to a lesser extent, Sierra Leone and Gambia. The ECOMOG intervention was strongly supported by the United States, which provided significant financial and diplomatic resources.

The prominent roles played by the United States and English-speaking African countries contributed to a new set of problems. France considered the ECOMOG operation further proof of Anglophone attempts to usurp its "traditional" sphere of influence in West Africa. French protégés in the region were hostile to American influence in Liberia and threatened by Nigeria's growing power. Burkina Faso and Côte d'Ivoire countered Anglophone dominance by supporting Taylor's rebel movement. President Blaise Compaoré (Burkina Faso) helped equip Taylor's men, allowed them to traverse his country en route to and from Libya, and sent Burkinabe soldiers to fight alongside Taylor's forces. President Félix Houphouët-Boigny (Côte d'Ivoire) allowed Taylor to use his country as a rear base and transfer point for weapons sent from Burkina Faso. Moreover, Ivoirian government officials and entrepreneurs made enormous profits by supplying Taylor with weapons and facilitating the illicit export of diamonds, gold, iron ore, timber, and rubber to finance his war effort.

As the peacekeeping operation floundered, Taylor further internationalized the war in March 1991 by opening a second front in Sierra Leone, where Joseph Momoh's government threatened his supply route. To undermine his nemesis, Taylor helped to organize, train, and equip a Sierra Leonean rebel organization, the Revolutionary United Front (RUF). Led by Taylor protégé Corporal Foday Sankoh, the RUF modeled its strategy and tactics on those of the NPFL. The rebels press-ganged boys and girls into RUF forces, where they were used as soldiers, porters, miners, cooks, and sex slaves. Brutalized RUF recruits were taught to abduct, rape, amputate, and kill, terrorizing the Sierra Leonean countryside. They killed chiefs, elders, traders, and agricultural development workers – anyone who was prosperous or associated with the Sierra Leonean government.

Meanwhile, in Liberia, it had become clear that ECOMOG was part of the problem. Although touted as a stabilizing force, ECOMOG soldiers sucked the country dry, absconding with railway cars, mining equipment, trucks, and natural resources – anything they could sell abroad. Unable to beat Taylor outright, ECOMOG had encouraged the establishment of new rebel groups and provided them with arms in exchange for booty. Because they profited from the prolongation of the war, ECOWAS countries could not be counted on to end it.

The most important of the anti-Taylor rebel movements was the United Liberation Movement of Liberia for Democracy (ULIMO), which was founded in 1991 by exiled Doe supporters. Although ULIMO included both Mandingos and Krahns, the Krahns were dominant. Within a year, ULIMO fractured as Mandingos and Krahns began killing one another. Nigeria formed alliances with Krahn warlords, while Guinea supported their Mandingo counterparts. Guinean government officials also engaged in diamond and arms trafficking, profiting from strong ties between Guinean and Liberian Mandingo traders who smuggled Liberian diamonds and foreign weapons across the porous border.[4]

By the early 1990s, the Liberian war was no longer primarily ethnic in character – it was a free-for-all among warlords, their

---

[4] In Guinea, the Mandingo are called the Malinke.

personal followers, and external backers, with plunder as its goal. For the remainder of the decade, Liberia was run by organized criminal gangs that controlled its vast mineral resources, timber, and rubber. During his warlord years, Taylor is estimated to have amassed a personal fortune worth nearly half a billion dollars. Diverse interests in Europe, the United States, and Japan bribed Taylor for the right to illegally exploit Liberian resources. French firms were particularly egregious in this regard. By 1991, NPFL-controlled areas served as France's third-largest source of tropical timber, and Taylor allowed a French company to assume control of the world's largest iron mine.

By 1995, Taylor realized that he could not become president of Liberia without Nigerian backing. Making peace with the regional powerhouse, Taylor signed an accord in August 1995 and was installed as Liberia's de facto ruler. Two years later, he was elected president by voters who feared that his defeat would mean a return to war. However, the killing did not stop. By the late 1990s, at least seven rebel factions were operating in Liberia. All had external backers, some of which were simultaneously providing soldiers to the ECOMOG "peacekeeping" forces. The rebels mimicked the NPFL in both method and objectives, engaging in massive human rights abuses against the civilian population as they plundered the country's riches.

By April 2003, rebel factions had seized 60 percent of Liberia, including most of its diamond-mining areas. During the ensuing siege of Monrovia, hundreds of civilians were killed and hundreds of thousands were forced to flee. Throughout the month of July, UN officials, African heads of state, and European diplomats urged the United States, as the de facto former imperial power, to take the lead in ending the crisis. Ignoring the long history of American support for a succession of oppressive Liberian regimes, the George W. Bush administration charged that Liberia was the responsibility of its West African neighbors and the UN – not the United States. As the battle for Liberia wound down, Washington remained largely on the sidelines. In August, Taylor resigned and accepted refuge in Nigeria. The following week, the warring parties signed a peace agreement that provided for an interim government, elections, and a new national army that incorporated both rebel and government soldiers.

The war was over, but the cost had been enormous. In the wars that had consumed the country since the 1980 coup, at least 250,000 Liberians had died, more than a million had been displaced, and tens of thousands of women and girls had been raped. The country's infrastructure and economy were devastated, and three-quarters of the population were living on less than one dollar a day. The country's $3.7 billion debt, much of it incurred by the Doe and Taylor regimes, was worth almost eight times the value of its annual gross domestic product.

Somalia

Across the continent in Somalia, another American client was also consumed by civil strife. During the Cold War, Siad Barre's regime had stifled political dissent and divided the opposition by encouraging clan rivalry. By the late 1980s, the divide-and-rule strategy had backfired. Clan-based militias and Islamic militants, who had been repressed by the Siad Barre dictatorship, began to compete for power. The regime cracked down hard, killing thousands of dissidents across the country. With the Soviet Union in dire straits, the Somali alliance was no longer critical to the United States. Washington distanced itself from the Somali dictator.

Without American support, Siad Barre was extremely vulnerable. In January 1991, the Hawiye clan–dominated United Somali Congress, led by former cabinet minister General Mohamed Farah Aideed, overthrew the Siad Barre regime. The congress's Ali Mahdi Mohamed was elected interim president. In 1991–92, a war between the Aideed and Ali Mahdi factions destroyed much of Mogadishu. As the central state collapsed, the formal economy ceased to function, and southern Somalia disintegrated into fiefdoms ruled by rival warlords and their militias. The war resulted in some 20,000 civilian casualties and one million displaced people.

One year after Siad Barre's ouster, the UN began to respond to the Somali crisis. In January 1992, the Security Council imposed an arms embargo, which prohibited the delivery of any weapons or military equipment to Somalia. Two UN military missions followed. In April, the United Nations Operation in Somalia (UNOSOM I) was established to monitor a ceasefire and to escort and protect aid convoys. However, the UN operation was of little help to thousands of starving Somalis. Warlords, who controlled Mogadishu's port and airport, confiscated food aid and manipulated supplies for political ends, doling it out to their supporters, denying it to those who opposed them, and selling the remainder to purchase weapons. In December, the

Security Council authorized the establishment of the multinational United Task Force (UNITAF) to work with UNOSOM I to secure ports, airports, warehouses, feeding centers, and roads so humanitarian relief could be delivered. The United States announced that it would take the lead in the task force action, which it dubbed "Operation Restore Hope." The UNITAF endeavor, which involved 28,000 American troops as well as personnel from other countries, operated under a narrow mandate. It was not authorized to disarm or demobilize warring parties, to confiscate heavy weapons, or to intervene to stop fighting between rival groups. Its mission was solely to ensure the delivery of humanitarian relief to the civilian population. This continued to be the public face of the mission even after the American role had changed substantially.

Both UNITAF and UNOSOM I concluded in May 1993 and were followed by UNOSOM II, which was also led by the United States. Comprising 18,000 peacekeepers, including 4,200 Americans, UNOSOM II was assigned a mission that was far removed from the traditional UN peacekeeping role. Believing that mass starvation could be averted only if local militias were neutralized, the UN leadership prescribed a course of action that included the forcible disarmament of Somali militias, particularly that of Mohamed Farah Aideed.

Tension between the UN and Aideed broke to the surface on June 5, when Aideed's militia ambushed and killed two dozen Pakistani peacekeepers who were attempting to inspect his radio station and weapons depots. The Security Council quickly expanded UNOSOM II's mandate, authorizing it to arrest, detain, try, and punish those responsible for the killings. Having moved from the original mission of protecting aid convoys and relief workers to capturing, disarming, and punishing one faction in the fighting, the UN crossed the line from humanitarian intervention to choosing sides in a deadly conflict. As the mission's chief advocate and leader, the United States had become deeply embroiled in Somalia's civil war.

On June 11–17, American soldiers manning AC-130 gunships and Cobra and Black Hawk helicopters attacked several Mogadishu compounds believed to hold weapons caches, as well as the radio station Aideed used to direct his militias and denounce the UN. UN troops fired on the angry crowds that poured into the streets, killing and maiming a large number of civilians. In July, a similar airborne force assaulted clan elders, religious leaders, intellectuals, and businessmen who were meeting to consider a UN peace initiative.

Sixteen prominent members of Aideed's party and dozens of others were killed, including many who opposed Aideed's stance and anxiously sought peace. The massacre generated strong anti-UN and anti-American sentiment among a population that had welcomed the international humanitarian mission only a year before. In the view of many Somalis, the United States and the UN had declared war; their soldiers were now perceived as an occupation force. Violent retaliation was directed at all foreigners, causing numerous relief organizations to withdraw their operations.

Although the delivery of food aid was the priority of American soldiers during the fall of 1992, it was not their objective one year later. From late August to early October 1993, the American armed forces were bent on capturing or killing Aideed and his top lieutenants. The final raid took place on October 3, 1993, when 120 elite U.S. Army Rangers and Delta Force troops attempted to capture key leaders of Aideed's militia in one of Mogadishu's most dangerous neighborhoods. The militia shot down two Black Hawk helicopters, which crashed into children in the streets below. Angry crowds attacked the soldiers who survived the crash and those who came to rescue them. In the fighting that ensued, eighteen American soldiers and some 500 Somali men, women, and children were killed. Within days, President Clinton announced that all U.S. troops would be withdrawn from Somalia by the end of March 1994. Without American backing, the UN was forced to terminate its operation. However, foreign intervention and internal strife continued to plague Somalia. Nearly two decades after the American and UN withdrawal, Somalia still lacked a functioning central government. The ongoing conflict attracted the attention of neighboring Ethiopia, which, with American support, invaded and occupied Somalia in 2006–9 in an attempt to install a compliant government; and of al-Qaeda, an international terrorist network that harnessed Somali anger at the violation of national sovereignty to its own quest for global jihad.

Sudan

From 1976 until the end of the Cold War, Sudan, like Liberia and Somalia, was an important American client. During the Carter years, Sudan was the largest beneficiary of U.S. aid in sub-Saharan Africa. The Reagan administration bolstered military aid to Khartoum in order to counter Qaddafi's expansion into East Africa and Soviet influence in Ethiopia. Similarly concerned about Qaddafi's designs on western Sudan and Soviet interest in the Horn, President Jaafar Nimeiri allowed the United States to use Sudan as a base for covert operations against Libya and as a regional center of operations during the Cold War. In exchange for American largesse, Nimeiri permitted the U.S. Army's Rapid Deployment Force, charged with protecting vital American interests in the Persian Gulf, to operate from Sudan.

Nimeiri also sought support from conservative Arab governments and turned to Sudanese Islamists in an attempt to strengthen his wavering domestic support.[5] In 1983, his government imposed Islamic law (sharia) throughout the country, sparking the resumption of a civil war that had long pitted the Muslim north against the predominantly Christian and animist south. Spearheaded by the Sudan People's Liberation Movement (SPLM), the southern struggle called for an end to northern and Islamic dominance and demanded greater southern control over the country's oil and mineral wealth, most of which was produced in the south. The SPLM's Marxist language and support from the Soviet Union, Cuba, and Ethiopia gave the United States the excuse it needed to continue its support for the Nimeiri regime.

The enormous costs of war, compounded by the worldwide economic crisis, triggered an economic meltdown in Sudan that was characterized by rising food and fuel prices, famine, and massive external debt. An IMF-imposed austerity program, implemented in exchange for new loans, resulted in protests, strikes, and, finally, the 1985 military coup that overthrew the Nimeiri regime. Following a brief return to civilian rule, Colonel Omar al-Bashir staged another military coup, toppling the civilian government in 1989.

Rising to power in the waning years of the Cold War, Bashir was more concerned about establishing his Islamist credentials at home and abroad than maintaining a relationship with the United States. He opened the country to radicals from across the Muslim world, including hundreds of mujahideen veterans of the 1979–89 Soviet-Afghan War, many of whom had been funded, trained, and equipped by the CIA.[6] Among these CIA protégés was Osama bin Laden, a Saudi

---

[5] Promoters of "political Islam" or "Islamism" believe that Islamic precepts should serve as the basis of the social and political order as well the personal lives of individual Muslims. They strive to establish Islamic as opposed to secular states.

[6] The Arabic term *mujahideen* is the plural of *mujahid* – that is, one who wages jihad, or holy war.

leader of the Afghan resistance and founder of al-Qaeda, an international terrorist network whose goal was to install Islamist governments throughout the Muslim world. Bin Laden established al-Qaeda training camps in Sudan and a network of cells and allied organizations that extended to nearly a dozen countries in East Africa and the Horn.

In 1991, the Soviet Union collapsed and the Ethiopian dictator, Mengistu Haile Mariam, was driven from power. The new Ethiopian government became Washington's strongest regional ally, while relations with Sudan deteriorated rapidly. In August 1993, the U.S. State Department designated Sudan a "state sponsor of terrorism" and imposed financial sanctions and an arms embargo. Following a 1995 assassination attempt against Egyptian President Hosni Mubarak, a staunch American ally, Washington supported the imposition of UN sanctions against Sudan, which was accused of harboring the culprits. Under enormous pressure from the United States, Saudi Arabia, and the UN Security Council, Khartoum expelled bin Laden and his al-Qaeda network from Sudan in 1996. Washington barred American businesses and nongovernmental organizations from working with the Sudanese government, prohibited the transfer of bank loans and technology, and seized Sudanese assets in the United States. However, the Clinton administration was convinced that Khartoum's links to al-Qaeda persisted. In August 1998, after al-Qaeda operatives bombed the U.S. embassies in Kenya and Tanzania, American missiles destroyed a Sudanese factory outside Khartoum. Although Washington charged that bin Laden was manufacturing chemical weapons components on the premises, independent investigators found no credible evidence to support the claim. Rather, they determined that the facility had been a pharmaceutical factory that produced the majority of Sudan's major medications, including veterinary, tuberculosis, and malaria drugs.

Increasingly isolated at home and abroad, Bashir was desperate for allies and international respectability. He desired an end to economic sanctions, which would open the door to foreign investment in Sudan's emerging oil industry and help pay down the country's $22 billion debt. Toward this end, Bashir sidelined some of his more radical Islamic associates, who were threatening his position both internally and externally, and began to cooperate with American counterterrorism initiatives. Following al-Qaeda's attacks on the United States in September 2001, this collaboration increased significantly. At Washington's request, the Bashir regime arrested foreign Islamists transiting Sudan and delivered them to the United States, helped the United States capture al-Qaeda operatives in Somalia, and permitted U.S. Special Operations Forces to detain alleged terrorists on Sudanese soil. However, as a result of Khartoum's ongoing atrocities against civilians in southern Sudan and, from 2003, in the Darfur region, Washington refused to lift sanctions or remove Sudan from its list of state sponsors of terrorism.[7]

Zaire

Bordering nine countries in a mineral-rich, strategic region, Zaire (formerly the Congo) was the largest, most populous country in Francophone Africa. During the Cold War, it served as a regional policeman for both the United States and France, which joined Belgium as major lenders and donors. All three countries helped the Mobutu regime quash antigovernment insurgencies in the 1970s. Mobutu allowed the United States to use the Kamina air base in Shaba Province to train and supply UNITA rebels, while Washington provided Zaire with more than $1 billion in military and economic aid between 1961 and 1990 and pressured the IMF and the World Bank to grant loans, reschedule debts, and relax lending conditions. Hoping to counter the regional influence of Anglophone Uganda, France also provided Zaire with generous loans, military hardware, and military training.

Like his counterparts in other American client states, Mobutu stood at the pinnacle of a corrupt patronage system. He treated Zaire's vast mineral resources, parastatal companies, central bank, and tax offices as his own and distributed the proceeds to family members and loyalists. During his thirty-two-year reign, he amassed a personal fortune worth an estimated $5 billion–$8 billion while Zaire's economy was ravaged by plummeting copper prices, food shortages, inflation, and an external debt that reached $10.2 billion in 1990. As the Cold War waned, Mobutu and his collapsing state were abandoned by important foreign sponsors. In 1990, Belgium ceased all military and economic assistance. In 1991, the United States suspended its aid programs, the IMF barred Zaire from receiving further loans, and the World Bank withdrew support for the country's development projects.

---

[7] Following a peace accord in 2005 and a popular referendum in January 2011, South Sudan became an independent state in July 2011. However, violent conflict between north and south continued.

As Mobutu's hold weakened, internal prodemocracy forces exerted enormous pressure on the regime. However, it was an externally backed insurgency that finally drove Mobutu from power. The insurgency and its aftermath were intimately linked to the 1994 Rwandan genocide, which had claimed some 800,000 lives. A longtime supporter of Rwanda's Hutu extremist regime, Mobutu opened Zaire's borders to more than a million Rwandan Hutus who fled the advancing RPF – the Uganda-backed Tutsi army that had stopped the genocide. Perpetrators of the genocide quickly asserted their dominance over the UN-administered refugee camps, controlling the distribution of food, medicine, and other humanitarian aid, while relief agencies paid them kickbacks as the price of doing business. Mobutu turned a blind eye as camp leaders trafficked in arms, conscripted and trained military cadres, and conducted raids into RPF-governed Rwanda. Mobutu's soldiers joined Hutu extremists in ethnically cleansing eastern Zaire, displacing tens of thousands of indigenous Tutsis and killing thousands more.

The anti-Tutsi pogroms and the security threat posed by Hutu extremists on the Rwandan border led to the First Congo War (1996–97), which would eventually embroil most countries in the Great Lakes region. Rwanda, Uganda, and, to a lesser extent, Burundi pushed their own agendas in Zaire – at great cost to the indigenous population. In October 1996, the Rwandan army launched a raid into Zaire to destroy UN refugee camps and to encourage Zairian Tutsis to rebel. The Alliance of Democratic Forces for the Liberation of Congo-Zaire (AFDL) was established a few weeks later. Rather than emerging from the local milieu, the rebel army was created by longtime Zairian exiles backed by the Rwandan government. It was trained, equipped, and led by the Rwandan army, and its spokesman, Laurent Kabila, was handpicked by the Kigali regime.

By November, the AFDL and its Rwandan backers controlled the borderlands from Uganda to Burundi. They quickly defeated Zaire's undisciplined army, which raped, looted, and killed as it retreated, and emptied the refugee camps, forcing as many as 700,000 Hutus back into Rwanda. Another 300,000 Hutus fled westward into the Zairian rainforest, pursued by AFDL and Rwandan forces, which slaughtered men, women, and children, making no distinction between former soldiers, government officials, and militia members, and innocent Hutu civilians. The response from the international community was muted, and the UN Security Council remained on the sidelines. Although France called for humanitarian and military intervention, Rwanda, Uganda, and the United States rejected its call. Paris's preoccupation with its loss of influence to Anglophone countries and its previous support for the Hutu extremist regime in Rwanda weakened its claim of humanitarian concern. Moreover, officials in the United States and Britain, remorseful for having failed to act in 1994, refused to countenance criticism of the RPF, which had halted the genocide as the world community stood by.

The war quickly became a regional one. As Kabila's rebel forces moved north and west, the Ugandan army moved in to assist them. As they approached Angola, UNITA guerrillas teamed up with Mobutu's army, drawing the MPLA government into war on the side of the AFDL. In response, Mobutu recruited European, South African, and Angolan mercenaries to bolster his undisciplined forces. Zaire's third-largest city, Kisangani, fell to the rebels in March 1997. A few days later, the rebels took Mbuji-Mayi, capital of the diamond-mining province of East Kasai, from which the government drew much of its revenue. In April, the AFDL arrived in Lubumbashi, Zaire's second largest city. Capital of the Shaba Province, Lubumbashi stood at the center of the country's copper and cobalt production.[8] American, Canadian, and South African mining interests initiated contacts with the AFDL. Zambia allowed the rebels to launch attacks from its territory, and Zimbabwe provided them with military equipment. By the middle of April 1997, Kabila, his army, and his foreign backers controlled all of Zaire's sources of revenue and foreign exchange.

Of Mobutu's many Western allies, only France supported him to the bitter end. The United States stood by while its longtime protégé floundered, ignoring pleas even for humanitarian intervention. In the final weeks, the Clinton administration urged Mobutu to step down. France, in contrast, embarked on a covert operation on the dictator's behalf. Vehemently opposed to Kabila, whom Paris considered a Ugandan proxy furthering Anglophone interests, Paris provided the Zairian regime with combat aircraft, pilots,

---

[8] During Mobutu's rule, the names of several cities and provinces were changed. Léopoldville became Kinshasa; Stanleyville became Kisangani; Elisabethville became Lubumbashi; Bakwanga became Mbuji-Mayi; and Katanga Province became Shaba. The rebellious province of South Kasai, which had rejected central government authority from 1960 to 1962, included parts of the provinces later known as East and West Kasai. Bakwanga (later Mbuji-Mayi) was the capital of both South and East Kasai.

and mechanics – as well as hundreds of French, Belgian, Serbian, Ukrainian, and South African mercenaries.

On May 17, 1997, Mobutu fled the country. Zairian soldiers, whose wages had been pocketed by their officers, refused to risk their lives to defend the capital, and the AFDL took Kinshasa without a fight. Kabila immediately declared himself president and changed the country's name to the Democratic Republic of Congo (DRC). He rejected the notion of a broad-based coalition government and refused to work with the internal opposition that had resisted Mobutu for years. Following Mobutu's lead, he outlawed opposition parties, prohibited public demonstrations, imprisoned opponents, and ruled by decree. Like Mobutu, Kabila ran the country through this relatives and cronies, among whom he divided the spoils. Nonetheless, the United States immediately rallied to Kabila and blocked UN Security Council condemnation of his regime.

The Second Congo War began in 1998, initiating more than a decade of violence and upheaval that claimed some 5.4 million lives, a 2002 peace agreement notwithstanding. Eight of the nine Great Lakes countries joined what came to be known as Africa's First World War – with only Tanzania refraining. During this round, Rwanda, Uganda, and Burundi turned on Kabila, disgruntled by his growing reluctance to follow their instructions. Determined to install a compliant regime that would allow them to protect their borders and divert DRC resources for their own development, Kabila's neighbors conspired to overthrow him. They backed disparate Congolese rebel factions with little popular support, including Congolese Tutsis linked to the Rwandan government, Mobutu cronies who hoped to return to power, disappointed office seekers denied positions in Kabila's government, and leftist intellectuals disenchanted with Kabila's corrupt personal rule.

As Rwanda, Uganda, and Burundi sought to undermine Kabila, a dozen African nations came to his rescue. Zimbabwe, Angola, and Namibia cited the Southern African Development Community (SADC) security pact as the basis for their intervention.[9] Zimbabwe sent 12,000 troops, funding its war effort with the DRC's own resources. Although Zimbabwe had no legitimate claim to security concerns in the DRC, it did have economic interests. Kabila was

---

[9] SADCC was reformulated as SADC in 1992, eventually broadening its membership to include fifteen African countries.

indebted to Zimbabwe for military equipment and supplies delivered during the 1996–97 war, and Zimbabwe was anxious for repayment. Moreover, the Zimbabwean regime hoped that unfettered access to the DRC's riches would appease powerful domestic constituencies that might otherwise protest their own government's failed policies. Zimbabwean political, economic, and military elites thus plundered the country's copper and cobalt wealth while Zimbabwean soldiers looted diamonds from Kasai and stashed profits from the illicit diamond trade in their private coffers.

If Zimbabwe did not have security interests in the DRC, Angola did. The MPLA government was anxious to protect Angola's oil and diamond regions, especially the oil-rich Cabinda Enclave, which was separated from the bulk of Angola by a wedge of Congolese territory. The Luanda government was concerned about collaboration between UNITA and anti-Kabila forces in western DRC, the threat of renewed attacks from Congolese soil, and UNITA's illegal mining of Congolese diamonds to finance its war against the MPLA. Beyond these immediate concerns, Angola was disturbed by the growing power of Uganda and Rwanda in the Central African region and their support for rebel forces that included Mobutu stalwarts. Namibia's concerns dovetailed with those of both Angola and Zimbabwe. Like Angola, Namibia was anxious to weaken UNITA, which supported a secessionist movement in the Caprivi Strip, while Namibian elites, like those in Zimbabwe, had developed extensive mining interests in the DRC.

Reminiscent of the Belgian colonial rulers in another era, the Great Lakes countries bled the DRC dry. The UN Security Council charged Rwanda, Uganda, and Burundi with the systematic looting of the country and implicated Zimbabwe in the depredations. Together with Congolese officials and rebel warlords, these countries stole billions of dollars worth of diamonds, gold, coltan, cobalt, copper, tin, timber, and cash crops. The wealth extracted from the eastern war zone was transmitted into the global economy through Rwanda and Uganda and used to finance their own development. From 1996 to 2009, Rwanda controlled the mineral-rich provinces of North and South Kivu – effectively integrating them into its domestic economy. In the same vein, Ugandan soldiers took control of gold-bearing regions in the east and forced the local population to extract the gold for Ugandan interests. Following the signing of peace accords in 2002, Rwanda and Uganda withdrew from the DRC but supported rebel proxies who continued to battle for control of the mines and trade routes.

The Global War on Terror (2001–10)

During the first post–Cold War decade, Africa was low on America's radar screen, even as former clients like Liberia, Somalia, Sudan, and Zaire descended into chaos. After the September 2001 terrorist attacks on the United States, however, existing policy was reevaluated. Economic deprivation and political chaos concerned the United States anew. Impoverished nations with weak state apparatuses were viewed as potential breeding grounds for political extremism – which during this era was understood to be terrorism rather than communism. As a result, Washington again sought to strengthen military alliances, provide financial assistance and training, and open military bases in dozens of African countries. The George W. Bush administration's "global war on terror" became the new anticommunism.

Just as domestic insurgencies sparked by local grievances were mistaken for "communist aggression" during the Cold War, the vague rubric of "international terrorism" was used to explain a range of civil disturbances in the early twenty-first century. African dictators who had appealed to the West by playing up the communist menace were replaced by a new generation of strongmen who won support by cooperating in the fight against terrorism. American foreign assistance became increasingly militarized. The Pentagon assumed responsibility for many humanitarian and development assistance programs previously under civilian authority, and the human security and human rights agenda of the U.S. Agency for International Development (USAID) was eclipsed by the counterterrorism program of the Defense Department. As war and instability engulfed the Middle East, America's access to its traditional sources of foreign oil were threatened. By the early twenty-first century, the United States had revised its Africa policy to focus on countries rich in oil and natural gas and those considered critical to the American war on terror.

Since September 2001, a cohort of American policy-makers have warned that "Islamic terrorism" is threatening American lives and security. However, the appellation is more confusing than enlightening. The Islamic groups designated "foreign terrorist organizations" by the U.S. secretary of state include diverse movements, organizations, cells, and individuals.[10] Many have local origins and grievances

---

[10] The criteria for and consequences of the designation "foreign terrorist organization" can be found on the website of the National Counterterrorism Center, http://www. nctc.gov/site/other/fto.html.

that have little if anything to do with the United States. However, the American security establishment has tended to view them as part of a vast, monolithic global conspiracy. As a result, the U.S. Special Operations Command, which coordinates the covert operations of all branches of the U.S. Armed Forces, has engaged in counterterrorism activities that have alienated local populations and undermined Washington's long-term security interests. In 2006, for instance, the CIA enlisted warlords in its fight against terror suspects on Somali soil, while U.S. Special Operations Forces participated in the Ethiopian invasion of Somalia that removed the popular Islamic Courts Union from power and sparked an antiforeign insurgency. The insurgency provided an opportunity for international terrorist organizations like al-Qaeda to embrace local Islamist groups that previously had been independent.

Hostility toward the West – and particularly the United States – stems from a number of issues. Many Muslims have been angered by the presence of American troops in Saudi Arabia, site of the holy cities of Mecca and Medina; the wars in Afghanistan, Iraq, and Somalia, which have resulted in the killing of hundreds of thousands of Muslims; and the decades-long plight of Palestinians in Israeli-occupied territories. Other Muslims resent American exploitation of Middle Eastern and African oil and U.S. support for repressive regimes that violently suppress local populations. From Egypt to Tunisia, Algeria, and Morocco, U.S.-allied governments have banned Islamic fundamentalist parties and arrested thousands of militants. In some instances, homegrown guerrilla organizations emerged from the outlawed parties. Only later did al-Qaeda seize the opportunity and offer its support.

The global war on terror radically transformed longstanding American practices. Among the first casualties was a decades-old ban on foreign political assassinations. In 1975, the U.S. Senate's Select Committee to Study Governmental Operations with Respect to Intelligence Activities published an in-depth investigation of American involvement in the assassination of foreign leaders. In response, President Ford issued a 1976 executive order that forbid U.S. government involvement in political assassinations abroad. For more than twenty-five years, this directive remained U.S. policy – at least, officially. However, shortly after the September 2001 attacks, President Bush issued an order that permitted the CIA and the Pentagon to ignore the assassinations ban and to capture or kill al-Qaeda militants worldwide. In the spring of 2004, the Bush administration authorized the U.S. Special Operations Command to conduct covert military operations to capture or kill suspected terrorist leaders anywhere in the world. The executive order granted U.S. forces the authority to engage in such activities in countries that were not at war with the United States – and without those countries' consent. The Pentagon subsequently sent Special Operations troops into African and Asian nations to collect intelligence and to capture or kill alleged terrorists – a practice that continued under the Obama administration. Repressive regimes played up the international terrorist threat as a means of obtaining American funds and military assistance – just as their predecessors exaggerated the communist menace during the Cold War. Security forces trained and financed by the United States were used to crack down on internal opposition and to fight regional wars. Rather than winning hearts and minds, American intervention often rendered local populations even more susceptible to the appeals of international terrorist organizations.

The new focus on counterterrorism also resulted in a surge of American military activity in Africa. East Africa and the Horn constituted Washington's first African front in the global war on terror. In 2002, a U.S. military base was established at Camp Lemonnier, Djibouti – the first American base to be opened in Africa since the Cold War. Strategically located at the juncture of the Red Sea and the Gulf of Aden – opposite Yemen and adjacent to Somalia – Camp Lemonnier was home to the new Combined Joint Task Force–Horn of Africa (CJTF-HOA), which included some 1,800 military and civilian personnel. CJTF-HOA's mission was to discover and destroy international terrorist networks in the Horn, East Africa, Yemen, and adjacent Indian Ocean islands. Toward that end, it conducted patrols of the Red Sea, Gulf of Aden, and Indian Ocean and assisted in training the military forces of Djibouti, Ethiopia, and Kenya. During the 2006 Ethiopian invasion of Somalia, the CJTF-HOA provided the Ethiopian army with satellite photos and other intelligence so it could locate Islamist fighters.

In 2003, the United States launched the East Africa Counterterrorism Initiative (EACTI), a $100 million program to combat terrorist activities in Kenya, Tanzania, Uganda, Eritrea, Ethiopia, and Djibouti. Personnel from these countries were trained in border, coastal, and aviation security and in general police work. EACTI also established programs to thwart money laundering and terrorist financing, as well as education programs to undermine the appeal of extremist ideologies. The United States counted on Ethiopia and Kenya to support its attacks on al-Qaeda suspects in Somalia, and U.S. Special Operations Forces launched numerous strikes from bases in those countries.

Washington identified the sparsely populated, lightly governed western Sahel as the second African front in the global war on terror. In 2002, the U.S. government launched the Pan-Sahel Initiative (PSI), which included Mauritania, Mali, Niger, and Chad. The PSI's mission was to coordinate and enhance border control against terrorist movement and arms and drug trafficking, which were believed to thrive in the Sahel's large "ungoverned" spaces. In 2005, the PSI program was extended and transformed into the five-year interagency Trans-Sahara Counterterrorism Initiative (TSCTI). Like its counterpart in East Africa, TSCTI's mission was to help countries with large Muslim populations curtail the proliferation of extremist ideologies and the appeal of terrorism by extending aid to the disaffected. TSCTI's military program, Operation Enduring Freedom–Trans Sahara (OEF-TS), provided equipment, logistical support, and training to regional forces in border control, rapid response capabilities, and terrorism prevention. Under these auspices, U.S. Special Operations Forces were widely reported to have engaged with their African counterparts in offensive operations as well as training operations. TSCTI's civil component included USAID programs to promote education and good governance; State Department programs to enhance airport security; Treasury Department aid to curb money laundering; and Federal Bureau of Investigation (FBI) assistance in tracking down illegal operatives. By 2010, the renamed Trans-Sahara Counterterrorism Partnership (TSCTP) included eleven North and West African countries, including Morocco, Algeria, Tunisia, Libya, Mauritania, Mali, Niger, Chad, Senegal, Nigeria, and Burkina Faso. A number of these countries joined the United States in military exercises, including Flintlock 2005, which was the largest joint military operation between the United States and Africa since World War II.

Washington's failure to understand the complex situation on the ground and its pursuit of short-term counterterrorism objectives over long-term human development goals embroiled American personnel in local conflicts that intensified anti-American feelings. Washington's bolstering of the Idriss Déby regime in Chad is a case in point. Notoriously repressive and corrupt – Transparency International designated Chad the world's sixth most corrupt country in 2010 – the military regime engaged in serious human rights abuses, including arbitrary arrests, torture, rape, and murder. Although foreign-backed rebels rather than international Islamic extremists were the regime's primary security threat, the United States justified its support on the grounds that it was helping Déby combat international terrorism. U.S. Army Special Forces trained Chadian military battalions, including one charged with protecting the Déby regime from a possible coup d'état. In essence, the United States helped a dictator maintain his hold on power under the guise of counterterrorism. U.S. military involvement in Mali and Niger also had unforeseen and problematic consequences. In 2007–8, U.S. Army Special Forces assisted the Malian government with combat support as it fought against a Tuareg insurgency that had emerged from local grievances, while American-trained troops in Niger engaged in atrocities against Tuareg civilians. Other consequences surfaced in March 2012, when Mali's democratically elected government was overthrown in a coup led by an American-trained army captain. Bolstered by weapons and fighters that had flooded Mali following the NATO-assisted overthrow of Qaddafi's Libyan regime in 2011, Tuareg rebels seized the opportunity presented by the coup to gain control of much of Mali's north and to announce the formation of a secessionist state. By June, Islamist factions, some of which were associated with Al-Qaeda in the Islamic Maghreb, had ousted the Tuareg nationalists and established a harsh regime that brutalized the civilian population.

Western diplomats, terrorism experts, and human rights organizations criticized American policies in the Sahel, charging that the terrorist threat in the region had been exaggerated. The vast majority of conflicts and insurgencies had local roots and little, if any, connection to international terrorist organizations. Many of the target groups blended religious fanaticism with illegal ventures such as drug and weapons trafficking, providing livelihoods to people with few alternatives. The dire political and economic conditions of Sahelian countries, long stricken by drought and famine, made it relatively easy for such groups to attract adherents. When U.S.-backed military operations removed their means of survival, Washington lost the battle to win their hearts and minds, and international terrorist organizations sometimes profited from the anger that ensued.

The capstone of America's increasingly militarized Africa policy was the U.S. Africa Command (AFRICOM). In February 2007, President Bush announced plans to create a unified military command that would oversee U.S. Army, Navy, Air Force, and Marine activities in Africa. This development was significant. During the Cold War and its aftermath, responsibility for American military activities on the continent had been divided between the European, Central, and Pacific Commands, attesting to Africa's adjunct status in the geopolitical arena. The European Command (EUCOM) had jurisdiction over forty-three African countries, most of which were in sub-Saharan Africa and all of which had been European colonies – with the exception of Liberia. The Central Command (CENTCOM) had jurisdiction over Egypt and the Horn, including Ethiopia, Eritrea, Somalia, Djibouti, Sudan, and Kenya, as well as the Middle East and Central Asia. The Pacific Command (USPACOM) covered the Asia-Pacific region, from the west coast of the United States to Madagascar, Seychelles, and the other Indian Ocean islands. Seen through the lens of U.S.-European relations or the Cold War, Africa as a self-contained entity was not high on the U.S. priority list. The establishment of AFRICOM was concrete evidence that Africa had migrated from the periphery to the core of American security concerns.

AFRICOM was also significant because of its new focus on interagency cooperation. Rooted in the security-development discourse that had come to characterize U.S. aid policy, AFRICOM's premise was that poverty, corruption, and failed states breed discontent and provide fertile ground for terrorism. To counter the threat effectively, the United States must link strategic and humanitarian interests. Stressing security, good governance, and development, AFRICOM's programs included personnel from the State Department and USAID as well as the Defense Department. However, Defense was by far the strongest partner in terms of resources and authority, and counterterrorism initiatives like CJTF-HOA and TSCTI continued to dominate AFRICOM's agenda.

Criticisms of AFRICOM have been many. As during the Cold War, target countries were chosen on the basis of political and economic interests, without regard for good governance or respect for democracy and human rights. AFRICOM's priorities were to secure American access to energy resources and to fight international terrorism. As a result, AFRICOM focused on countries that were rich in oil, natural gas, or uranium; in close proximity to strategic communications routes; or near sites of Islamist activities. Its detractors warned that if military priorities dominated the agenda, humanitarian initiatives would be suspect, and the long-term objective of winning hearts and minds would be undermined by short-term military considerations. They charged that AFRICOM had militarized police and development functions that were better left to civilian authorities. As the Pentagon took over humanitarian and development initiatives previously under the domain of USAID, soldiers engaged in activities for which they were not trained – and trained experts were shunted aside. Critics asserted that AFRICOM personnel frequently conflated local unrest with international terrorism and strengthened the military capacity of countries whose armed forces were used to attack civilians. In resource-rich countries, AFRICOM enhanced military capabilities without addressing the inequitable distribution of wealth, thereby harming rather than helping African peoples. Because American rather than African security concerns dominated the agenda, AFRICOM and its constituent programs risked intensifying rather than reducing international terrorist threats. These criticisms will bear ever greater scrutiny as U.S.-Africa policy evolves during the second decade of the twenty-first century.

Beyond the War on Terror

Despite their prominence in American military strategy, the global war on terror and the systematization of U.S. military involvement through AFRICOM were not the defining features of foreign military intervention in Africa during the first decade of the twenty-first century. This period witnessed a wide range of interventions, including bilateral operations by African and non-African countries and multilateral actions by global, continental, and regional organizations. In many cases, the lines between intervention on behalf of political and economic interests and those based on humanitarian and peacemaking concerns were blurred. A more detailed examination of these interventions and their implications is the subject of a future book, but it is worth noting here three of their most salient characteristics.[11]

First, with the formation of the African Union in 2002 and the expansion of regional organizations such as ECOWAS, SADC, and the Intergovernmental Authority on Development (IGAD), African international organizations, often in collaboration with UN or ad hoc

---

[11] See Elizabeth Schmidt, *From State Collapse to the War on Terror: Foreign Intervention in Africa after the Cold War* (Athens: Ohio University Press, in progress).

international initiatives, played a more prominent role in both diplomacy and peacekeeping efforts. Although African organizations could boast some success, their activities were frequently hampered by a lack of resources, discordant interests among the states involved, and problematic resolutions that opened the door to future conflict. In 2004, for instance, the African Union and IGAD worked with the UN and the European Union to establish a central government in Somalia, and the African Union contributed peacekeeping troops. However, the transitional government had virtually no support inside Somalia, and many Somalis considered the African Union troops to be unwelcome intruders. The African Union and IGAD also helped to negotiate the 2005 peace agreement that ended Sudan's civil war. However, the agreement was rife with unresolved problems, and it paved the way for further strife.[12] The African Union was also involved in attempts to settle the Darfur conflict in western Sudan. In 2004, it sent an underfunded and ill-equipped peacekeeping force to the region to monitor a ceasefire agreement. Three years later, the ineffective force was bolstered by an infusion of UN aid and the establishment of a joint African Union–UN mission. A peace agreement was signed in 2011, but it failed to include the most significant rebel groups, thus ensuring further conflict. In West Africa, a UN-backed ECOWAS mission in Côte d'Ivoire was authorized to enforce a 2004 ceasefire between the government and rebel forces and to protect civilian and humanitarian workers. In 2008 and 2009, SADC played a key role in conflict resolution during crises of governmental authority in Zimbabwe and Madagascar, respectively. A notable UN initiative involving African, Asian, and Western nations was the Contact Group on Piracy off the Coast of Somalia, established in 2009 to suppress activities that threatened international shipping, humanitarian relief, and human security. In contrast to organizations focusing on counterterrorism, the contact group recognized piracy as a symptom of the general breakdown of Somali society and emphasized the need to address such issues as illicit fishing and toxic waste disposal in Somali waters as contributory factors to the development of an outlaw economy.

---

[12] The agreement provided for a referendum on self-determination that led to the independence of South Sudan in 2011. Unresolved disputes over boundaries and the division of oil revenues gave rise to renewed violence shortly after South Sudan's independence.

Second, emerging powers such as China, India, Brazil, Turkey, and the Middle Eastern Gulf states increased their economic involvement in Africa during the first decade of the twenty-first century. Although these countries initially played only limited diplomatic and military roles, their presence gave African states more flexibility and opportunity in forming international alliances. These benefits did not always trickle down to the general population. Interested in African oil, minerals, and agricultural land, the emerging powers often dealt with repressive regimes that promoted their own interests at the expense of the population at large. In some instances, however, outside powers used their influence to persuade their allies to compromise. Such was the case in the 2012 conflict between Sudan and South Sudan, which threatened to escalate into a wider war. With significant oil and infrastructure investments in both countries, Beijing joined the African Union, the United States, and other powers in pressuring both sides to pursue peace.

Third, the growth of public pressure for "humanitarian intervention" in response to African crises became a significant factor in political decision making. In the United States, this phenomenon was best illustrated by the campaigns of the Save Darfur Coalition, a broad-based movement that sought international intervention to stop atrocities in Darfur, and the nonprofit organization Invisible Children, which mobilized support for action against Joseph Kony's brutal Lord's Resistance Army in Central Africa. Although their advocacy emerged from a humanitarian impulse, similar to that underlying the UN R2P resolution, these groups generated criticism as well as praise. Although both organizations brought mass atrocities to world attention and rallied support for action to protect civilians, critics claimed that they oversimplified complex issues, ignored human rights abuses committed by individuals and entities they supported on the ground, and proposed military solutions that could have adverse effects on civilian populations. Detractors warned that the organizations' support for foreign military intervention, in particular, risked perpetuating a trend toward simplistic military solutions that failed to address the fundamental political, economic, and social issues underlying the crises.

By the end of the first decade of the twenty-first century, there was little consensus in ongoing debates about foreign intervention in Africa. In the United States, those who shaped Africa policy did not speak with one voice. As was the case during the years of decolonization and the Cold War, advocates of caution and negotiation were often found among Africa specialists in the State Department, while those who supported counterterrorism and counterinsurgency measures were generally found in other sectors of the State Department, in the Pentagon, and in the various national security agencies. The resulting policies were criticized both domestically and internationally. Some critics warned that aggressive intervention could be counterproductive, fomenting rather than reducing antiforeign sentiment and deepening regional insecurity. Others charged that American responses to terrorism or to humanitarian crises were too timid.

As calls for multilateral diplomacy evolved into appeals for military intervention under the mantle of responsibility to protect, there was sharp disagreement over the motives of those intervening, the means used, and whether the outcomes provided protection or increased insecurity. Some multilateral interventions gained widespread support from the UN and from African regional organizations, while others were weakly supported or opposed. In countries and regions affected by conflict, people and governments were often divided on the merits of outside intervention, whether by neighboring states, international organizations, or external powers. When outside entities supplied arms and training to repressive regimes beset by rebel insurgencies, African commentators and civil society groups demanded that all parties responsible for human rights abuses be held accountable – governments as well as rebel movements. They remained skeptical of outsiders' motives and their capacity to bring peace, even when their actions were part of an approved multilateral initiative. These concerns did not diminish as the new century's second decade began.

Suggested Reading

Several works establish a framework for better understanding the events that transpired in post–Cold War Africa. Michael Clough's *Free at Last? U.S. Policy toward Africa and the End of the Cold War* (New York: Council on Foreign Relations Press, 1992) lays the groundwork with an overview of U.S.-Africa policy during the Cold War and its effects, examining the "dismal balance sheet" in six countries where the United States spent the most resources. Nicolas van de Walle's *African Economies and the Politics of Permanent Crisis, 1979–1999* (New York: Cambridge University Press, 2001) examines the African economic crisis that began in the 1970s, which is critical to understanding post–Cold War political events. For a fascinating case study, see Isaac A. Kamola's "The Global Coffee Economy and the Production of Genocide in Rwanda," *Third World Quarterly* 28, no. 3 (2007): 571–92, which analyzes the 1994 Rwandan genocide in the context of the international coffee economy, economic crisis, and structural adjustment.

A number of books explore state collapse, warlordism, and political violence in the 1990s. Especially recommended is William Reno's *Warlord Politics and African States* (Boulder, CO: Lynne Rienner, 1998), which offers important insight into the failure of the bureaucratic state in post–Cold War Africa and its replacement by warlords whose goal was to control economic resources rather than to mobilize citizens. See also the chapter "Warlord Rebels" in his book *Warfare in Independent Africa* (New York: Cambridge University Press, 2011). Mary Kaldor's *New and Old Wars: Organized Violence in a Global Era* (Stanford, CA: Stanford University Press, 1999) explores the causes of increased ethnic violence in the 1990s and the reasons the international community failed to stop it. Continuing the focus on the international community, Adekeye Adebajo's *UN Peacekeeping in Africa: From the Suez Crisis to the Sudan Conflicts* (Boulder, CO: Lynne Rienner, 2011) examines UN peacekeeping missions in Africa since the end of the Cold War, exploring the reasons for their success or failure. Elizabeth Schmidt's *From State Collapse to the War on Terror: Foreign Intervention in Africa after the Cold War* (Athens: Ohio University Press, in progress) examines intra- and extracontinental intervention in African political and economic affairs during the two decades following the Cold War.

The following sections offer suggestions for the cases studies of Liberia, Somalia, Sudan, and Zaire. For Liberia, besides Reno's *Warlord Politics and African States* (mentioned above), Stephen Ellis's *The Mask of Anarchy: The Destruction of Liberia and the Religious Dimension of an African Civil War*, 2nd ed. (New York: New York University Press, 2006) is especially recommended. Ellis's book explains the origins and process of the Liberian civil war, focusing on corruption, the collapse of the state bureaucracy and patrimonial political system, the manipulation of ethnicity by politicians and warlords, and the role of indigenous religious belief systems. Bill Berkeley's *The Graves are Not Yet Full: Race, Tribe and Power in the Heart of Africa* (New York: Basic Books, 2001), a clearly written journalistic account, also explores the ways in which Doe and Taylor manipulated ethnicity to gain access to power and resources and pays special attention to the role of the United States in the Liberian catastrophe. Mark Huband's *The Liberian Civil War* (Portland, OR: Frank Cass, 1998) is a riveting personal memoir of the early years of the Liberian civil war by a journalist who was captured by Taylor's forces. The related war in Sierra Leone is examined in David Keen's *Conflict and Collusion in Sierra Leone* (Oxford, UK: James Currey; New York: Palgrave Macmillan, 2005), which investigates the crisis of the patronage-based political and economic system and the response of the dispossessed. Lansana Gberie's *A Dirty War in West Africa: The RUF and the Destruction of Sierra Leone* (Bloomington: Indiana University Press, 2005), an insider account by a Sierra Leonean journalist-historian, offers insights into the disintegration of the state, the nature of the RUF, the role of Liberia, and the impact of British and UN intervention.

For Somalia, several works examine the failed U.S.-UN intervention in the early 1990s. Mohamed Sahnoun's *Somalia: The Missed Opportunities* (Washington, DC: U.S. Institute of Peace Press, 1994), written by the senior UN representative in Somalia in 1992, provides a critical account of the failed UN operation. For the perspective of Robert B. Oakley, the U.S special envoy for Somalia in 1992–94, who led the humanitarian phase of the operation, see John L. Hirsch and Robert B. Oakley, *Somalia and Operation Restore Hope: Reflections on Peacemaking and Peacekeeping* (Washington, DC: U.S. Institute of Peace Press, 1995). For a critical account of the operation's misunderstandings, missteps, and failures by a humanitarian relief worker, see Kenneth R. Rutherford, *Humanitarianism under Fire: The US and UN Intervention in Somalia* (Sterling, VA: Kumarian Press, 2008). Mark Bowden's *Black Hawk Down: A Story of Modern War* (New York: Atlantic Monthly Press, 1999), based on interviews and primary documents, offers a gripping account of the failed October 1993 U.S. Army Ranger Task Force operation.

For Sudan, besides Berkeley (mentioned above), several books are especially recommended. Douglas H. Johnson's *The Root Causes of Sudan's Civil Wars* (Bloomington: Indiana University Press, 2007) provides a historical overview of north-south conflicts; differential distribution of power and resources; manipulation of ethnicity and religion; and the role foreign governments, institutions, and aid organizations. Peter Woodward's *US Foreign Policy and the Horn of Africa* (Burlington, VT: Ashgate, 2006) examines the evolution of U.S. policy toward the Horn of Africa, with special emphasis on Somalia, Sudan, and Islamist movements. Donald Petterson's *Inside Sudan: Political Islam, Conflict and Catastrophe* (Boulder, CO: Westview Press, 1999), an insider account by the American ambassador to Sudan from 1992 to 1995, covers such topics as U.S. relations with Sudan, civil war, terrorism, and Islamic fundamentalism. Two recommended books focus on Darfur. Gérard Prunier's *Darfur: A 21st Century Genocide*, 3rd ed. (Ithaca, NY: Cornell University Press, 2008) is a highly accessible comprehensive account of the Darfur conflict, its historical underpinnings, and the key players. Julie Flint and Alex de Waal's *Darfur: A New History of a Long War*, revised and updated (New York: Zed Books, 2008) introduces the history of the conflict, the main participants, and the response of the African Union and the broader international community.

Three recommended books focus on the Congo/Zaire/DRC. Crawford Young and Thomas Turner's *The Rise and Decline of the Zairian State* (Madison: University of Wisconsin Press, 1985) provides an overview of Zairian politics from the Belgian colonial state through the Mobutu regime. It examines the transformation of the colonial bureaucracy into a corrupt, personalized, patrimonial state and explores the consequences of economic decline and the role of Western countries and corporations. Michael G. Schatzberg's highly accessible *Mobutu or Chaos: The United States and Zaire, 1960–1990* (Lanham, MD: University Press of America, 1991) focuses on U.S. policy toward Zaire from independence to the end of the Cold War. Georges Nzongola-Ntalaja's *The Congo from Leopold to Kabila: A People's History* (New York: Zed Books, 2002), written by a Congolese scholar and activist, offers a valuable historical overview that includes a detailed history of the Congolese prodemocracy movement.

Four recent books explore late-twentieth-century political violence and wars in Central Africa and the Great Lakes region, with particular emphasis on the DRC, Rwanda, and Burundi. They focus on the causes, internal dynamics, and effects of the conflicts, as well as the role of outside powers and corporations. See René Lemarchand, *The Dynamics of Violence in Central Africa* (Philadelphia: University of Pennsylvania Press, 2008); Gérard Prunier, *Africa's World War: Congo, the Rwandan Genocide, and the Making of a Continental Catastrophe* (New York: Oxford University Press, 2009); Filip Reyntjens, *The Great African War: Congo and Regional Geopolitics, 1996–2006* (New York: Cambridge University Press, 2010); and Jason K. Stearns, *Dancing in the Glory of Monsters: The Collapse of the Congo and the Great War of Africa* (New York: Public Affairs, 2012).

Several works focus on the militarization of U.S.-Africa policy in the early twenty-first century. Robert G. Berschinski's *AFRICOM'S Dilemma: The "Global War on Terrorism," "Capacity Building," Humanitarianism, and the Future of U.S. Security Policy in Africa* (Carlisle, PA: Strategic Studies Institute, U.S. Army War College, November 2007), http://www. strategicstudiesinstitute.army.mil/, critiques the United States' post-9/11 model of military engagement in Africa, military involvement in humanitarian and development operations, and Washington's misunderstanding of many antigovernment movements. Malinda S. Smith's edited collection, *Securing Africa: Post–9/11 Discourses on Terrorism* (Burlington, VT: Ashgate, 2010), which includes contributors from several continents, focuses on the impact of the war on terror on African societies across the continent. John Davis's edited collection, *Africa and the War on Terrorism* (Burlington, VT: Ashgate, 2007), explores the evolution of the war on terror in Africa, with special attention paid to the role of the African Union and U.S. Special Forces. Daniel Volman and William Minter's "Making Peace or Fueling War in Africa," *Foreign Policy in Focus*, March 13, 2009, http://www.fpif.org critiques Washington's emphasis on the strengthening of bilateral military ties and its reduction of resources for the UN and other multilateral institutions, as well as its focus on counterterrorism and access to natural resources, rather than humanitarian concerns.

Four recommended books focus on militant Islam and U.S. policy in the Horn of Africa, which is considered the African front line in the American war on terror. Besides Woodward (mentioned above), Alex de Waal's edited collection, *Islamism and Its Enemies in the Horn of Africa* (Bloomington: Indiana University Press, 2004), examines the emergence of new forms of radical Islam and their relation to American political and economic power, the wars in Afghanistan and Iraq, and U.S. intervention in the Horn. Robert I. Rotberg's edited collection, *Battling Terrorism in the Horn of Africa* (Washington, DC: Brookings Institution Press and the World Peace Foundation, 2005), focuses on the Horn as a front line in the American war on terror and Washington's use of regional powers to promote U.S. interests. Gregory A. Pirio's *African Jihad: Bin Laden's Quest for the Horn of Africa* (Trenton, NJ: Red Sea Press, 2007) offers a narrative account of al-Qaeda's presence in East Africa and the Horn, focusing especially on Sudan, Somalia, Kenya, and Tanzania.

Conclusion

This book has demonstrated that during the period of decolonization and the Cold War (1945–91) and the first two decades of its aftermath (1991–2010), foreign intervention in Africa strongly influenced the outcome of conflicts and the fate of African nations. However, foreign powers did not simply impose their will on a passive continent or use African actors as proxies for their own interests. Rather, external powers interacted in complex ways with African societies. While foreign governments took advantage of divisions within African societies to promote their own interests, African actors also used external alliances for their own ends. The scale and character of the interventions varied across time and space, reflecting both the interests and concerns of foreign powers and the regional and national contexts in which they occurred. Although most interventions during the Cold War and decolonization period were perpetrated by extracontinental powers, African nations also embroiled themselves in their neighbors' affairs. During the period of state collapse (1991–2001), the most serious instances of foreign intervention involved intracontinental powers, which in turn implicated regional and extracontinental peacekeeping forces. The narrative of the global war on terror emerged during the first decade of the twenty-first century (2001–10), focusing on real or imagined threats from Islamist extremists in several parts of the continent. However, this period also witnessed an array of interventions that were unrelated to the war on terror, as global, continental, and regional organizations became involved in African conflicts on behalf of political and economic interests and for humanitarian and peacemaking purposes. In many instances, the boundaries between conflicting objectives were muddled.

Although varying in their specifics, the case studies presented in this book support four general observations. First, both colonial and Cold War powers attempted to control the decolonization process in ways that would advance their interests. While Britain, France, Belgium, and Portugal tried to influence political and economic practices in their former colonies, France, more than any other power, engaged in military actions to protect its interests. The colonial powers hoped to establish neocolonial regimes that would function much as before, operating on behalf of external political and economic interests. The Cold War superpowers looked forward to a new international order in which they would play the leading roles. When their interests converged, the United States preferred to let European powers take the lead in their former colonies, as in the case of Belgium in the Congo and Britain in Rhodesia. However, when old-style imperialist policies threatened to provide opportunities for the Soviet Union, the United States opposed its NATO allies, as it did during the Suez Crisis and the Algerian independence war. The Soviet Union generally increased its involvement in response to intervention by the United States and its associates, as it did in the Congo and Angola. However, Moscow was sometimes drawn into regional conflicts when its African allies were threatened by outside forces, as in the case of Ethiopia after the 1977 Somali invasion. Although viewed by the West as a Soviet proxy, Cuba often navigated its own course, as it did in Angola and Eritrea. Hostile to Moscow after the Sino-Soviet split, China promoted political movements that rivaled those backed by the Soviet Union, throwing its support to ZANU in Zimbabwe and the FNLA and UNITA in Angola.

The second observation suggests that conflicts during the Cold War and decolonization period, free market austerity policies imposed by international financial institutions, and weak postcolonial states led to deadly struggles over power and resources in the post–Cold War period. The cases of Liberia, Somalia, and Zaire demonstrate the ways in which Cold War era despots who repressed their citizenry and plundered their countries' resources were vulnerable to political pressures once their sponsors abandoned them. In the case of Sudan, a weakened dictator sought support from radical Islamists, which resulted in retaliatory action by the United States. As dictators were driven from power, indigenous strongmen and neighboring states intervened to further their own interests, while international peacekeeping forces sometimes ameliorated and in other instances exacerbated the crises.

The third observation is that Washington's global war on terror resulted in increased foreign military presence on the continent and renewed support for repressive regimes. Concerned about U.S. energy and physical security, Washington focused on countries rich in energy resources and those considered vulnerable to terrorist infiltration. U.S. military aid, combined with commercial sales and arms left over from the Cold War, contributed to an escalation of violence in many parts of Africa. Rather than promoting security, American military and covert operations in the Horn and the Sahel often provoked intensified conflict and undermined the prospects for peace negotiations. A notable exception during this period was in Sudan, where international peace efforts supported by the African Union, the United States, and other international forces resulted in a fragile peace accord that led to the independence of South Sudan in 2011. Despite this success, serious differences were not resolved, and the region continued to be wracked by violence.

Although American counterterrorism initiatives cast a large shadow, they were not the only foreign interventions in Africa during the first decade of the twenty-first century. Together with the UN, the African Union and various regional organizations played a growing role in diplomacy and peacekeeping initiatives, which sometimes led to multilateral military action. Emerging powers such as China, India, Brazil, Turkey, and the Middle Eastern Gulf states, which were heavily invested in African oil, minerals, and agricultural land, exerted increased political influence. Although these countries often reinforced the powers of repressive regimes, in some instances they used their authority to promote peace and security efforts. Public pressure for "humanitarian intervention" in response to African crises also contributed to new foreign involvement. Although activist groups in Western countries put the spotlight on mass atrocities and mobilized support for action to protect African civilians, they often oversimplified complex issues and proposed the kinds of military solutions that historically have had negative effects on civilian populations.

The fourth and final observation suggests that during the period under consideration (1945–2010), foreign intervention in Africa generally did more harm than good. External involvement often intensified conflicts and rendered them more lethal. Even humanitarian and peacekeeping missions, which were weakened by inadequate mandates, funding, and information and undermined by conflicting interests, sometimes hurt the people they were intended to help. At the close of the first decade of the twenty-first century, the merits and demerits of foreign intervention remained hotly contested, while the consequences of failure to intervene were also the subject of much debate. As the second decade opened with no clear path for moving forward, it became increasingly imperative that the voices of African civil society be heard and that in future debates over foreign involvement, the people of the affected countries set the agenda.

Index

Abidjan, 174
Addis Ababa, 150, 159, 160
Adoula, Cyrille, 68–70, 85. *See also*
    Congo (Belgian)
Afewerki, Isaias, 160. *See also*
    Eritrea; Eritrean People's
    Liberation Front (EPLF)
Afghanistan, 154. *See also* al-Qaeda;
    bin Laden, Osama; mujahideen;
    Soviet-Afghan War (1979–1989)
    and the Soviet Union, 154, 155,
    206–207
    and the United States, 206–207,
    214
Africa Cell. *See* France
African Americans, 24–25, 103
    anti-apartheid movement, 25, 103,
    104
    anticolonial solidarity movements,
    24–25, 29
African Democratic Rally (RDA),
    170–172, 182. *See also* Boda,
    Biaka; Communist Party;
    General Confederation of Labor
    (CGT); Houphouët-Boigny,
    Félix; Nigerien Democratic
    Union; Senegalese Democratic
    Union; Union of the Peoples of
    Cameroon (UPC)

Bamako Congress, 170–171
    coordinating committee,
    171
    expulsions, 171
    and French Communist Party,
    171
    membership, 170–171
    program, 171
    repression of, 171
African Financial Community
    (CFA), 177–178
    convertibility, 177–178, 189
    devaluation, 178, 189
African National Congress (ANC),
    106, 112–113, 114, 115. *See also*
    anti-apartheid movement;
    Congress Alliance; Mandela,
    Nelson; South Africa;
    Umkhonto we Sizwe
    African support, 113, 130
    armed struggle, 112, 118
    communism, 112–114
    and Frontline States, 129
    humanitarian aid, 113
    military aid, 113, 130
    military bases, 113, 129
    sanctions, 106
    terrorism, 113–114
    and the United States, 113–114

African Party for the Independence
of Guinea and Cape Verde
(PAIGC), 89–90, 158. *See also*
Cape Verde; Portuguese
Guinea
African involvement, 80, 90–91
and China, 90
communist influences, 89
and Cuba, 90, 91
and Guinea, 90
and Morocco, 90
Nordic countries, 80, 90
and the OAU, 90
and the Soviet Union, 90, 91
and the United Nations, 80, 91
and the United States, 90–91
and the World Council of
Churches, 80, 90
African Union, xiii, 194, 219–220,
229. *See also* Organization of
African Unity (OAU)
peacekeeping, 2, 11, 194, 219–221,
227–229
African unity, 150
Africanization, 59–60
Africa's First World War. *See* Second
Congo War (1998–2002)
Afrikaners, 19, 105. *See also* South
Africa
Afro-Asian Peoples' Solidarity
Organization, 36, 173
Ahidjo, Ahmadou, 182. *See also*
Cameroon
Aideed, Mohamed Farah, 156, 203,
204–205. *See also* Somalia;
United Somali Congress
Algeria, 19, 28, 30, 73, 168. *See also*
Communist Party; Egypt;
National Liberation Front
(FLN)
aid to liberation movements,
53–54, 90, 113, 173, 182
and Bandung Conference, 35–36
Battle of Algiers, 49–50
Evian Accords (1962), 52–53
and France, 30, 48, 49, 52–53, 79,
84, 180

and French Communist Party, 48,
52
French economic interests, 46
independence, 52–53
independence war, 13, 20, 35, 46,
48, 52–53, 60, 173, 180
Islamic militants, 48, 214
military accords, 52
and NATO, 45–46, 49, 50–51
oil, 36, 45, 46, 52
provisional government, 51, 52, 53
referendum, 52
settlers, 19, 46, 103
and the Soviet Union, 30, 45–46,
48, 51–52, 53, 54
and the United Nations, 49, 51
and the United States, 30, 45–46,
48–50, 51, 52, 54, 214, 216, 228
Algerian Communist Party. *See*
Communist Party
Allegheny Ludlum, 118. *See also*
Rhodesia lobby
Alliance of Democratic Forces for
the Liberation of Congo-Zaire
(AFDL), 209–211. *See also*
Kabila, Laurent;
Zaire/Democratic Republic of
Congo (DRC)
al-Qaeda, 205, 207, 208, 214, 216,
217. *See also* Al-Qaeda in the
Islamic Maghreb; bin Laden,
Osama; global war on terror;
mujahideen; Soviet-Afghan War
(1979–1989); Sudan; terrorism;
terrorist attacks
Al-Qaeda in the Islamic Maghreb,
217
Alvor Accord. *See* Angola
American Committee on Africa,
104. *See also* anti-apartheid
movement
Amhara, 145, 151, 159. *See also*
Ethiopia
Anglo-Iranian Oil Company, 36. *See*
also Iran
Anglophone Africa, 165, 181, 182,
184, 188, 200–201, 208, 210

Angola, 30, 79, 104, 129. *See also*
National Front for the
Liberation of Angola (FNLA);
National Union for the Total
Independence of Angola
(UNITA); Popular Movement
for the Liberation of Angola
(MPLA)
aid to liberation movements, 113,
119, 122, 129
Alvor Accord, 93–94, 96
assimilados, 81
Benguela railroad, 132
Bicesse Accords (1991), 132
Cabinda Enclave, 88, 93, 95, 212
and China, 8–9, 92, 93
coffee, 84, 92
and Cuba, xii, 92, 93, 96–98,
125–126, 132, 155, 228
Cuito Cuanavale, 126
destabilization, 128, 129, 130,
131–133, 193
diamonds, 92, 95, 133, 212
elections, 132–133
independence, 89, 92, 94, 96–98,
122
liberation movements, 53, 81,
83–84, 92–94, 122
liberation struggle, 26, 81, 83–84,
92–98
mercenaries, 95–98, 210
mestiços, 81, 84
oil, 88, 92, 93, 95, 133, 212
sanctions, 132–133
settlers, 19, 81, 84, 103
and South Africa, xii, 9, 92,
95–97, 98, 106–107, 123,
125–127, 129, 130, 131–132
and the Soviet Union, xii, 26, 31,
92, 96, 98, 126, 155, 228
and SWAPO, 95, 122, 125, 129,
131–132
and the United States, xii, 8–9, 31,
87, 92–93, 94, 95, 98, 126, 199,
208, 228
and Zaire, 92, 95, 187–188, 208,
210, 211–212

animism. *See* Sudan
anti-apartheid movement, 135. *See
also* African Americans
British, 134–135
U.S., 25, 103–104, 113, 114–115
world, 103, 104, 106, 133–135
anticolonial activities, xi, 6–7, 18, 21,
22, 25, 82, 83, 134, 166–167,
168, 172–173, 197
apartheid. *See* South Africa
Arab League, 51, 149, 157
Arab states, 40, 49, 51, 53, 149, 152,
157, 158, 159, 206. *See also*
pan-Arab movement
Arabian Peninsula, 4–5
Arab-Israeli War (1973), 44, 88,
181–182. *See also* Egypt; Israel;
Sadat, Anwar
Arabs, 4–5, 186
armed struggle, 13, 18, 19, 20,
79–80, 85, 89, 91, 105, 118–119,
120, 122, 173, 185, 197, 198. *See
also* Algeria; Angola;
Mozambique; Namibia;
Portuguese Guinea; Rhodesia;
South Africa
arms embargo. *See* sanctions;
United Nations
arms trafficking. *See* illicit activities
Asia, xi, 7–8, 22, 25, 27–28, 29, 36,
38, 42, 44, 49, 51, 82, 84, 90,
105, 134, 167–168, 169, 172,
214–215, 218, 220, 221
Asia-Pacific region, 218
Asmara, 145, 158, 159
Assab, 158
Atlantic Charter (1941), 48–49,
167–168, 169
Atlantic Ocean, 181
Azores, 84. *See also* Portugal
air base, 84–85, 86, 88, 90
islands, 84, 89

Ba'ath Party. *See* Iraq
Baghdad Pact, 37–38, 43
Bakongo, 81, 93. *See also* Angola
Bakwanga, 210. *See also* Mbuji-Mayi

balkanization, 150. *See also* decolonization

Ball, George, 85. *See also* United States; U.S. Department of State

Bamako, 170

Bamako Congress (1946), 170–171. *See also* African Democratic Rally (RDA)

Bandung Conference (1955), 27–28, 36, 38, 59

Bank of France, 175, 177–178

Bashir, Omar al-, 206–208. *See also* Sudan

Baudouin, King, 59. *See also* Belgium

Bay of Pigs, 72. *See also* Central Intelligence Agency (CIA); Cuba

Beira, 132

Belgium, 18, 20, 22, 92, 108. *See also* Congo (Belgian); Lumumba, Patrice
colonialism, 5–6, 7, 20, 59, 181, 212
decolonization, 7, 19, 20, 30, 66–68, 79, 228
economic interests in the Congo, 20, 30, 57, 60, 212
mercenaries, 60, 72, 210–211
military intervention in the Congo, 19, 30, 57–60, 63–66, 68, 71–73, 86
political intervention in the Congo, 58, 69, 73–74
settlers in the Congo, 19, 30, 59–60

Ben Bella, Ahmed, 53. *See also* Algeria

ben Yusuf, Mohammed, 46, 47. *See also* Morocco

Benin, 175, 180, 188

Berbera, 149, 151, 155

Berlin Conference (1884–1885), 5

Berlin Crisis (1961), 51–52, 84, 85

Biafran secession. *See* Nigeria

Biko, Steve, 109. *See also* South Africa

bin Laden, Osama, 206–207. *See also* Afghanistan; al-Qaeda; global war on terror; mujahideen; Soviet-Afghan War (1979–1989); Sudan; terrorism; terrorist attacks; United States
CIA support, 206–207

Black Consciousnesss Movement. *See* Biko, Steve; South Africa

Boda, Biaka, 171. *See also* African Democratic Rally (RDA); Côte d'Ivoire

Bokassa, Jean-Bédel, 184–185. *See also* Central African Republic

Bolshevik Revolution, 112

Bongo, Omar, 184. *See also* Gabon

Botha, P. W., 110, 123, 128. *See also* Constellation of Southern African States (CONSAS); South Africa
total onslaught, 128
total strategy, 128–129

Botha, Roelof "Pik," 110–111. *See also* South Africa

Botswana, 104, 119, 128, 129

Bourguiba, Habib, 46, 47. *See also* Tunisia

Bowles, Chester, 85. *See also* United States; U.S. Department of State

Brazil, 221, 229

Brazzaville Conference (1944), 168

Brezhnev, Leonid, 26. *See also* Soviet Union

Britain, 6, 18, 21, 22, 48–49, 57, 150, 168, 175. *See also* Congo (Belgian); South Africa; Suez
Africa policies, 32, 79
Colonial Office, 19
decolonization, 7, 19–20, 30, 68, 79, 167–168, 228
economic interests, 57, 92, 106, 121, 123
empire, 20, 167
mercenaries, 72
military intervention, 32, 40–42, 43, 60
oil interests, 36–37, 40, 43

and Portugal, 84, 86
repression, colonial, 18, 19
socialism, 134
trust territories, 21
and the United Nations, 61, 84, 86, 108
British East Africa, 150. *See also* Kenya
British Secret Intelligence Service, 36–37, 41
British Somaliland. *See* Somalia
Brzezinski, Zbigniew, 154–155. *See also* United States
Bulgaria, 175
Burkina Faso, 175, 188, 200–201, 216
Burundi, 73, 181. *See also* Zaire/Democratic Republic of Congo (DRC)
Bush, George H. W., 155. *See also* United States
administration, 155, 156, 159
Bush, George W., 202, 217–218. *See also* global war on terror; United States
administration, 202, 213, 214–215
Byrd Amendment, 118. *See also* Rhodesia; United States
Byrnes, James F., 21. *See also* United States; U.S. Department of State

Cabinda Enclave. *See* Angola
Cabral, Amílcar, 80, 89, 90. *See also* African Party for the Independence of Guinea and Cape Verde (PAIGC); Cape Verde; Portuguese Guinea
assassination, 90–91, 92
Caetano, Marcello, 87. *See also* Portugal
Cameroon, 168. *See also* Cameroon, British; Cameroon, French
dictatorship, 182
German colony, 168, 172
independence, 182
national conference, 188
and RDA, 170–171

Cameroon, British, 172, 182–189
League of Nations mandate, 172
UN trust, 172
Cameroon, French, 18, 172, 177. *See also* Union of the Peoples of Cameroon (UPC)
communism, 171–172
French military intervention, 165–166, 180, 181, 182
French repression, 165, 171–173, 175
and French Union, 171–172
independence struggle, 168–169, 171–173, 182
League of Nations mandate, 172
UN trust, 168, 170, 172, 175
Camp Lemonnier, 215. *See also* Combined Joint Task Force–Horn of Africa (CJTF-HOA); Djibouti
Canada, 62, 121, 123, 154, 210
Cape Verde, 79, 80. *See also* African Party for the Independence of Guinea and Cape Verde (PAIGC); Portugal; Portuguese Guinea
capitalism, 20, 22, 23, 25, 27, 29, 48
free market economics, 9–10, 20, 22, 26, 35, 48–49, 167–168, 196–197, 228
privatization, 9–10
Caribbean, 134
Carter, Jimmy, 109, 110, 111, 120, 153. *See also* United States
administration, 22, 109–110, 118, 147, 154–155, 205
and Ethiopia, 147
human rights, 109–110, 147, 155
and Rhodesia, 118, 120–121
and Somalia, 154–155
and South Africa, 109–110
Castro, Fidel, 29. *See also* Cuba
Catholic Church, 132
Central Africa, 26, 30, 31, 57, 60, 79, 212, 221
Central African Empire. *See* Central African Republic

Central African Federation, 57–58, 60, 69. *See also* Northern Rhodesia; Nyasaland; Rhodesia
Central African Republic, 165, 175, 180
coup d'état, 184–185
diamonds, 182, 184
dictatorship, 184–185
French military intervention, 165, 180, 181–182, 184–185
national conference, 188
uranium, 181–182, 184
Central Asia, 218
Central Intelligence Agency (CIA), xii, 23, 37, 41, 43, 63, 64, 65, 68, 72, 73, 85, 86, 91, 92, 93, 94, 95, 97–98, 113, 184, 187, 198, 199, 206, 214. *See also* United States
Central Intelligence Organisation, 120–121, 130. *See also* Mozambique National Resistance (RENAMO); Rhodesia
CFA franc. *See* African Financial Community (CFA)
Chad, 175, 180
armed conflict, 185–187
Christians, 185
colonial legacy, 185
corruption, 216–217
coup d'état, 186, 217
dictatorship, 185, 187, 216–217
ethnic conflict, 186
French military intervention, 165, 180, 181–182, 185–187
human rights abuses, 216–217
and Libya, 185–187
Muslims, 185, 186
national conference, 188
OAU, 186–187
oil, 181–182, 185
and the United States, 186, 187, 216, 217
uranium, 181–182, 185
and Zaire, 187
Chamoun, Camille, 42–43. *See also* Lebanon

child soldiers, 199, 201. *See also* National Patriotic Front of Liberia (NPFL); Revolutionary United Front (RUF)
China, ancient, 4
China, People's Republic of, xi, 3, 18, 27, 29, 39–40, 51, 63, 153, 154, 168, 175, 182, 184, 221, 229. *See also* Angola; Communist Party; Sino-Soviet split; Soviet Union
and Bandung Conference, 27–28, 38
civil war, 27
Cold War, 27–29, 87
economic aid, 27–28
ideology, 27–28, 89, 119
military aid, 28, 29, 31, 73, 83, 104, 113, 119, 155, 157, 182
Soviet Union, friendship with, 27
Soviet Union, rivalry with, 7, 8–9, 27, 28–29, 228
and the United States, 8–9, 29
China, Republic of (Taiwan), 39–40
Chirau, Jeremiah, 120. *See also* Rhodesia; Zimbabwe
Christianity, 4, 42–43, 103, 132, 145, 151, 157–158, 185, 199–200, 206
civil rights movement. *See* United States
civilizing mission, 24
Clark Amendment, 98, 126. *See also* Angola; United States
Clinton, Bill, 207. *See also* United States
administration, 207, 210–211
and Somalia, 205
and Sudan, 207
Cold War, xi, 1, 2, 3, 7, 8, 11, 12–13, 18, 19, 21, 30–31, 36, 83, 103, 112, 128, 131, 134, 135, 143, 145, 154–155, 156, 169, 193–195, 197–198, 208, 215, 218, 222, 227. *See also* China, People's Republic of; Cuba; Soviet Union; United States
actors, xi–xii, 1–2, 3, 7, 13, 22–29, 35, 167, 194, 197, 205–206, 228

détente, 96
regional policemen, 8, 87, 198,
    208
colonial powers. *See* imperial powers
colonialism, xi, 12–13, 73, 185. *See
    also* decolonization; liberation
    movements
conquest, 5–6
extraction, 6, 11, 27, 57, 59, 60,
    79, 92, 128–129
reform, 35, 45, 46, 166, 167–168,
    173
repression, 18, 59, 66, 80, 84
resistance, 6, 8, 18–19, 27–28,
    35–36, 66, 68, 80, 82
Combined Joint Task Force–Horn of
    Africa (CJTF-HOA), 215, 218.
    See also global war on terror
Commonwealth, 19, 21, 42, 46,
    105–106, 114, 116, 120, 134
communism, xi, 7, 8–9, 14, 24, 26,
    35, 59, 60, 68, 73, 80, 81, 82, 83,
    84, 85, 103, 109, 112–115, 118,
    119, 128, 131, 134, 143, 145, 152,
    153, 158, 159, 165, 166–167, 169,
    170, 171–172, 180, 182, 185, 186,
    187, 188, 195, 213, 215. *See also*
    Communist Party
Communist Party, 38
    Algerian, 48
    Chinese, 27, 134
    Egyptian, 38, 43
    French, 45, 48, 52, 165, 166–167,
        171, 182
    Portuguese, 81, 88–89
    South African, 112–115
    Soviet, 25, 26, 48, 154
Community of Sant'Egidio, 132. *See
    also* Mozambique
Comoros, 180
Compaoré, Blaise, 200–201. *See also*
    Burkina Faso
Comprehensive Anti-Apartheid Act
    (1986), 25, 114. *See also*
    anti-apartheid movement; South
    Africa; United States
Conakry, 90–91, 174. *See also*
    Guinea

Conference of Asian and African
    States. *See* Bandung Conference
    (1955)
Conference of Nationalist
    Organizations of the Portuguese
    Colonies (CONCP), 82. *See also*
    African Party for the
    Independence of Guinea and
    Cape Verde (PAIGC); Front for
    the Liberation of Mozambique
    (FRELIMO); Organization of
    Solidarity with the Peoples of
    Asia, Africa, and Latin America;
    Popular Movement for the
    Liberation of Angola (MPLA);
    Tricontinental Conference
    (1966)
Congo (Belgian), 13, 19, 20, 21, 30,
    81, 85, 143, 181. *See also*
    Belgium; Katanga lobby;
    Lumumba, Patrice; Mobutu,
    Joseph-Désirée; Zaire/
    Democratic Republic of Congo
    (DRC)
    African involvement in, 57, 63, 64,
        68, 73
    army mutiny, 59
    and Belgium, 58–60, 62–66,
        71–73
    and Britain, 59–61, 69, 71–72,
        74
    commercial interests, 57, 58,
        59–60, 61, 69
    Congo Crisis, 57–58, 65
    coup d'état, 58, 63, 69, 70, 74
    and Cuba, 58, 68, 71–72, 73–74
    independence, 20, 58, 59
    Katanga Province and secession,
        57–58, 59–60, 62, 63, 64–65, 69,
        70, 84, 208
    mercenaries, 60, 69, 72, 73, 74
    mineral wealth, 57, 58–59
    parliament, 63, 68
    People's Republic, 72–73
    political unrest, 58, 69, 70
    rebellion, 58, 70–74
    South Kasai, 57, 60, 62, 63, 70,
        210

Congo (Belgian) (*cont.*)
  and the Soviet Union, 26, 30, 57,
    60, 61, 62, 63, 64, 65, 68, 73,
    228
  Stanleyville raid, 72–74, 86
  and the United Nations, 57,
    60–62, 63, 64, 69, 70
  and the United States, 30, 57, 58,
    59–61, 62, 65–66, 68–69, 70, 71,
    72–73, 228
  uranium, 21, 57, 59
  Western powers, 58, 61–62, 71–72
Congo, Democratic Republic of. *See*
    Zaire/Democratic Republic of
    Congo (DRC)
Congo, Republic of, 73, 175, 180,
    188
Congo-Brazzaville. *See* Congo,
    Republic of
Congolese National Movement
    (MNC), 59, 69
Congress Alliance, 112, 113. *See also*
    African National Congress
    (ANC)
Congressional Black Caucus, 25. *See
    also* United States
Constellation of Southern African
    States (CONSAS), 128–129.
    See also Botha, P. W.; South
    Africa
constructive engagement. *See*
    Reagan, Ronald
Contact Group on Piracy off the
    Coast of Somalia, 220. *See also*
    Somalia
Cordier, Andrew, 63. *See also* United
    Nations; United States
Côte d'Ivoire, 18, 175–177, 180, 184,
    199, 200–201
  and ECOWAS, 219–220
  French military intervention, 180,
    195
  French repression, 171
  UN intervention, 195, 219–221
Council on African Affaairs, 103. *See
    also* anti-apartheid movement;
    United States

Crèvecoeur, Jean-Marie, 66. *See also*
    Congo (Belgian); Tshombe,
    Moïse
crimes against humanity, 12, 194.
    See also genocide; human rights;
    war crimes
Crocker, Chester, 111, 124–125. *See
    also* Reagan, Ronald; United
    States; U.S. Department of
    State
Cuba, xi–xii, 18. *See also* Castro,
    Fidel; Eritrea; Ethiopia;
    Guevara, Ernesto "Che";
    Tricontinental Conference
    (1966)
  African solidarity, 29, 83, 90, 92,
    113, 122, 149, 151, 153, 158, 182,
    206
  and Angola, xii, 92, 93, 96–98,
    125–126, 132, 155, 228
  anti-Castro Cubans, 68, 72, 73,
    126
  Cold War, 29–30
  and Congo, 58, 68, 71–72, 73–74
  Cuban revolution, 29, 89
  soldiers in Africa, 31, 68, 72, 73,
    96–97, 125, 126, 131, 132, 151,
    152, 165, 166
  and the Soviet Union, 8–9, 29, 96,
    98, 151, 228
  and the United States, 29
Cuban Missile Crisis (1962),
    86
Cuito Cuanavale. *See* Angola
Czechoslovakia, 7, 63, 90, 175
  arms deals, 39

Dacko, David, 184–185. *See also*
    Central African Republic
Dahomey. *See* Benin
Dakar, 174
Darfur, 12, 194, 220–221. *See also*
    Sudan
  and the African Union, 219–221
  ethnic cleansing, 194
  human rights abuses, 208
  and the United Nations, 220

Dayal, Rajeshwar, 75. *See also* Congo (Belgian); United Nations

de Gaulle, Charles, 51, 52, 168, 173–174, 183, 184. *See also* France

Déby, Idriss, 187, 216–217. *See also* Chad

decolonization 1, 2, 3, 6–7, 8, 12–13, 18, 19, 24, 25–26, 27, 29, 30–31, 44, 66–68, 83, 84, 134, 143, 150, 179, 222, 227–229. *See also* liberation movements

Defense Appropriations Bill (1976). *See* Tunney Amendment

democracy, 6, 10, 218. *See also* good governance; prodemocracy movements

Democratic Movement for Malagasy Restoration (MDRM), 170. *See also* Madagascar

Democratic Republic of Congo (DRC). *See* Zaire/Democratic Republic of Congo (DRC)

Denmark, 82, 90, 92. *See also* Nordic countries

diamonds, 57, 92, 95, 122, 133, 182, 184, 201, 202, 210, 212

Diego Garcia, 147

Dien Bien Phu, 46. *See also* Indochina; Viet Minh; Vietnam

Diori, Hamani, 182–184. *See also* Niger

Djibouti, 148, 153, 168, 180, 189, 215, 218

Doe, Samuel, 198–200, 201, 203. *See also* Liberia

drug trafficking. *See* illicit activities

Dulles, John Foster, 157. *See also* United States; U.S. Department of State

East Africa, 4, 57, 206–207, 215

East Africa Counterterrorism Initiative (EACTI), 215–216. *See also* global war on terror

Eastern Bloc, 7, 47, 92, 134, 154, 166, 172, 175, 182

Eastern Europe, xi, 31, 152, 153, 172
aid to liberation movements, 31, 93, 104, 113, 122

Economic Community Monitoring Group (ECOMOG), 200, 201, 202. *See also* Economic Community of West African States (ECOWAS)

Economic Community of West African States (ECOWAS), 200, 201, 219–220. *See also* Economic Community Monitoring Group (ECOMOG)

economy, 166. *See also* African Financial Community (CFA); capitalism; colonialism; International Monetary Fund (IMF); neocolonialism; World Bank
balance of trade, 9
colonial, 5–6, 8–9, 11
commodity prices, 9, 196, 208
corruption, 1, 8–11, 195, 197–198, 218
debt crisis, 1–2, 10–11, 196, 206–208
economic crisis, 2, 6–7, 8–11, 13–14, 166, 178, 188, 193, 195–198, 203, 206, 208, 213, 217, 218, 221, 228
oil price increase, 9, 196
unequal exchange, 9, 11

Egypt, 4, 13, 28, 42, 43, 51. *See also* Nasser, Gamal Abdel; Suez; United Arab Republic
aid to liberation movements, 53, 113
and Algeria, 40, 44
arms deal, 38–39
Aswan High Dam, 39–40, 44
and Baghdad Pact, 37–38, 44
and Bandung Conference, 36, 38
and Britain, 30, 35, 37, 38–42
and France, 40, 42, 44
Islamic militants, 37, 46, 214

Egypt (*cont.*)
and Israel, 37, 39, 40, 42, 44
and Lebanon, 42
and Palestine, 54
radical nationalism, 35, 36, 37, 42,
43, 44, 48, 50, 53–54
and the Soviet Union, 26, 30, 38,
39, 40, 42, 43–44
and the United States, 30, 37,
38–42, 44, 187, 207, 214,
217–218
Eisenhower, Dwight D., 22. *See also*
United States
administration, 22, 24, 37–38,
39–40, 45, 46, 49–50, 51, 52, 58,
62, 65, 68, 83, 113
Eisenhower Doctrine, 42–43
Elisabethville, 210. *See also*
Lubumbashi
empire. *See* Britain; France
Eritrea, 21. *See also* Ethiopia
annexation by Ethiopia, 21, 31,
145, 157, 160
and Britain, 21, 157
Christians, 158
and Cuba, 144, 158, 228
federation with Ethiopia, 21, 145,
157, 160
human rights abuses, 160
independence referendum, 157,
160
independence struggle, 21, 31,
143, 145, 154, 156–160
and Israel, 158
Italian colony, 21, 144, 156–157
liberated areas, 158
Muslims, 157, 158
and the Soviet Union, 143, 157,
158
and the United Nations, 21, 145,
157, 160
and the United States, 21, 145,
157, 215–216, 217–218
Eritrean Liberation Front (ELF),
157, 158, 159. *See also* Eritrea
external assistance, 157–158
Eritrean Liberation Movement, 157

Eritrean People's Liberation Front
(EPLF), 158, 159, 160. *See also*
Eritrea
external assistance, 158, 159
Marxism, 158, 159
Eritrean-Ethiopian War
(1998–2000), 160
Ethiopia, 4, 21, 22, 26, 149. *See also*
Eritrea; Somali-Ethiopian War
(1977–1978)
aid to liberation movements, 113,
157, 206
and Britain, 21, 144–145, 150, 152
and China, 153, 157
Christians, 145, 151
coup d'état, 26, 143, 146
and Cuba, 31, 158
Derg, 146–147, 149, 153, 158
economic crisis, 146
empire, 144, 150, 151, 156, 157
and Eritrea, 144–145, 151,
156–160
ethnic minorities, 151
famine, 145–146, 154
feudalism, 21, 143, 145, 146
human rights abuses, 145–146,
147, 153, 154, 160
insurgencies, 31, 151, 154, 159
internal dissent, 145, 146, 151
and Israel, 152, 158, 159
and Italy, 21, 144–145, 152
Kagnew communications station,
145, 147
Marxism-Leninism, 26, 143, 146,
149, 151, 153, 154, 158, 159
Muslims, 145, 151
and the OAU, 150–151
Ogaden and Haud, 21–22,
144–145, 149–150, 151, 152, 154,
155, 158–159
overthrow of Haile Selassie, 146
overthrow of Mengistu Haile
Mariam, 154
prodemocracy movement, 146
Red Terror, 146, 153, 154
separatist movements, 31,
143–144, 145

socialism, 146, 153
and Somalia, 21, 31, 143, 150–153
and the Soviet Union, 26, 31, 143,
  147, 149, 151–152, 153–154, 155,
  158–159, 206, 228
and the United Nations, 21
and the United States, 26, 30–31,
  143, 144–147, 150, 152, 153, 154,
  156, 159–160, 207, 215, 216,
  217–218
and World War II, 21, 144–145,
  150
Ethiopian People's Revolutionary
  Party, 146
Ethiopian Popular Revolutionary
  Democratic Front (EPRDF),
  159. See also Ethiopia
ethnic conflict, 1, 186, 193, 198
ethnic cleansing, 12, 193, 194, 209
European Community, 114
European Economic and Monetary
  Union, 189
European Economic Community,
  177
European Union, 220
Evian Accords (1962). See Algeria
External Documentation and
  Counterespionage Service
  (SDECE), 175, 176, 179, 182,
  183, 184, 185. See also France

failed states. See state collapse
Faisal II, King, 37–38. See also
  Iraq
Fanon, Frantz, 52. See also Algeria
Farouk, King, 37. See also Egypt
Fashoda complex, 181. See also
  France
Federal Bureau of Investigation
  (FBI), 216
Federal Republic of Germany. See
  Germany, West
Finland, 82, 90. See also Nordic
  countries
First Congo War (1996–1997),
  209–211. See also Alliance of
  Democratic Forces for the

Liberation of Congo-Zaire
  (AFDL); Hutu; Rwanda; Tutsi;
  Uganda; Zaire/Democratic
  Republic of Congo (DRC)
Flintlock 2005, 216. See also global
  war on terror; Trans-Sahara
  Counterterrorism Initiative
  (TSCI)
Foccart, Jacques, 176, 183, 184, 185.
  See also France
Foote Mineral, 118. See also
  Rhodesia lobby
Ford, Gerald, 214–215. See also
  Kissinger, Henry; United States
administration, 23, 83, 92, 94, 98,
  109, 147
and Rhodesia, 119–120
foreign intervention, 18, 19. See also
  African Union; Belgium; Cuba;
  Economic Community of West
  African States (ECOWAS);
  Ethiopia; France; Libya;
  Rwanda; Somalia; South Africa;
  Soviet Union; Uganda; United
  Nations; United States
economic, 5–6, 8–11
extracontinental, xi–xiii, 1–3, 7,
  12, 13, 227–228, 229–230
humanitarian, xiii, 2, 12, 221,
  227–228, 229–230
intracontinental, xi–xiii, 2, 3,
  13–14, 227–228, 229
military, 1, 2–3, 4–5, 6, 7, 12, 13,
  19, 31–32, 227–230
peacekeeping, 2, 3, 227–228,
  229–230
political, 1, 2–3
precolonial, 4–5, 12
proxy forces, xii–xiii, 7, 13–14, 23,
  94, 125–126, 130, 131, 186, 187,
  198, 210–211, 212, 227, 228
Four Freedoms, 169. See also
  Roosevelt, Franklin D.
Fourteen Points, 169–172. See also
  Wilson, Woodrow
franc zone. See African Financial
  Community (CFA)

France, 6, 7, 11, 13, 18, 20, 21, 22,
   150. *See also* Bank of France;
   Brazzaville Conference (1944);
   Cameroon, French; Central
   African Republic; Chad;
   Communist Party; External
   Documentation and
   Counterespionage Service
   (SDECE); Fashoda complex;
   Franco-African summits;
   French Community; French
   Union; Gabon; Guinea;
   Indochina; Madagascar; Niger;
   Nigeria; Rwanda; Socialist
   Party; South Africa; Vichy;
   Zaire/Democratic Republic of
   Congo (DRC)
1946 Constituent Assembly, 170
1946 constitution, 168–169, 170
1958 constitution, 20, 51, 173
Africa Cell, 176–177
Africa policies, 31, 79, 165, 166,
   176–177, 188–189
Anglophone menace, 13, 165, 166,
   172, 180–181, 182–183, 184, 188,
   200–201, 208, 210
Arab threat, 180, 181, 185
and Britain, 180–181
chasse gardée, 181
civilizing mission, 168
colonial development, 173, 185
communism, 8–9, 165, 166–167,
   170, 171, 172, 180, 181, 182–184,
   185, 187, 188
and Congo (Belgian), 59, 69,
   71–72
cooperation agreements, 20, 31,
   176–180, 184
coup attempt, 51
decolonization, 7, 19, 20, 30, 68,
   79, 165, 166–168, 169–175,
   179–180, 228
democracy, 166, 188–189
dictators, 166, 176, 182–189
economic agreements, 13, 20, 31,
   175, 176, 177–178, 184, 228

economic interests, 46, 106, 117,
   122, 123, 176, 177, 178, 181–182,
   183, 184, 185, 187, 189
economy, 166–167, 173, 189
empire, 20, 46, 49, 51, 167–168,
   173, 175, 181
Fifth Republic, 20
and Germany, 45, 53
loi-cadre, 173
mercenaries, 60, 72, 188, 210–211
military agreements, 13, 20, 31,
   175, 176, 178–180, 184
military aid, 93, 186, 187, 189,
   208
military bases, 180, 183, 184, 189
military intervention, 13, 31, 40,
   42, 50, 59, 165–166, 176, 177,
   178, 180–188, 210–211, 228
Nazi occupation and resistance,
   166
neocolonialism, 165, 175–180, 228
overseas territories, 51, 168–169,
   171, 173
personalization of politics, 176,
   177
and Portugal, 82, 84, 86
pré carré, 181
referendums, 51, 170, 173–174
reforms, colonial, 20, 46, 51, 165,
   168, 173
repression, colonial, 18, 46, 49–50,
   165, 167, 170, 171–173
soldiers in Africa, 165, 179–180,
   182, 183, 184, 185, 186, 187–188,
   189
and the Soviet Union, 45, 52, 185,
   187–188
Treasury, 177–178
UN trust territories, 168, 170–172,
   175–176
and the United Nations, 61, 84,
   86, 108
and the United States, 44–45, 46,
   49–50, 51–52, 54, 108, 165, 166,
   167–168, 169–170, 179–181, 184,
   185

and World War II, 166, 167–168,
169
Franco-African summits, 176,
188–189
Francophone Africa, 13, 22, 35, 40,
165, 170, 173, 176–177, 181,
187–189, 208. *See also*
prodemocracy movements
francophonie, la. *See* Francophone
Africa
Free French, 51, 168. *See also* France
Free South Africa Movement, 25,
104, 135. *See also* anti-apartheid
movement
French Community, 51, 173, 174,
175, 177. *See also* France
French Equatorial Africa, 20, 168,
170, 175
French Guiana, 168
French Guinea. *See* Guinea
French North Africa, 44
    and the Soviet Union, 45
    and the United States, 45, 46
French Republic. *See* French
Union
French Somaliland. *See* Djibouti
French Soudan. *See* Mali
French Union, 46, 168, 169, 170,
171, 172, 173, 175. *See also*
France
associated territories and states,
168–169, 170
French Republic, 46, 168, 170–171
metropolitan France, 168
overseas departments, 168
overseas territories, 51, 168–169,
171, 173
secession, 168–169, 173–174
French West Africa, 20, 168, 170,
175
Front for the Liberation of
Mozambique (FRELIMO), 28,
80–81, 131, 158. *See also*
Mozambique
and Britain, 131
and China, 28, 91, 92

and the Soviet Union, 28, 92
and the United States, 86, 92
Front for the Liberation of the
Enclave of Cabinda, 93. *See also*
Angola
Front for the National Liberation of
Chad (FROLINAT), 185. *See
also* Chad
Frontline States, 104, 119, 120, 129
aid to liberation movements, 104,
119, 129

Gabon, 175, 176–177, 180, 189
and Biafran secession, 184
coup d'état, 184
dictatorship, 184
French military intervention, 165,
180, 181–182, 184
national conference, 188
oil, 181–182, 184
uranium, 181–182, 184
Gambia, 200
Gaza Strip, 37
Gbenye, Christophe, 71. *See also*
Congo (Belgian); Simba
rebellion
General Confederation of Labor
(CGT), 171. *See also* African
Democratic Rally (RDA);
Communist Party; France
General Motors, 106. *See also* South
Africa; United States
Geneva Conference. *See* Rhodesia
genocide, xii, 2–3, 11–12, 181, 193,
194, 195, 208–209. *See also*
crimes against humanity; human
rights; war crimes
German Democratic Republic. *See*
Germany, East
Germany, 5–6, 11, 45, 121, 167, 168
Germany, East, 7, 73, 95, 122, 149,
152, 158, 159
Germany, West, 52, 53, 82, 89, 91,
92, 105, 106, 115, 122, 123, 125,
148, 152, 175. *See also* Berlin
Crisis (1961)

Ghana, 28, 175
aid to liberation movements,
53–54, 90, 173, 182
and Congo (Belgian), 61, 63–64,
65–66, 73
and ECOWAS, 200
and neocolonialism, 9
Gio, 199–200. See also Liberia
Giscard d'Estaing, Valéry, 186. See
also France
Gizenga, Antoine, 68–69. See also
Congo (Belgian)
deputy prime minister, 68
rebel regime, 68, 69
and the Soviet Union, 68
global war on terror, 1, 2, 3, 12,
13–14, 195, 212–219, 227–229.
See also Combined Joint Task
Force–Horn of Africa
(CJTF-HOA); East Africa
Counterterrorism Initiative
(EACTI); Flintlock 2005;
Operation Enduring
Freedom–Trans Sahara
(OEF-TS); Pan-Sahel Initiative
(PSI); Trans-Sahara
Counterterrorism Initiative
(TSCI); Trans-Sahara
Counterterrorism Partnership
(TSCTP); terrorism; terrorist
attacks; U.S. Africa Command
(AFRICOM); U.S. Special
Operations Command
assassinations, 214–215
executive orders, 214–215
impact on local populations,
12, 13–14, 215, 216–217,
218–219
militarization of U.S. aid,
13–14, 195, 213, 215–219,
228–229
U.S. counterterrorism initiatives,
xiv, 195, 207–208, 213, 214–219,
221–222, 228–229
good governance, 178, 197, 216, 218,
219. See also democracy;
Franco-African summits;

International Monetary Fund
(IMF); prodemocracy
movements; World Bank
Gorbachev, Mikhail, 154. See also
Soviet Union
Goukouni Oueddei, 186–187. See
also Chad
Great Britain. See Britain
Great Lakes countries, 209, 211,
212–213
Greater Zaire, 93
Greece, empire, 3–5
Guadeloupe, 168
guerrilla warfare. See armed
struggle; liberation movements
Guevara, Ernesto "Che," 71, 73, 74.
See also Congo (Belgian); Cuba;
Kabila, Laurent; Simba
rebellion
Guinea, 28, 201–206
aid to liberation movements,
90–91, 173
and Congo (Belgian), 61, 63–64,
73
and ECOWAS, 200
French retaliation, 165, 174–175
independence referendum,
173–174, 175
and Liberia, 200, 201
and PAIGC, 89–91
Portuguese invasion, 90
and the Soviet Union, 26, 90
Guinea-Bissau, 91. See also
Portuguese Guinea
Gulf of Aden, 147, 149, 150, 215
Gulf Oil, 88. See also Angola

Habré, Hissène, 186–187. See also
Chad
Haig, Alexander, 110–111, 124–125.
See also United States
Hammarskjöld, Dag, 62, 64. See also
Congo (Belgian); United
Nations
Haud. See Ethiopia
Hawiye, 203. See also Somalia
Herero, 122. See also Namibia

HIV/AIDS pandemic, 11
Ho Chi Minh, 169–172. *See also* Viet Minh; Vietnam
Horn of Africa, 4, 13, 26, 31, 143–145, 148, 151, 153, 154, 160, 206, 207, 215, 218, 229. *See also* Djibouti; Eritrea; Ethiopia; Somalia
al-Qaeda, 206–207
Cold War intervention, 13, 142–143, 144, 160, 205–206
destabilization, 13, 144, 160
Marxist-Leninist confederation, 153
militarization, 144
regional rivalries, 13, 143, 144, 156, 160
Houphouët-Boigny, Félix, 171, 200. *See also* African Democratic Rally (RDA); Côte d'Ivoire
human rights, 135, 155. *See also* crimes against humanity; genocide; humanitarian intervention; United Nations; war crimes
abuses, xiii, 12, 110, 145–146, 147, 154, 170, 171, 172–173, 182, 187, 193, 201, 202, 203, 209, 216–217, 221, 222, 229
and French policy, 188–189
and U.S. policy, 109, 110, 111, 147, 167–169, 213, 218–219
humanitarian intervention, xiii, 2, 12, 221, 227–228, 229
Hungary, 40
Hutu, 181, 208–210. *See also* Rwanda; Zaire/Democratic Republic of Congo (DRC)

Idi Amin, xii, 32. *See also* Uganda
illicit activities, 133, 193, 194, 197, 201–202, 209, 211–213, 215–216, 217, 219–221
imperial powers, xi–xii, 1–2, 6–7, 8–9, 13, 18, 19, 20, 21, 22, 30, 31, 35, 40, 60–61, 69, 83, 167, 168, 176, 179, 202, 228. *See also* Belgium; Britain; France; Portugal
imperialism, 5–6, 10, 27, 35, 38, 48, 59, 60, 66, 83, 112, 166, 168, 173. *See also* Belgium; Britain; France; Portugal
U.S., 48
Western, 25–26, 27, 38, 60, 65
independence, African, 6–7, 8, 18, 19, 20, 21, 24, 61, 66–68, 77, 79, 83, 88, 94, 103, 104, 109, 121, 145, 147, 157, 165, 166, 168, 170, 172, 173–174, 175–176, 179, 180, 182–189, 219–220
India, 3–5, 75, 134, 221, 229
Indian Ocean, 3–5, 143, 147, 149, 150, 157, 169–170, 180, 215, 217–218. *See also* Comoros; Diego Garcia; Madagascar; Réunion; slave trades; trade
Indochina, 20, 27, 46, 60, 166, 167, 168, 169–172, 173. *See also* Vietnam
Indonesia, 4, 27, 51
Indus Valley, 4
industrial revolution, 5–6
Intergovernmental Authority on Development (IGAD), 219–221
internal settlement. *See* Namibia; Rhodesia
International Court of Justice, 122
international law, 12, 117–118, 123, 194–195
International Monetary Fund (IMF), 8–10, 178. *See also* capitalism; neocolonialism; World Bank
neoliberal norms, 9–10
and South Africa, 111–112
structural adjustment programs, 9–10, 196–197, 206, 228
and Zaire, 208
International Security Assistance and Arms Export Control Act (1976). *See* Clark Amendment

international terrorism. *See* global
war on terror; terrorism;
terrorist attacks
Invisible Children, 221. *See also*
Kony, Joseph; Lord's Resistance
Army; Uganda
Iran, 152, 155. *See also* Mossadegh,
Mohammad
American hostages, 155
and Britain, 36–37
coup d'état, 36–37
oil, 36–37
revolution, 155
Shah, 155
and the United States, 36–37, 155
Iraq, 51, 157–158
anticommunism, 43
Ba'ath Party coup d'état, 43
Baghdad Pact, 37–38, 43, 44
and Britain, 43
Egypt, rivalry with, 37
and Israel, 43
monarchy, 37–38
oil, 43
opposition movements, 43
pro-Nasser coup d'état, 43
pro-Western regime, 37–38, 42,
43
and the United States, 43, 214
Ireland, 113
Islam, 4, 216–217. *See also* Islamism
Algeria, 48
Egypt, 46
Somalia, 153, 155, 156, 203
Sudan, 206–208
Islamic Courts Union, 214. *See also*
Somalia
Islamism, 46, 156, 160, 201, 203,
206–208, 213–214, 215, 216,
217, 218–219, 227–228. *See also*
jihad
Israel, 7, 30, 32, 40, 44, 54, 72–73.
See also Egypt; France; South
Africa
Arab-Israeli War (1973), 88, 106,
179–185

and Egypt, 7, 37, 38–39, 40–42,
44
and Ethiopia, 152, 158, 159
occupied territories, 214
Six-Day War (1967), 7, 44, 106
and South Africa, 7, 31, 106–107
Suez War (1956), 7, 30
Italian East Africa. *See* Italy
Italian Somaliland. *See* Somalia
Italy, 18, 21, 72, 91, 113, 132, 148,
150, 152. *See also* Eritrea; Libya;
Somalia; World War II
African colonies, 5–6, 18, 21–22,
144–145, 147, 150, 151, 157
decolonization, 21–22, 31, 157
and Ethiopia, 21, 144–145, 152

Japan, 105, 114, 168, 169, 202
jihad, 205, 206–207. *See also*
Islamism
Johnson, Lyndon B., 22. *See also*
United States
administration, 22, 24–25, 70–71,
83, 86–87, 92, 108, 116
and Congo (Belgian), 70–74
and Portugal, 83, 86–87
Jordan, 37–38, 51
opposition movements, 42–43
pro-Western regime, 42–43
Judaism, 4

Kabila, Laurent, 71. *See also* Alliance
of Democratic Forces for the
Liberation of Congo-Zaire
(AFDL); Congo (Belgian);
Simba rebellion;
Zaire/Democratic Republic of
Congo (DRC)
corruption, 211
dictator, 211
and First Congo War, 209–211
Guevara's assessment of, 73
overthrow of Mobutu, 74, 211
rebel leader, 71, 73, 209, 210–211
and Second Congo War, 211–212
and the United States, 211

Kagnew communications station.
See Ethiopia
Kamerun. See Cameroon;
Cameroon, British; Cameroon,
French
Kasavubu, Joseph, 63, 64. See also
Congo (Belgian)
Katanga lobby, 69, 70, 85, 118. See
also Congo (Belgian)
Katanga secession. See Congo
(Belgian); Katanga lobby
Kaunda, Kenneth, 134. See also
Zambia
Kennedy, John F., 50. See also
United States
administration, 22, 24–25, 43, 52,
64–65, 66–69, 82, 83–86, 87, 90,
92, 107–108, 111, 115, 148
Africa policy, 66–68, 83, 86, 87,
92, 107, 108, 109, 115
and Algeria, 50
and Congo (Belgian), 64–65,
68–69, 70, 83
and Portugal, 83–86, 87, 90
and South Africa, 107–108
Kenya, 19, 32, 73, 148, 150, 207,
215, 216, 217–218
Khartoum, 207
Khrushchev, Nikita, 25, 38, 40, 60.
See also Soviet Union
peaceful coexistence, 27
Kinshasa, 208, 211. See also
Léopoldville
Kisangani, 210. See also Stanleyville
Kissinger, Henry, 86–87, 88–89, 94,
147. See also United States; U.S.
Department of State
and Angola, 94
National Security Study
Memorandum 39, 87
and Rhodesia, 119–120
Kolingba, André, 185. See also
Central African Republic
Kolwezi, 187–188
Kony, Joseph, 221. See also Lord's
Resistance Army; Uganda

Korea, North, 51, 93, 122
Korean War, 153
Kosygin, Alexei, 26. See also Soviet
Union
Krahn, 198–200, 201. See also
Liberia
Kremlin. See Soviet Union
Kuwait, 149

La Baule. See Franco-African
summits
Lake Tanganyika, 73–74
Lancaster House Agreement. See
Rhodesia
Lancaster House Conference. See
Rhodesia
land, xii, 6, 221, 229
Latin America, xi–xii, 8, 22, 25, 27,
29, 36, 61, 181
law, international. See international
law
League of Nations, 121. See also
Cameroon, British; Cameroon,
French; Namibia; Togo
mandates, 121–122, 168, 172
Lebanon, 38, 51
Christians, 42–43
domestic unrest, 42–43
Muslims, 42–43
opposition movements, 42–43
pro-Western regime, 42–43
U.S. invasion, 42–43, 51, 84
Leopold II, King, 5–6. See also
Belgium
Léopoldville, 63. See also Kinshasa
Lesotho, 128–129
liberation movements, 7, 8, 21, 26,
27, 79–82, 87, 89, 92–94, 103,
104, 105, 109, 112, 113, 119, 122,
128, 129, 130, 134, 135, 154, 157,
158, 168
external assistance, 7–8, 30–31, 51,
53–54, 89, 103, 104, 118–119,
128, 129, 134
and the OAU, 8, 83, 90, 92, 113,
119

Liberia, 175, 195, 197–198
  Americo-Liberians, 198–199
  army, 198–199, 202
  Christians, 199–200
  civil war, 11–12, 199–203
  class conflict, 199
  corruption, 198–199, 201–202,
    228–229
  coup d'état, 198–199
  dictatorship, 198–199, 228–229
  economic crisis, 195, 198–199,
    202–203
  and ECOWAS, 200–201, 202
  elections, 202
  ethnic conflict, 198–200, 201–202
  and France, 200–202
  and Francophone countries,
    200–201
  Muslims, 199, 200
  and Nigeria, 200–201, 202
  peace agreement, 202
  rebel groups, 199–202, 203
  religious conflict, 199–200
  repression, 198–200
  resources, 200, 201–202, 228–229
  and the United States, 198,
    199–200, 201–202, 213,
    217–218, 228–229
Libya, 51, 185. See also Chad;
    Sudan; World War II
  aid to African insurgencies,
    185–187, 199, 200
  Cold War, 21
  coup d'état, 185
  independence, 21, 145, 157
  and Italy, 21
  NATO air strikes, 195, 217
  oil, 36
  overthrow of Qaddafi, 217
  pan-Arabism, 185–186
  and the Soviet Union, 21, 186
  and the United Nations, 21, 157,
    195
  and the United States, 44, 186,
    187, 199, 205–206, 216
linkage. See Reagan, Ronald
Lobito, 132

local autonomy. See self-government
loi-cadre. See France
Lord's Resistance Army, 221. See
    also Uganda
Luanda, 81, 83, 94, 95, 96, 97
Lubumbashi, 210. See also
    Elisabethville
Lumumba, Patrice, 59, 64. See also
    Congo (Belgian)
  assassination, 58, 62–63, 64–65
  and Belgium, 58–59, 60, 62–63,
    64–65, 66
  capture, 64
  coup d'état, 58, 63
  house arrest, 63, 64
  independence day speech, 59
  prime minister, 58, 59
  and the Soviet Union, 62, 63, 64,
    65
  and the United Nations, 60,
    61–62, 63, 64–65
  and the United States, 59, 62–63,
    64
Lumumbists, 69, 70, 71, 72
Lunda, 95. See also Angola
Lutheran church, 122, 134

Machel, Samora, 92. See also Front
    for the Liberation of
    Mozambique (FRELIMO);
    Mozambique
Macmillan, Harold, 6. See also
    Britain
Madagascar, 18, 168, 175, 180, 200,
    218
  French military intervention, 170,
    180
  French repression, 165, 167, 170
  independence struggle, 169–170
  national conference, 188
  parliamentarians, 170
  revolt, 170
Maghreb, 4
Malagasy. See Madagascar
Malawi, 128–129. See also Central
    African Federation; Nyasaland
Malaysia, 134

Mali, 26, 28, 175, 188
al-Qaeda, 217
coup d'état, 217
Tuareg insurgency, 217
and the United States, 216, 217
Malinke. See Mandingo
Malloum, Félix, 186. See also Chad
Mandela, Nelson, 112–113, 114, 115.
See also African National
Congress (ANC); South Africa;
Umkhonto we Sizwe
Mandingo, 199–200, 201. See also
Liberia
Mano, 199–200. See also Liberia
Mao Zedong, 27. See also China,
People's Republic of
Maoist ideology, 28, 81, 119, 153
Marshall Plan, 45
Martinique, 168
Marxism-Leninism. See communism
Massawa, 145, 158, 159
Mau Mau insurgency. See Kenya
Mauritania, 175, 180, 188, 216
M'ba, Léon, 184. See also Gabon
Mbuji-Mayi, 210. See also Bakwanga
Mbundu, 81. See also Angola
Mecca, 44, 214
Medina, 214
Mediterranean Ocean, 5
Meles Zenawi, 160. See also
Ethiopia; Tigray People's
Liberation Front (TPLF)
Menelik II, Emperor, 144. See also
Ethiopia
Mengistu Haile Mariam, 146, 147,
153, 154, 160, 207. See also
Ethiopia
mercantilism. See France;
neocolonialism
mercenaries, 60, 69, 72, 73, 74,
95–97, 98, 188, 194, 210–211.
See also Angola; Belgium;
Britain; Congo (Belgian);
France; Portugal; Rhodesia;
Serbia; South Africa; Ukraine;
Zaire/Democratic Republic of
Congo (DRC)

Middle Congo. See Congo, Republic
of
Middle East
and Africa, 220–221, 229
Cold War, 35, 36, 38–39, 40, 42,
44–45, 84–85, 143, 145, 198
colonialism, 21
decolonization, 36, 38–39, 44–45
nationalism, 35, 42, 44, 45, 214
oil, 36, 44–45, 143, 147, 151, 155,
213, 214
pan-Arabism, 36, 185–186
repressive regimes, 35, 42–43, 214
Middle Passage. See slave trades
Military Procurement Authorization
Act (1971). See Byrd
Amendment
militias, 156, 160, 203, 204, 205,
209
minerals. See illicit activities;
resource wars; resources,
African
missionaries, 69
Mitterrand, François, 186, 188–189.
See also France
Mobutu, Joseph-Désiré, 59, 64, 208,
211, 212. See also Congo
(Belgian); First Congo War
(1996–1997); Zaire/Democratic
Republic of Congo (DRC)
army chief of staff, 59, 63
corruption, 208–209
coup d'état, 63, 69, 70, 74
dictatorship, 74, 181, 208–209
and FNLA, 81, 93
and France, 187–188, 208,
209–211
overthrow of, 209, 210–211
and the United States, 63, 70, 73,
74, 188, 208, 210–211
Mobutu Sese Seko. See Mobutu,
Joseph-Désiré
Mogadishu, 149, 151, 155, 203,
204–205
Mohamed, Ali Mahdi, 203. See also
Somalia; United Somali
Congress

Momoh, Joseph, 201. *See also* Sierra
  Leone
Mondlane, Eduardo, 80. *See also*
  Front for the Liberation of
  Mozambique (FRELIMO);
  Mozambique
  assassination, 92
  and the United States, 80, 86, 92
money laundering. *See* illicit
  activities
Monroe Doctrine, 181
Monrovia, 200
Morocco, 4, 51, 63, 168, 187–188
  aid to liberation movements, 113
  independence, 46–47
  Islamic militants, 46–47, 214
  political unrest, 46
  repression, colonial, 46
  and the Soviet Union, 46–47
  and the United States, 44, 47, 214,
    216
Mossadegh, Mohammad, 36–37. *See
  also* Iran
Mozambique, 19, 21, 30, 79, 104,
  117, 129. *See also* Front for the
  Liberation of Mozambique
  (FRELIMO); Mozambique
  National Resistance
  (RENAMO)
  and African National Congress,
    130, 131
  aid to liberation movements, 118,
    119, 130
  Beira oil pipeline and refinery, 130
  and Britain, 131
  destablization, 120, 128, 129,
    130–131, 193
  elections, 132
  independence, 88
  liberated zones, 91
  liberation movements, 80
  liberation struggle, 28, 80, 89,
    91–92, 93
  Nkomati Accord (1984), 131
  Rome General Peace Accords
    (1992), 132

settlers, 19, 103
socialism, 130
  and South Africa, xii, 129,
    130–131
  and the Soviet Union, xii, 26, 28,
    131
  and the United States, xii, 87, 92,
    131
Mozambique National Resistance
  (RENAMO), 130–131. *See also*
  Front for the Liberation of
  Mozambique (FRELIMO);
  Mozambique; RENAMO lobby
  and Rhodesia, 130
  sabotage, 130–131
  and South Africa, 130, 131
  terror tactics, 130–131
Mubarak, Hosni, 207. *See also*
  Egypt
mujahideen, 206–207. *See also*
  Afghanistan; al-Qaeda; bin
  Laden, Osama; Islamism;
  Soviet-Afghan War (1979–1989);
  Sudan
  CIA support, 206–207
Mulele, Pierre, 71. *See also* Congo
  (Belgian); Simba rebellion
Muzorewa, Abel, 120–121. *See also*
  Rhodesia; United African
  National Council; Zimbabwe

Namibia, 107, 211–212. *See also*
  South West Africa National
  Union (SWANU); South West
  Africa People's Organization
  (SWAPO)
  African reserves, 121
  and Angola, 122, 123, 212
  apartheid, 121
  Caprivi Strip, 212
  constituent assembly, 127
  constitution, 124–125, 127
  diamonds, 121–122
  elections, 123–125, 127
  foreign investment, 121, 123
  German colony, 121

illegal occupation, 26, 31, 92, 95,
103, 105, 119, 122–123, 131
independence, 104, 122, 124–128,
134
internal settlement, 122–124
League of Nations mandate,
121–122
liberation struggle, 13, 26, 105,
124–125, 128
minerals, 121–122
sanctions, 121–123
settlers, 19, 26, 31, 104
and South Africa, 26, 31, 92, 95,
103, 111–112, 121–128, 131, 134
and the Soviet Union, 26, 31, 122,
125–126
Turnhalle Conference (1975),
122–123
and the United Nations, 122–125,
126–127, 134
uranium, 122
U.S. investments, 122
U.S. policies, 31, 124–125,
134–135
Western Contact Group, 123–125
Nasser, Gamal Abdel, 13, 37, 40, 53,
59. See also Bandung
Conference (1955); Communist
Party; Egypt; Non-Aligned
Movement; Suez
anticommunism, 38, 43–44
coup d'état, 37
neutralism and nonalignment, 13,
38
pan-Arabism, 36, 46, 59
national conferences. See
prodemocracy movements
National Front for the Liberation of
Angola (FNLA), 81. See also
Angola; Zaire/Democratic
Republic of Congo (DRC)
anticommunism, 81
attack near Luanda, 83–84, 94–97
and China, 29, 93, 97, 228
ideology, 81
membership, 81, 94

and MPLA, 81–82, 85, 94
racism, 81
and South Africa, 95, 98
and the United States, 29, 85, 86,
92–95
National Liberation Front (FLN),
44, 47–54. See also Algeria
anticommunism, 48, 54
radical nationalism, 44
National Patriotic Front of Liberia
(NPFL), 199–200, 201, 202. See
also Liberia; Taylor, Charles
and Francophone countries,
200–201
and Libya, 199, 200
and Revolutionary United Front,
201
Small Boy Units, 199
national security advisor, 86–87, 94,
154
National Security Council. See
United States
National Security Study
Memorandum 39 (NSSM 39),
87
National Union for the Total
Independence of Angola
(UNITA), 29, 81, 93–96, 210.
See also Angola; Clark
Amendment; Tunney
Amendment; UNITA lobby;
Zaire/Democratic Republic of
Congo (DRC)
anticommunism, 81
and China, 29, 93, 228
ideology, 81
Maoism, 81
membership, 81, 94
and MPLA, xii, 81–82
and Portugal, 81–82
racism, 81
sabotage, 132
and South Africa, 95, 98, 125,
131–133
and the United States, 29, 85, 95,
126, 132, 199, 208

nationalism, 12–13, 197. *See also* Afro-Asian Peoples' Solidarity Organization; Bandung Conference (1955); Conference of Nationalist Organizations of the Portuguese Colonies (CONCP); Non-Aligned Movement; Organization of African Unity (OAU); Organization of Solidarity with the Peoples of Asia, Africa, and Latin America; pan-African movement; pan-Arab movement; pan-Islamic movement; Tricontinental Conference (1966)

   African, 6, 18, 19, 20, 22, 24, 50, 66, 81, 85, 87, 157

   radical, 7, 8–9, 13, 24, 30, 35–37, 42–43, 44, 46, 53–54, 58–61, 68, 71, 83, 84, 85, 103, 123, 165, 166–175

natural resources. *See* resources, African; resource wars

Ndebele, 119. *See also* Rhodesia

neocolonialism, 1–2, 9–10, 28, 30, 73, 79, 165, 175–180, 228. *See also* capitalism; International Monetary Fund (IMF); World Bank

neoliberalism. *See* International Monetary Fund (IMF); World Bank

Netherlands, the, 90, 92, 113

Neto, Agostinho, 81, 93. *See also* Angola; Popular Movement for the Liberation of Angola (MPLA)

New World, 5

Niger, 175

   coup d'état, 182

   French military intervention, 165, 180–188, 189

   human rights abuses, 217

   national conference, 188

   rebellion, 182–183

Tuaregs, 217

and the United States, 216, 217

uranium, 181–184

Nigeria, 120, 149, 181, 187

   Biafran secession, 181, 184

   civil war, 32, 181, 184

   and ECOWAS, 200–202

   French involvement, 181, 182, 183, 184

   Trans-Sahara Counterterrorism Partnership, 216

Nigerien Democratic Union, 171, 182. *See also* African Democratic Rally (RDA); Niger; Sawaba

Nimeiri, Jaafar, 157, 206. *See also* Sudan

Nixon, Richard M., 23. *See also* Kissinger, Henry; United States administration, 23, 82, 83, 86–88, 109, 117–118

   and China, 29

   and Portugal, 86–89, 90

   and Rhodesia, 117–118

Nkomati Accord. *See* Mozambique

Nkrumah, Kwame, 9–10, 53–54, 59, 64, 66, 150. *See also* Ghana

Non-Aligned Movement, xi, 8, 13, 36, 38, 42, 59, 64, 65, 92, 120, 158. *See also* Afro-Asian Peoples' Solidarity Organization; Bandung Conference (1955); Nasser, Gamal Abdel; Organization of Solidarity with the Peoples of Asia, Africa, and Latin America

nongovernmental organizations, 9, 31, 80, 82, 90, 133–134, 135, 207

   humanitarian relief, 194, 203–204, 205, 209, 220

Nordic countries, 129

   aid to liberation movements, 8, 31, 82, 93, 103, 113, 119, 122, 134

   socialism, 134

North Africa, 4–5, 13, 21, 26, 30, 35–54, 57, 143, 169, 180

North America, 5, 113
North Atlantic Treaty Organization
(NATO), 7, 30, 35, 45, 46, 49,
50, 51, 58, 60, 79, 80, 82,
84–86, 88, 92, 108, 181, 195,
217, 228
North Korea. *See* Korea, North
North Vietnam. *See* Vietnam,
North
Northern Frontier District, 150. *See
also* British East Africa; Kenya;
Somalia
Northern Rhodesia, 28, 58, 77. *See
also* Central African Federation;
Zambia
Norway, 82, 90, 92. *See also* Nordic
countries
Nujoma, Sam, 127. *See also*
Namibia; South West Africa
People's Organization
(SWAPO)
Nyasaland, 58, 80. *See also* Central
African Federation; Malawi
Nyerere, Julius, 134. *See also*
Tanzania

Obama, Barack, 215. *See also* United
States
administration, 215
targeted assassinations, 215
Ogaden. *See* Ethiopia
oil, 91, 132, 229. *See also* Algeria;
Angola; Chad; economy;
Gabon; Iran; Iraq; Libya;
Middle East; sanctions; Sudan
embargo, 117–118, 124, 133,
181–182
price increase, 9, 146, 196
resources, 12, 14, 36–37, 40, 42,
43, 44–45, 46, 52, 88, 92, 93, 95,
106, 130, 133, 143, 147, 151, 155,
176, 178, 181, 182, 184, 185, 196,
206, 207, 212, 213, 214, 218,
220, 221, 229
Omega navigation station, 198. *See
also* Liberia

Operation Enduring Freedom–Trans
Sahara (OEF-TS), 216. *See also*
global war on terror; Pan-Sahel
Initiative (PSI); Trans-Sahara
Counterterrorism Initiative
(TSCI); Trans-Sahara
Counterterrorism Partnership
(TSCTP)
Operation Restore Hope, 204. *See
also* Somalia; United Nations
Operation in Somalia
(UNOSOM); United Task
Force (UNITAF)
Organization of African Unity
(OAU), 8, 83, 98, 108, 120,
150–151, 152, 194. *See also*
African Union
charter, 150–151, 155
colonial boundaries principle,
150–151
Haile Selassie influence, 150–151
Liberation Committee, 8, 83, 90,
92, 113, 119
peacekeeping, 186–187
Organization of Solidarity with the
Peoples of Asia, Africa, and
Latin America, 29, 36, 82. *See
also* Tricontinental Conference
(1966)
Oromo, 154, 159. *See also*
Ethiopia
Oromo Liberation Front, 159. *See
also* Ethiopia
Ottoman Empire, 4. *See also*
Turkey
Ovimbundu, 81, 84. *See also*
Angola

Pakistan, 204
Palestine, 42, 54, 214
Pan Africanist Congress, 113, 115.
See also South Africa
pan-African movement, 59. *See also*
nationalism
pan-Arab movement, 36, 59, 181,
185–186. *See also* nationalism

pan-Islamic movement, 158
Pan-Sahel Initiative (PSI), 216. *See
    also* global war on terror;
    Operation Enduring
    Freedom–Trans Sahara
    (OEF-TS); Trans-Sahara
    Counterterrorism Initiative
    (TSCI); Trans-Sahara
    Counterterrorism Partnership
    (TSCTP)
Paris Peace Conference (1919), 169
Patriotic Front, 120–121. *See also*
    Rhodesia; Zimbabwe;
    Zimbabwe African National
    Union (ZANU); Zimbabwe
    African National
    Union–Patriotic Front
    (ZANU-PF); Zimbabwe African
    People's Union (ZAPU)
Peace Corps, 148
Pentagon. *See* United States
People's Democratic Republic of
    Yemen. *See* Yemen, South
People's Republic of Angola. *See*
    Angola
People's Republic of China. *See*
    China, People's Republic of
Persia, empire, 4
Persian Gulf, 4, 5, 155, 206, 221, 229
Persian Plateau, 4
petroleum. *See* oil
Phoenicia, 4
Poland, 40
political Islam. *See* Islamism
politics of exclusion, 193
Popular Movement for the
    Liberation of Angola (MPLA),
    81. *See also* Angola
    attack on Luanda, 83
    and China, 93
    communism, 81
    and Cuba, 93, 96–98, 126
    and FNLA, 81, 85, 94–95
    membership, 81, 94–95
    and South Africa, 95, 98
    and the Soviet Union, 29, 93–94,
        95, 125

territory controlled, 94–95, 96–97,
    98
and UNITA, 81, 95–96, 212
and the United States, 85, 93, 94,
    98
and Yugoslavia, 93
and Zaire, 94, 95, 187–188
Portugal, 6, 18, 20–21. *See also*
    Angola; Azores; Cape Verde;
    Communist Party; Guinea;
    Mozambique; Portuguese
    Guinea; Socialist Party; São
    Tomé and Príncipe
African colonies, 6, 13, 79–80, 88,
    143
African Wars, 13, 21, 28, 30,
    79–80, 82, 83–84, 88–89, 90–91
colonialism, 20–21, 58, 60, 68, 69,
    79, 83
coup d'état, 21, 88, 91, 92, 93
decolonization, 7, 13, 19, 20–21,
    26, 79–80, 93–94, 97, 109, 128,
    132, 228
dictatorship, 79
economy, 79, 88
liberation movements, 80–82
mercenaries, 95–97
and NATO, 30, 82–83, 84–86, 88,
    92
secret police, 82, 91–92, 130
settlers in African colonies, 30, 81,
    84
and the Soviet Union, 82, 83, 84
and the United Nations, 84, 86,
    88, 91, 108
and the United States, 30, 79–80,
    82, 83–89, 91, 92, 94, 108
Portuguese Africa. *See* Angola; Cape
    Verde; Mozambique; Portugal;
    Portuguese Guinea; São Tomé
    and Príncipe
Portuguese Guinea, 21, 26, 30,
    79–80, 158. *See also* African
    Party for the Independence of
    Guinea and Cape Verde
    (PAIGC); Cape Verde;
    Guinea-Bissau; Portugal

dockworkers' strike, 89
independence, 89, 91
liberated areas, 89–90, 91
liberation movements, 80, 82,
   89–92
liberation struggle, 26, 80, 82,
   89–91
and the Soviet Union, 26
private military companies. *See*
   mercenaries
prodemocracy movements, 2, 166,
   188, 193, 197–198, 209. *See also*
   democracy; good governance
Francophone Africa, 166,
   188–189, 209
proxy wars. *See* Foreign
   Intervention

Qaddafi, Muammar al-, 185–187,
   199, 205–206, 217. *See also*
   Libya
Qasim, Abd al-Karim, 43. *See also*
   Iraq
Quiwonkpa, Thomas, 199. *See also*
   Liberia

racial conflict, 87, 121, 193
racism. *See* white minority
rapid deployment force, 180, 206
Reagan, Ronald, 113, 124, 132. *See
   also* Clark Amendment;
   Mozambique National
   Resistance (RENAMO);
   National Union for the Total
   Independence of Angola
   (UNITA); RENAMO lobby;
   UNITA lobby
administration, 23, 110–114,
   124–127, 131, 132, 155, 187, 199,
   205
and Angola, 125–126, 132
constructive engagement, 111–112,
   127
linkage policy, 125–126
and Namibia, 124–127
and South Africa, 110–114,
   124–127, 131–132

rebel movements, xii, xiii, 3, 58, 68,
   69, 71–74, 128–133, 181,
   186–187, 188, 193, 194, 195,
   199–203, 208–212, 217, 220,
   222
Red Sea, 21, 143, 144, 147, 150, 151,
   156–157, 158, 215
regime change, 12, 35, 43, 133–134,
   160, 184, 195
religions, 4. *See also* Christianity;
   Islam; Judaism
religious conflict, 1, 193, 197–198
religious right. *See* United States
RENAMO lobby, 131, 132. *See also*
   Mozambique; Mozambique
   National Resistance
   (RENAMO); Reagan, Ronald;
   United States
resource wars, 3, 11, 13–14, 193–194,
   198, 202, 211–212, 228–229
resources, African, 5–6, 8, 11, 12, 14,
   20, 57, 58–59, 60, 84, 92,
   116–118, 121–122, 176, 181–189,
   196, 202, 208, 210, 219, 229.
   See also diamonds; land; oil;
   resource wars; uranium
responsibility to protect. *See* United
   Nations
Réunion, 168, 180
Revolutionary United Front (RUF),
   201. *See also* child soldiers;
   Sierra Leone; Taylor, Charles
Rhodesia, 19, 28, 30, 58, 60, 77,
   80–81, 104. *See also* Byrd
   Amendment; Central African
   Federation; Patriotic Front;
   Rhodesia lobby; Zimbabwe;
   Zimbabwe African National
   Union (ZANU); Zimbabwe
   African People's Union
   (ZAPU)
African reserves, 115
and Britain, 31, 105, 116–117,
   120–121, 228
Central Intelligence Organisation,
   120–121, 130
and Commonwealth, 116, 134

Rhodesia (*cont.*)
  communist threat, 7, 115, 118–119,
    130, 134
  elections, 121
  and France, 117
  and Frontline States, 117, 118,
    119, 120
  Geneva Conference, 120
  internal settlement, 120, 123
  Lancaster House Agreement
    (1979), 121, 131
  Lancaster House Conference
    (1979), 120–121
  liberation struggle, 26, 28, 29, 105,
    115–121
  majority rule, 6–8, 104, 105, 116,
    120, 121, 134
  mercenaries, 60, 72
  minerals, 116–118
  and Portugal, 117
  repression, 115
  sanctions, 105, 116–119, 120–121
  security forces, 118
  settlers, 19, 103, 115–116, 118
  and South Africa, 117, 119
  and the Soviet Union, 26, 30–31
  Unilateral Declaration of
    Independence (UDI), 116–117,
    119
  and the United Nations, 105,
    116–117, 119
  and the United States, 31, 69,
    115–121, 228
Rhodesia lobby, 118, 120
Rhodesian Front, 121. *See also*
  Smith, Ian
Rhodesian Information Office, 118
Rhodesian Security Forces. *See*
  Rhodesia
Roberto, Holden, 81, 85–86, 88. *See*
  also Angola; National Front for
  the Liberation of Angola
  (FNLA)
Roberts Field, 198, 199. *See also*
  Liberia
Romania, 93
Rome, empire, 4

Rome General Peace Accords
  (1992). *See* Mozambique
Roosevelt, Franklin D., 169. *See also*
  United States
Rusk, Dean, 108. *See also* United
  States; U.S. Department of State
Russia. *See* Soviet Union
Rwanda, 180. *See also* First Congo
  War (1996–1997); Second
  Congo War (1998–2002)
  and France, 180–181, 188,
    209–210
  genocide, xii, 12, 181, 194,
    209–210
  Hutu regime, 181, 209–210
  intervention in Zaire/DRC, 181,
    188, 211–212
  and Uganda, 181, 209
Rwandan Patriotic Front (RPF),
  181, 188, 209–210. *See also*
  Rwanda; Uganda;
  Zaire/Democratic Republic of
  Congo (DRC)

Sadat, Anwar, 44. *See also* Egypt
Saddam Hussein, 43. *See also*
  Iraq
Sahara, 4–5, 45, 46, 216
Sahel, 216–217, 229
  economic crisis, 217
  ungoverned spaces, 216
Sakiet Sidi Youssef, 50. *See also*
  Tunisia
Salazar, António, 79, 84–85, 87. *See*
  also Portugal
sanctions, 120–121, 122, 132,
  207–208. *See also* African
  National Congress (ANC);
  Angola; Namibia; Rhodesia;
  South Africa; Sudan; United
  Nations; Zimbabwe African
  National Union (ZANU);
  Zimbabwe African People's
  Union (ZAPU)
  arms embargo, 86, 88, 104, 106,
    108–110, 114, 116–118, 124, 133,
    203, 207

economic, 87, 104, 105, 106, 107,
    108–111, 114, 116–118, 120, 121,
    123, 124, 132–133, 207
oil, 124, 133
Sankoh, Foday, 201. *See also*
    Revolutionary United Front
    (RUF); Sierra Leone
São Tomé and Príncipe, 79. *See also*
    Portugal
Sara, 185–186. *See also* Chad
Saudi Arabia, 42, 51, 149, 152, 155,
    206–207, 214
American troops, 214
pro-Western regime, 42
Save Darfur Coalition, 221. *See also*
    Darfur
Savimbi, Jonas, 81, 96, 132–133. *See
    also* Angola; National Union for
    the Total Independence of
    Angola (UNITA)
Sawaba, 182–183. *See also* Niger;
    Nigerien Democratic
    Union
Anglophone connection, 182–183
communism, 182–183
external support, 182–183
Schlesinger, James, 89. *See also*
    United States
Scramble for Africa, 6, 144, 150
Second Congo War (1998–2002),
    211–212. *See also* Rwanda;
    Southern African Development
    Community (SADC); Uganda;
    Zaire/Democratic Republic of
    Congo (DRC)
death toll, 211
regional involvement, 211–212
resource plunder, 212
segregation. *See* United States
Selassie, Haile, 21, 26, 143, 145–146,
    147, 149, 150–151, 157–158. *See
    also* Ethiopia
self-determination, 6, 49, 50, 52, 68,
    83, 85–86, 156, 159, 167–168,
    169, 220
self-government, 49, 167–168, 172
British colonies, 19, 168

French colonies, 20, 45, 46, 50–51,
    52, 167–168, 171, 172, 173
Senegal, 90, 171, 175, 177, 180, 189,
    216
Senegalese Democratic Union, 171.
    See also African Democratic
    Rally (RDA)
Serbia, 210–211
mercenaries, 210–211
settler colonies. *See* white minority
Seychelles, 218
Shaba. *See* Zaire/Democratic
    Republic of Congo (DRC)
sharia, 206. *See also* Islam; Islamic
    Courts Union; Islamism
Shermarke, Abdirashid Ali, 148. *See
    also* Somalia
Shona, 119. *See also* Rhodesia
Siad Barre, Mohamed, 26, 143,
    148–149, 152, 155–156, 203. *See
    also* Somalia
Sierra Leone, 200–201. *See also*
    Revolutionary United Front
    (RUF)
Simba rebellion, 71–74. *See also*
    Congo (Belgian)
Sinai Peninsula, 42. *See also* Egypt;
    Israel; Suez
Sino-Soviet split, 7, 27, 28, 93, 228.
    See also China, People's
    Republic of; Soviet Union
Sithole, Ndabaningi, 120. *See also*
    Rhodesia
Six-Day War (June 1967), 7, 44. *See
    also* Egypt; Israel
slave trades, xi, xii, 12, 144
Arab, 5
East Africa, 5, 144, 148
indigenous, 5
North Africa, 5
trans-Atlantic, 5
West Africa, 5
Small Boy Units. *See* National
    Patriotic Front of Liberia
    (NPFL)
Smith, Ian, 116–121. *See also*
    Rhodesia; Rhodesian Front

smuggling. *See* illicit activities
socialism, 8, 25, 26, 28–29, 64, 80,
    128, 130, 134, 143, 146–148, 151,
    153, 154, 158, 167
Socialist Party
    French, 167, 186
    Portuguese, 88–89
Société Générale de Belgique, 57.
    See also Belgium; Congo
    (Belgian)
Somali Bantu, 148. *See also* Somalia
Somalia, 21, 26, 31, 143–144, 198,
    215, 218. *See also* Operation
    Restore Hope; Somali-Ethiopian
    War (1977–1978); United
    Nations Operation in Somalia
    (UNOSOM); United Somali
    Congress; United Task Force
    (UNITAF)
    and the African Union, 219–221
    and al-Qaeda, 205, 208, 214, 216
    Arab influence, 153
    and Britain, 21, 31, 147, 150
    clan rivalry, 147–148, 156, 203
    corruption, 148, 195, 228
    coup d'état, 148, 203
    and Cuba, 149, 151
    dictatorship, 148, 155–156, 203,
        228
    economic crisis, 155–156, 195, 203
    and Ethiopia, 21, 31, 143, 148,
        150–153
    Ethiopian invasion (2006), 205,
        214–215
    ethnic minorities, 148
    expansionist aims, 143, 145, 148,
        149–151
    famine, 149, 156, 203
    and France, 150
    Greater Somalia, 151
    human rights abuses, 148–149,
        155–156
    humanitarian relief, 203–204, 205
    independence, 31, 145, 147, 150, 157
    insurgencies, 155–156, 160, 214
    Islam, 153, 160, 214
    Islamic militants, 156, 203, 205,
        214, 216
    and Italy, 21, 144–145, 148, 150
    military facilities, 149, 151, 155
    militias, 155–156, 160, 203–205
    National Security Service, 149
    Ogaden and Haud, 22, 144–145,
        149–153, 155, 158–159
    overthrow of Siad Barre, 156
    piracy, 220
    political opposition, 148–149,
        156
    socialism, 26, 143, 148, 153
    and the Soviet Union, 26, 31, 143,
        147–153, 154, 228
    and the United Nations, 203–205,
        220
    and the United States, 31, 143,
        147, 148, 150, 154–156, 159–160,
        203–205, 213–214, 218, 228
    warlords, 156, 160, 203, 214
Somali-Ethiopian War (1977–1978),
    31, 150–153, 154, 155, 158–159,
    228. *See also* Ethiopia; Somalia;
    Western Somali Liberation
    Front (WSLF)
Soumaliot, Gaston, 71. *See also*
    Congo (Belgian); Simba
    rebellion
South Africa, 9, 19, 31, 57–58, 60,
    68, 69, 80, 103, 104, 105. *See
    also* African National Congress
    (ANC); Afrikaners; Angola;
    anti-apartheid movement;
    Commonwealth; Communist
    Party; Comprehensive
    Anti-Apartheid Act (1986);
    Constellation of Southern
    African States (CONSAS);
    France; International Monetary
    Fund (IMF); Israel;
    Mozambique; Namibia; Pan
    Africanist Congress; Reagan,
    Ronald; Rhodesia; South
    African Defence Force (SADF);
    United Nations; United States

African reserves, 105–109
apartheid, 7, 9, 31, 95, 97–98,
103–115, 121, 127–129, 132–135
border war, 131
and Britain, 31, 105–106, 108, 115,
123, 124, 125
communist threat, 103, 106,
112–115, 119, 125, 128, 130, 134
destabilization, xii, 30–31, 60, 72,
104, 105, 127–133
economic interests, regional, 60,
117, 121–122, 127–130, 210
economy, 105–106, 107, 115,
127–129
foreign investment, 105–106, 135
and France, 31, 105–106, 108, 114,
123–125
and Israel, 7, 31, 106–107
liberation movements, 54, 103,
112–113, 128–129
liberation struggle, 13, 26
majority rule, 8, 104
mercenaries, 60, 70, 72, 210–211
military, 106–107, 108, 111, 114,
123–127, 131–132
minerals, 105–106, 108, 110
National Party, 110
Nazi sympathizers, 110
nuclear collaboration, 106–107,
109, 111, 114
sanctions, UN, 105, 106, 108–110,
115, 122–124
sanctions, U.S., 107, 108, 110,
114–115, 132
settlers, 7, 19, 26, 69, 103–104
and the Soviet Union, 21, 26, 128
state of emergency, 114
and the United Nations, 91, 105,
106, 108, 109–110, 115, 121–127,
134
uranium, 109, 114
U.S. bank loans, 106, 114
U.S. collaboration, 9, 95–98,
110–112, 123–127, 131–133
U.S. investments, 69, 105–106,
109, 114

U.S. policies, 31, 103–104,
105–115, 123–127
South African Communist Party.
See Communist Party
South African Defence Force
(SADF), 95–96, 107, 118,
126–127. See also South Africa
South Kasai. See Congo (Belgian)
South Sudan, 208, 220, 221, 229.
See also Sudan; Sudan People's
Liberation Movement (SPLM)
South West Africa. See Namibia
South West Africa National Union
(SWANU), 122. See also
Namibia
and China, 122
South West Africa People's
Organization (SWAPO), 95. See
also Namibia
and Angola, 95, 122, 125, 129,
131–132
armed struggle, 122, 125
and Eastern Europe, 122
and FNLA, 95
and Frontline States, 125, 129
and Lutheran churches, 122,
134
and Nordic countries, 122, 134
and South Africa, 95, 125
and the Soviet Union, 122
and the United Nations, 122–127
and UNITA, 95
and the World Council of
Churches, 122
Southeast Asia, 169, 198
Southern Africa, 24, 26, 79
Cold War intervention, 30–31, 87,
133–134, 143–144
decolonization, 7–8, 30–31, 60,
103, 133–135, 143
destabilization, 30, 104, 105,
111–112, 120, 127–133, 193
settlers, 6–7, 13, 30, 103, 104, 109,
118
solidarity movements, 103,
133–135

Southern African Development
Community (SADC), 211,
219–220. *See also* Southern
African Development
Coordination Conference
(SADCC)
Southern African Development
Coordination Conference
(SADCC), 129–130, 211. *See
also* Constellation of Southern
African States (CONSAS);
South Africa; Southern
Africa
Southern Rhodesia. *See* Rhodesia
sovereignty, 4
state, 9, 10, 12, 47, 49, 51, 53, 97,
194, 205
Soviet Union, xi–xii, 2–3, 7–9, 11,
18, 21, 25–26. *See also*
Afghanistan; Algeria; Angola;
Communist Party; Congo
(Belgian); Cuba; Egypt; Eritrea;
Ethiopia; France; Front for the
Liberation of Mozambique
(FRELIMO); Libya; Lumumba,
Patrice; Mozambique; Namibia;
Popular Movement for the
Liberation of Angola (MPLA);
Portugal; Sino-Soviet split;
Somalia; South Africa; South
West Africa People's
Organization (SWAPO); United
Nations; Zimbabwe African
People's Union (ZAPU)
and China, 8–9, 25–29, 153
Cold War, 2–3, 7–9, 11, 25–29,
37–38, 84–85, 115
decolonization, 7, 8–9, 25–26, 35,
38, 65, 175
disintegration, 11, 132, 154, 156,
159, 193, 197, 207
economic aid, 25–26
economic model, 8–9, 26–27
and Ghana, 26
ideology, 28
military aid, 26, 29, 38, 39, 44, 90,
91, 104, 113, 119, 122, 147, 148,

149, 151–152, 153, 154, 157,
158–159, 182, 206
military bases, 21, 44, 149, 151,
155
and Portuguese Guinea, 26
World War II, 25
Soviet-Afghan War (1979–1989),
206. *See also* Afghanistan;
mujahideen
Spain, 6
Spencer, John H., 157. *See also*
Ethiopia; United States
Stalin, Joseph, 38. *See also* Soviet
Union
Stanleyville, 63, 68, 72–73, 86, 210.
See also Kisangani
state collapse, 1, 2, 3, 11, 13–14,
193–198, 203. *See also* economy;
illicit activities; International
Monetary Fund (IMF);
resource wars; World Bank
popular uprisings, 11, 13–14,
197–198, 213, 218
Stevenson, Adlai, 85–86. *See also*
United Nations; United States
structural adjustment programs. *See*
capitalism; International
Monetary Fund (IMF); World
Bank
sub-Saharan Africa, 13, 110, 149,
155, 165, 170, 173, 175–176, 180,
195–196, 199, 205, 218
Sudan, 4, 12, 51, 73, 157–158, 195,
198. *See also* Darfur; South
Sudan; Sudan People's
Liberation Movement (SPLM)
and al-Qaeda, 206–208
animists, 157–158, 206
and Arab states, 206
and Chad, 186
Christians, 157–158, 206
civil war, 206, 220–221
coup d'état, 157–158, 206
economic crisis, 206–207
and Ethiopia, 157–158, 207
Fashoda, 181
human rights abuses, 208

Islamic law, 206
Islamists, 206–208, 228
and Libya, 206
mineral resources, 206
Muslims, 206
oil, 206–207, 220–221
peace agreement, 206, 220,
229
referendum, 206, 220, 229
regional conflicts, 206, 221
sanctions, 207–208
southern secession, 157–158
terrorism, 207–208
and the United States, 147, 187,
205–208, 213, 218, 221,
228–229
U.S. air strikes, 207
Sudan People's Liberation
Movement (SPLM), 206. See
also Sudan; South Sudan
communist support, 206
Marxism, 206
Suez, 40. See also Egypt; Nasser,
Gamal Abdel
Canal and Canal Company,
39–41, 155
Canal Zone, 37
Crisis (1956), 22, 45, 59–60, 71,
84, 228
War (1956), 7, 30, 40–42, 45
Swaziland, 128–129
Sweden, 82, 90, 92, 93. See also
Nordic countries
Syria, 38, 43, 51, 157–158
and Lebanon, 42–43
pro-Nasser government, 38,
42–43

Tanganyika. See Tanzania
Tanzania, xii, 28, 73, 80, 83, 91, 129,
207, 211, 215. See also Frontline
States
aid to liberation movements, 104,
113, 119, 134
British military intervention,
32
Zanzibar revolt, 32

Taylor, Charles, 199–203. See also
Liberia; National Patriotic Front
of Liberia (NPFL);
Revolutionary United Front
(RUF)
terrorism, xiii, 14, 110, 113, 195, 213,
218–222, 229. See also al-Qaeda;
global war on terror
financing, 215–216
foreign terrorist organizations,
205, 207, 213–214, 215, 217
Islam and terrorism, 213–214
state sponsors of terrorism, 186,
199, 207–208
terrorist attacks, 195
in Kenya and Tanzania, 207
in the United States, 2, 14, 195,
207–208, 213–214
Thatcher, Margaret, 120, 131. See
also Britain
Third World, 25–27, 44, 52, 154
Tigray, 154, 159. See also Eritrea;
Ethiopia
Tigray People's Liberation Front
(TPLF), 159–160. See also
Ethiopia
Tigrinya-speakers, 158–159. See also
Eritrea; Ethiopia
Togo, 180
German colony, 168
League of Nations mandate, 168
national conference, 188
UN trust, 168, 170, 175
Tolbert, William, 198. See also
Liberia
Tombalbaye, Ngartha François,
185–186. See also Chad
Touré, Sékou, 53–54, 58, 90, 150,
174. See also Guinea
Trade. See also colonialism;
economy; neocolonialism;
slave trades
ancient, 4
"legitimate," 5
trade unions, 68, 104, 113, 115–116,
134, 146, 166, 171–173, 188
trafficking. See illicit activities

Transitional Government of
    National Unity (GUNT), 186.
    See also Chad
Transjordan. See Jordan
Transparency International,
    216–217
Trans-Sahara Counterterrorism
    Initiative (TSCTI), 216, 218.
    See also global war on terror;
    Operation Enduring
    Freedom–Trans Sahara
    (OEF-TS); Pan-Sahel Initiative
    (PSI); Trans-Sahara
    Counterterrorism Partnership
    (TSCTP)
Trans-Sahara Counterterrorism
    Partnership (TSCTP), 216. See
    also global war on terror;
    Operation Enduring
    Freedom–Trans Sahara
    (OEF-TS); Pan-Sahel Initiative
    (PSI); Trans-Sahara
    Counterterrorism Initiative
    (TSCI)
Tricontinental Conference (1966),
    29, 82. See also Organization of
    Solidarity with the Peoples of
    Asia, Africa, and Latin
    America
Tripartite Agreement (1988),
    126–127, 132. See also Angola;
    Cuba; South Africa
Truman, Harry, 169. See also United
    States
    administration, 24, 169
Tshombe, Moïse, 65. See also Congo
    (Belgian)
    and Belgium, 70–72
    Lumumba assassination, 65, 70
    prime minister, 70–71
    secessionist leader, 60, 65–66,
    70–71
    and the United States, 70–72
Tuareg, 217. See also Mali; Niger
Tubman, William, 198. See also
    Liberia

Tubu, 186. See also Chad
Tunisia, 18, 51, 63, 168
    and Algeria, 47
    and France, 46–47, 50
    independence, 47
    Islamic militants, 46, 47, 214
    political unrest, 46–47
    reforms, colonial, 46–47
    repression, colonial, 46
    self-government, 46–47
    and the Soviet Union, 47–48
    and the United States, 47–48, 214,
    216
Tunney Amendment, 98. See also
    Angola; United States
Turkey, 37, 221, 229. See also
    Ottoman Empire
Turnhalle Conference (1975). See
    Namibia
Tutsi, 181, 209, 211. See also
    Rwanda; Zaire/Democratic
    Republic of Congo (DRC)
Tutu, Desmond, 110. See also South
    Africa

Ubangi-Shari. See Central African
    Republic
Uganda, xii, 73, 181, 208–212, 215.
    See also First Congo War
    (1996–1997); Second Congo
    War (1998–2002)
    aid to liberation movements, 113
    British military intervention, 32
    Idi Amin coup, xii, 32
    intervention in Zaire/DRC, 181,
    188, 209–212
    and Rwanda, 181
Ukraine, 210–211
    mercenaries, 210–211
Umkhonto we Sizwe, 112, 113. See
    also African National Congress
    (ANC); South Africa
    military camps, 113
Unilateral Declaration of
    Independence (UDI). See
    Rhodesia

Union Carbide, 118. *See also*
Rhodesia lobby
Union Minière du Haut Katanga,
57. *See also* Belgium; Congo
(Belgian)
Union of Peoples of Angola. *See*
National Front for the
Liberation of Angola (FNLA)
Union of Soviet Socialist Republics
(USSR). *See* Soviet Union
Union of the Peoples of Cameroon
(UPC), 171–173. *See also* African
Democratic Rally (RDA);
Cameroon, French
Anglophone connection, 172
armed struggle, 173, 182
banning of, 172–173, 182
communism, 171–172, 182
exile, 173
expulsion from the RDA, 171,
182
external support, 172, 173
program, 172
repression of, 172–173, 182
UNITA lobby, 126, 132. *See also*
Angola; National Union for the
Total Independence of Angola
(UNITA); Reagan, Ronald;
United States
United African National Council,
120–121. *See also* Rhodesia;
Zimbabwe
United Arab Republic, 43, 64, 73,
173. *See also* Egypt; Syria
United Kingdom. *See* Britain
United Liberation Movement of
Liberia for Democracy
(ULIMO), 201. *See also* Liberia
United Nations, xiii–xiv, 3, 21, 50,
203. *See also* Algeria; Britain;
Congo (Belgian); Côte d'Ivoire;
Eritrea; Ethiopia; France;
Lumumba, Patrice; Namibia;
Portugal; Rhodesia; sanctions;
Somalia; South Africa; Suez;
United Nations Operation in

Somalia (UNOSOM); United
Task Force (UNITAF)
African members, 61, 64, 108
African troops, 63–64
Afro-Asian bloc, 42, 49, 51, 57, 62,
63–64, 69, 84
aid to liberation movements, 8, 31,
122
charter, 12, 169, 172, 194
decolonization, 21, 83, 134, 157
General Assembly, 12, 42, 61, 62,
64, 122, 157, 172
General Assembly resolutions, 12,
68, 83, 91, 122, 124, 172,
194–195
peacekeeping, xiii–xiv, 3, 11–12,
127, 132, 194, 203–205,
219–220, 229
refugee camps, 209
responsibility to protect, xiii, 12,
194–195, 221–222
sanctions, 86, 105–111, 115–119,
122–124, 132–133, 203, 207
Secretariat, 63–64
Security Council, 42, 62, 64,
116–117, 122–125, 127, 203–204,
207, 209, 211–212
Security Council resolutions, 42,
61, 62, 69, 84, 86, 108–110, 115,
123–127, 211
and the Soviet Union, 60–64,
69
Special Committee against
Apartheid, 134
trust territories, 21, 168, 170–173,
175–176
and the United States, 21–22, 30,
41–42, 52, 60–63, 69, 83–84, 86,
88, 91, 109–110, 120, 123–125,
134, 157, 202
and the Western powers, 21,
61–62, 64, 105, 123
United Nations Operation in
Somalia (UNOSOM), 203–205.
See also Somalia; United Task
Force (UNITAF)

United Somali Congress, 203–205.
  See also Somalia
United States, 7, 18, 21, 22–23, 24,
  25, 175. *See also* African
  Americans; Algeria; Angola;
  anti-apartheid movement; Byrd
  Amendment; capitalism; Carter,
  Jimmy; Central Intelligence
  Agency (CIA); Clark
  Amendment; Comprehensive
  Anti-Apartheid Act (1986);
  Congressional Black Caucus;
  Congo (Belgian); Egypt;
  Eisenhower, Dwight D.;
  Ethiopia; Ford, Gerald; France;
  global war on terror; Iran; Iraq;
  Johnson, Lyndon B.; Katanga
  lobby; Kennedy, John F.;
  Lebanon; Mobutu;
  Joseph-Désiré; Namibia; Nixon,
  Richard M.; Portugal; Reagan,
  Ronald; RENAMO lobby;
  Rhodesia; Rhodesia lobby;
  Somalia; South Africa; Sudan;
  Suez; Truman, Harry; UNITA
  lobby; U.S. Department of
  State; Zaire/Democratic
  Republic of Congo (DRC)
anticommunism, 7, 8–9, 22–23,
  24, 38, 43, 46–48, 60–61, 69, 70,
  71–72, 83, 85, 87, 103, 106, 108,
  109, 112–114, 118, 125, 126, 130,
  145, 166, 168, 169, 186, 195,
  206, 213, 215
civil rights movement, 24–25, 86,
  103–104, 107–108, 109, 114,
  120, 134
Cold War, xi, 11, 21–25, 31, 35, 37,
  40–42, 57–58, 60, 83, 92, 104,
  106, 134–135, 145, 154–155,
  166–167, 169, 195, 197–198, 205,
  208, 213, 215
Commerce Department, 23,
  108
Congress, 23–25, 39–40, 50, 70,
  85, 98, 108, 114, 118, 120, 126,
  131, 156

decolonization, 7, 23, 35, 38, 45,
  48–49, 60–61, 65, 66–68, 69,
  116, 167–168, 169–170
Defense Department, 23, 69, 84,
  85, 87, 89, 108, 131, 155,
  213–219, 222
Democrats, 23, 50
economic aid, 11, 23, 36, 66, 88,
  129, 148, 155, 156, 166–167, 195,
  197, 199, 208, 213
economic interests, 37, 58–61, 69,
  87, 88, 92, 106, 117–118, 123,
  168, 210, 213, 218–219
executive branch, 23
Joint Chiefs of Staff, 155
military aid, 23, 43, 48–49, 68,
  72–73, 83–86, 88, 92, 94–95,
  126, 145, 147–148, 153, 155–156,
  187, 195, 197–200, 205, 208,
  213, 215, 219, 229
military bases, 35, 44–45, 47, 145,
  147, 155, 167, 198–199, 213, 215
military intervention, xiii, 3,
  42–43, 203–205, 213–219
National Security Council, 23,
  87
oil interests, 36, 40, 42–43, 213,
  218
religious right, 131, 199–200
Republicans, 23, 50
segregation, 24, 69, 85, 108, 118
Treasury Department, 23–24,
  216
U.S. Africa Command
  (AFRICOM), 217–219. *See also*
  global war on terror
U.S. Agency for International
  Development (USAID), 213,
  216, 218–219. *See also* human
  rights; United States
human security/human rights
  agenda, 213, 216
security/development agenda, 216,
  218
U.S. Armed Forces, 200, 205, 214.
  See also U.S. Army
Air Force, 218

Marine Corps, 42–43, 51, 200, 218
Navy, 200, 218
U.S. Army, 205–206, 217–218
Delta Force, 205
Rangers, 205
Special Forces, 217, 225
U.S. Central Command (CENTCOM), 218. See also U.S. Africa Command (AFRICOM)
U.S. Department of State, 22–23, 38, 86–87, 108, 110–111, 207, 216, 218
Africanists, 22–24, 84–87, 94, 107–108, 222
assistant secretaries of state for African Affairs, 85, 87, 107, 111
Bureau of African Affairs, 24, 69
Bureau of European Affairs, 69, 84
Bureau of International Organization Affairs, 69
Europeanists, 69, 84–86, 108
secretaries of state, 84, 87, 94, 108, 110–111, 155, 157, 213
U.S. European Command (EUCOM), 218. See also U.S. Africa Command (AFRICOM)
U.S. Pacific Command (USPACOM), 218. See also U.S. Africa Command (AFRICOM)
U.S. Senate, Committee on Foreign Relations, 124
U.S. Senate, Committee on Foreign Relations, Subcommittee on United Nations Affairs, 50
U.S. Senate, Committee on the Judiciary, Subcommittee on Security and Terrorism, 113. See also African National Congress (ANC)
U.S. Senate, Select Committee to Study Governmental Operations with Respect to Intelligence Activities, 214

U.S. assassination of foreign leaders, 214
U.S. Special Operations Command, 214–215. See also global war on terror
U.S. Special Operations Forces, 208, 214, 216. See also U.S. Army
United Task Force (UNITAF), 204. See also Somalia; United Nations Operation in Somalia (UNOSOM)
Upper Volta. See Burkina Faso
uranium, 21, 57, 59, 109, 114, 122, 178, 181–185, 218. See also Central African Republic; Chad; Congo (Belgian); Gabon; Namibia; Niger; South Africa; Zaire/Democratic Republic of Congo (DRC)

Vance, Cyrus, 155. See also United States; U.S. Department of State
Vichy, 168, 169. See also France
Viet Minh, 46, 168, 169. See also Dien Bien Phu; Indochina; Vietnam
Vietnam, 51, 83, 86, 169. See also Dien Bien Phu; Indochina; Viet Minh
Vietnam, North, 51, 182
Voice of America relay station, 198. See also Liberia
Vorster, John, 110, 119, 123. See also South Africa
regional détente, 119, 122–123, 128

war crimes, 12, 194. See also crimes against humanity; genocide; human rights
war on terror. See global war on terror
warlords, 3, 11, 156, 160, 166, 193–194, 197–198, 199, 201–203, 209, 212, 214, 228–229

Washington Consensus. *See*
 International Monetary Fund
 (IMF); World Bank
weapons influx, 5, 7, 11
West Africa, 4–5, 26, 30, 79, 198,
 200, 202, 216, 220
Western alliance, 7, 50, 52, 84
Western civilization, 103
Western Contact Group. *See*
 Namibia
Western Europe, 5, 61–62, 129, 154.
 See also anti-apartheid
 movement
Africa solidarity movements, 103,
 104
Western Somali Liberation Front
 (WSLF), 151. *See also* Somalia;
 Somali-Ethiopian War
 (1977–1978)
white man's burden, 24
white minority, 57. *See also* Algeria;
 Angola; Belgium; Central
 African Federation;
 Mozambique; Namibia;
 Portugal; Rhodesia; South
 Africa; Southern Africa
regimes, 6–7, 25–26, 57, 58–59,
 60, 69, 87, 98, 103, 104, 105,
 109, 111–112, 116, 118, 119,
 133–134, 143
rights, 23, 24, 59, 61, 119, 121,
 124–125, 135
rule, 7–8, 13, 23–26, 28–31,
 103–105, 112, 115, 120–121,
 127–128, 130, 134
settlers, xii, 23–26, 30–31, 69, 77,
 103, 105–109, 115
Williams, G. Mennen, 85, 107, 108.
 See also United States; U.S.
 Department of State
Wilson, Harold, 116. *See also*
 Britain
Wilson, Woodrow, 169. *See also*
 United States
wind of change, 6. *See also*
 Macmillan, Harold
World Bank, 9, 178. *See also*
 capitalism; International

Monetary Fund (IMF);
 neocolonialism
neoliberal norms, 9–10
structural adjustment programs,
 9–10, 178, 196–197, 228
and Zaire, 208
World Council of Churches
aid to liberation movements, 8, 31,
 80, 82–83, 90, 92, 113, 119, 122
Programme to Combat Racism,
 82–83, 135
World War I, 121, 169
World War II, 6, 18, 22, 25, 35, 51,
 106, 110, 115, 166–169, 172, 175.
 See also France; Italy; South
 Africa; Viet Minh
African role, 6, 167–168
Allied powers, 21, 144–145, 157
anti-Nazi alliance, 134, 166
Axis powers, 49
East Africa Campaign, 21,
 144–145, 150, 157
North Africa Campaign, 21, 44
United States, 25, 35, 44,
 167–168

Yaoundé Convention (1963), 177
Yemen, 51, 215
opposition movements, 42
pro-Western regime, 42
Yemen, South, 153, 157–159
Young, Andrew, 109, 120. *See also*
 United Nations; United States
Yugoslavia, 93, 154
independent foreign policy, xi, 7,
 93

Zaire/Democratic Republic of
 Congo (DRC), 92, 149, 198,
 211. *See also* Angola; Congo
 (Belgian); First Congo War
 (1996–1997); International
 Monetary Fund (IMF); Kabila,
 Laurent; Mobutu,
 Joseph-Désiré; Second Congo
 War (1998–2002); World Bank
army, 210, 211
and Belgium, 208

and Britain, 210
and Burundi, 209, 211, 212
corruption, 208, 211–212, 228
diamonds, 182, 210, 212
East Kasai Province, 210, 212
economic crisis, 195, 208
ethnic cleansing, 209
and FNLA, 93–97
foreign mining interests, 210,
 212
and France, 208, 209–210
French military intervention,
 165–166, 180–182, 187–188,
 208, 209–211
human rights abuses, 209
insurgencies, 208, 209, 228
Kamina air base, 199, 208
Kivu Provinces (North and
 South), 212
mercenaries, 210–211
mineral resources, 181–182,
 187–188, 208, 210–212
national conference, 188
overthrow of Mobutu, 209, 210,
 211
prodemocracy movement, 188,
 209, 211
regional war, 209–212
and Rwanda, 209–212
Shaba invasions, 187–188
Shaba Province, 208, 210
and Uganda, 208–212
and UNITA, 93, 95, 132, 199,
 208, 210, 212
and the United States, 93–95, 188,
 199, 208, 209–210, 213, 228
uranium, 181–182
and Zimbabwe, 210–212
Zambia, 28, 104, 129, 210. *See also*
 Central African Federation;
 Frontline States; Northern
 Rhodesia

aid to liberation movements, 113,
 118–119, 129, 134
destabilization, 120, 128–130, 132
Zanzibar. *See* Tanzania
Zimbabwe, 104, 115, 120–121,
 128–130, 154, 160, 210–212,
 220. *See also* Rhodesia;
 Zimbabwe African National
 Union (ZANU); Zimbabwe
 African People's Union (ZAPU)
independence, 121, 128, 130
Zimbabwe African National Union
 (ZANU), 28, 115–116, 118–119,
 121. *See also* Rhodesia
and China, 28–29, 119, 228
and Frontline States, 119
and Mozambique, 118–120, 129,
 130
and Nordic countries, 119
and the OAU, 119
sanctions, 117
and the United States, 115–116
and the World Council of
 Churches, 119
Zimbabwe African National
 Union–Patriotic Front
 (ZANU-PF), 121. *See also*
 Rhodesia; Zimbabwe
Zimbabwe African People's Union
 (ZAPU), 115, 118–119, 121. *See
 also* Rhodesia
and ANC, 118
and Frontline States, 119
and Nordic countries, 119
and the OAU, 119
sanctions, 117
and the Soviet Union, 29, 119
and the United States, 115–116
and the World Council of
 Churches, 119
and Zambia, 118, 120, 129
Zimbabwe-Rhodesia. *See* Rhodesia

Printed in the United States
By Bookmasters